DRAWN

TO THE

RHYTHM

Sara Hall

DRAWN

TO THE

RHYTHM

A Passionate Life Reclaimed

W. W. Norton & Company

New York London

"The Journey" from *Dream Work*, copyright © 1986 by Mary Oliver. Used by permission of Grove/Atlantic, Inc., and the author.

For information about permission to reproduce selections from this book, write to Permissions, W. W. Norton & Company, Inc., 500 Fifth Avenue, New York, NY 10110

The text of this book is composed in Centaur MT
Composition by Gina Webster
Manufacturing by Quebecor World Fairfield
Book design by Judith Stagnitto Abbate
Production manager: Andrew Marasia

Library of Congress Cataloging-in-Publication Data

Hall, Sara, 1953–
Drawn to the rhythm : a passionate life reclaimed / Sara Hall.
p. cm.
ISBN 0-393-04940-X
I. Hall, Sara, 1953– 2. Rowers–United States—Biography. 3. Women rowers—United States—Biography. 4. Middle aged women—United States—Biography. 5. Self-realization—United States. I. Title.

GV790.92.H35 A3 2002
797.1'4'092—dc21
[B]   2001044565

W. W. Norton & Company, Inc., 500 Fifth Avenue, New York, N.Y. 10110
www.wwnorton.com

W. W. Norton & Company Ltd., Castle House,
75/76 Wells Street, London WIT 3QT

1 2 3 4 5 6 7 8 9 0

for Robert Tucker Hall

The names of my children have been changed to protect their privacy. Sara Hall is my maiden name. While these events took place, I used my name as it was during my marriage.

The Journey

One day you finally knew
what you had to do, and began,
though the voices around you
kept shouting
their bad advice—
though the whole house
began to tremble
and you felt the old tug
at your ankles.
"Mend my life!"
each voice cried.
But you didn't stop.
You knew what you had to do,
though the wind pried
with its stiff fingers
at the very foundations,
though their melancholy
was terrible.
It was already late
enough, and a wild night,
and the road full of fallen
branches and stones.

But little by little,
as you left their voices behind,
the stars began to burn
through the sheets of clouds,
and there was a new voice,
which you slowly
recognized as your own,
that kept you company
as you strode deeper and deeper
into the world,
determined to do
the only thing you could do—
determined to save
the only life you could save.

—*Mary Oliver*

Contents

Preface 1 3

Chapter One First Race 1 9

Chapter Two Being a Fish 3 3

Chapter Three Mine Is to Serve 4 6

Chapter Four Falling in Love 5 8

Chapter Five Bathed in the Salty Waters 6 3

Chapter Six Hearing the Voices 8 9

Chapter Seven Heeding the Call 9 9

Chapter Eight The Shining Arrow 1 0 8

Chapter Nine Striking Gold 1 2 5

Chapter Ten The Edge 1 4 2

Chapter Eleven Letting Go 1 5 4

Chapter Twelve The Single 1 6 2

Chapter Thirteen Moving On 1 8 2

Contents

198   *Chapter Fourteen*   Contact

208   *Chapter Fifteen*   The Big A

224   *Chapter Sixteen*   Resolute

241   *Chapter Seventeen*   Fire and Water

264   *Chapter Eighteen*   The Final

275   *Afterword*

283   *Acknowledgments*

Photographs appear between pages 128 and 129.

I began learning to row nearly forty years before I saw a single shell for the first time. When I was a little girl, my mother practiced the piano every afternoon—usually some jazz, something twelve-tone and indecipherable, but always she added a Bach toccata in an eternal evolution toward perfection. I liked to lie on my back under the piano and imagine the throb from the pale wood sounding board of the big mahogany Steinway over my head beating like a heart. My mother's hands moved over the keyboard, her body swayed on the padded piano bench, and the impetus of the counterpoint made my teeth vibrate thrillingly. It was all about rhythm, about the sweet cyclical singing lines that made my heart squeeze, the endless repetitive honing of a phrase. That's where I got the basics of the stroke.

I couldn't play Bach until forty years later, on the water, an oar in each hand. In a boat I found the throb I knew as a child: in the quiet solitary moments on the dark harbor before daylight, in the first sear of competitive heat. In the single shell I found my instrument, the rhythm of the stroke animating my body to move the blades, heart beating a chant of breath and exultation, shell home to the sweetest song and hardest labor I'd ever known.

Mine is not the story of a career athlete, a woman driven by a lifelong dream of racing the single shell in a World Championship. Not an account of a woman who spends years tirelessly driving herself toward the moment when she stands exhausted on the medal stand. Not the story of a woman whose quest is thwarted by disability or illness. Not a woman destined to win against all odds.

This is the story of the girl who lay under a piano all those years ago, a woman in midlife mired in a long and painful marriage, full-time mother to three small children. A woman lugging twenty extra pounds from her last baby and enough hurt and doubt to fill the cargo hold of a Suburban, her education and aspirations long since packed away in the attic, her life circumscribed by pediatrician appointments, grocery runs, and volunteer work. A woman who fell in love one early spring evening, when the last rays of sun gleamed on the riffled waters of a harbor. A woman transfixed by the sight of one tiny, fragile boat—a single shell—rhythmically working its way up the shoreline in slow, steady stokes, framed by nodding sedge grasses and egrets picking through the tidal flats.

This is the story of a woman in her forties who heard, that evening on the harbor, the calling of a passionate self she left behind. Who saw, in the vision of a shining little craft, the means to find her way back to a place where her heart could speak, her rhythms sing. It is a story of a woman filled with longing who, from that moment, sought the skill to row the most technically difficult, fiendishly unstable boat in the world; the courage to hear her truth, and face the truth of her marriage; and the strength to win, three years later, a World Masters title in the single shell. Most of all, it is the journey of a woman who rowed her way home. This is my story.

DRAWN

TO THE

RHYTHM

Chapter One

F I R S T

R A C E

That morning in June 1996 when I pushed my
tiny borrowed racing shell away from the launch
dock for the thousand-meter journey down
to the start line, I thought I might faint.
The voice shouting encouragement from shore
as I took my first strokes downstream was not my
mother calling from the knot of swim team moms,
a memory from thirty years before, but the reedy
voice of my own eleven-year-old daughter, Janie,
dressed in pale yellow overalls and a white
T-shirt, pigtails flying behind her as she ran
through the spectators along the bank of the
Hudson in downtown Albany. "Go, Mommy, go
get 'em!" The wind blew her little voice to me in gusts.
Go, Mommy. I was about to race for the first time
in thirty years, the first time since 1966, when
I had pulled on my red rubber swim cap,

adjusted my black Speedo, and crouched on the block for the start of the fifty-meter butterfly, my face expectant and upturned, a thirteen-year-old girl eager for the gun and the plunge into adolescence. Now, after the currents of adulthood, marriage, and motherhood had carried me thousands of miles from that starting block on the pool's edge, I was finally ready to put myself on the line once again, this time in a racing shell—a woman of almost forty-three with three days of lessons, a year of solitary practice, and a borrowed boat. It was the most frightening thing I'd ever done. Ever.

Rowing away from the dock that early morning in June, I felt unreal, disembodied. Like eleven years before when they had wheeled me into the operating room to give birth to my first child, Janie, by Caesarian, and I thought, You have no choice, this is going to happen whether you're brave or not, and the obstetrician had said, "You're going to feel a little pinch," which meant, "Now I'm going to stick a long needle into your spine and it's going to hurt like hell." You've chosen this, I told myself, so summon courage, take a deep breath. Race this race.

I'd first picked up an oar almost exactly a year before. In the winter after that first summer of floundering and thrashing, flipping the boat again and again like every other novice, I discovered that I was more deeply in love with rowing than anything but the sight of my newborn's face, and that something long hidden and long waiting in myself was urging—no, demanding—that I race the single shell. It was as if I were suddenly locked onto a course newly discovered but eternally fated for me, like a Greek hero setting out on the journey that will ultimately transform and define him even though he might rather stay home pressing olives. What was I thinking of, I wondered in the months leading to Albany, I who had convinced myself that the small contentments of getting my library books in on time and keeping my roses free of Japanese beetles were reward enough in a life that had become far tighter and smaller than I could bear to recognize?

With my three lessons, a year of reading all the books on rowing my reference librarian could get me from the New York State interlibrary loan system, and a season of earnestly hacking at the water of my home harbor, my skill and balance were still marginal: for me, a good workout was one in which I didn't capsize or run broadside into a moored fishing boat. Yet I was planning to race a twenty-seven-foot, ten-inch-wide boat up a swollen river littered with half-submerged logs and old tires, threading my way past safety buoys marking a course between a pair of massive railroad pylons. Where was the ancient robed chorus telling me: "Go back! Go back before it's too late"?

As I rowed to the start and began to feel the ticking of minutes and seconds accelerating toward the moment in which I would sit in that fragile boat on the line, I told myself that the task was to stay upright and cross the finish. That's it. Beating someone was, if not the last thing on my mind, at least far down on the list. Higher was fear of the infamous physical pain of racing a shell and a nagging conviction that if I'd never been brave enough to stand up for myself at home, how could I have what it took to go the distance on a race course.

And there were other very real worries: muscle failure at fifteen hundred meters from maintaining a death hold on the oar handles; broken bones and boat damage from rowing full-steam into a monumentally unyielding stone bridge abutment; or, finally, "catching a crab," the term for feathering an oar too soon, flipping the boat, and catapulting the rower into icy waters.

When I look back, I remember with an ache how ardent, earnest, and frighteningly incompetent I was in Albany.

The day before the race, Janie and I drove down to the boathouse on Lloyd Harbor, Long Island, and loaded *S4*, the sturdy fiberglass, club-owned boat which was my daily companion, on top of our faded blue station wagon. We strapped down the old-fashioned macon oars with blue bungee cords, and taped a red bandana as tail flag on *S4*'s tapered stern. When the moment came an hour later to kiss the baby and eight-year-old goodbye, I felt like a woman in the first stages of labor, wanting to cry, *No, this is too frightening, there's too much risk, I want everything to stay as it is.* But Janie, who was excited about her new responsibilities as my support crew, had a firm grip.

"Okay, Mommy," she said as we stood next to the car in the driveway of our suburban house on Long Island. "I've got enough Diet Coke and Janet Jackson tapes for about three hours. And I've got my retainer and my overnight bag." I looked at her overnight bag. It was pink and had a picture of ballet slippers on the front. "You have all your stuff, Mom? Your racing shirt, the tape for your knees?" I did. So I gave the baby-sitter the emergency numbers one last time, then we were off: past the library, past the elementary school, past the mouth of our safe little harbor.

Just past the New Hyde Park exit on the Long Island Expressway, when we had been underway about twenty minutes, I burst into tears. It seemed I had waited for this moment since standing on the starting block on the edge of the pool. Adolescence and adulthood had been a confusion of sorrow and self-doubt, yet here I was, finally, my red tail flag flying, my bow jauntily plowing through the humid June afternoon. Janie opened a can of Cherry Coke, handed it to me, and put on a tape. We opened the windows and sang at the top of our lungs. Silly things—old Beatles, Janet Jackson. We sang and sang, laughed and laughed, lost our way past the George Washington Bridge and decided to cut from the Palisades Parkway to the New York Thruway on a two-lane road.

Suddenly we found ourselves in a quiet, luminously verdant forest in the New Jersey countryside. The two-lane road we chose led us winding up steep hillsides and down into misted green vales, a mythic landscape suspended between city and highway. Janie and I fell silent with the mystery of it, *S4* still tracing its course over our heads. It was like a dream, as if we had been blessed by the Good Witch of the East and were following a yellow brick road to some long-sought home of the heart, a path sometimes placid, sometimes frightening, sometimes ethereally beautiful.

Then suddenly there was the thruway—the toll booths, the crowded rest stops with their Cinnabon shops and McDonald's. We stopped to come to terms with all that Cherry Coke. When we got back on the highway, we decided Janie's job was to watch for tour buses and tractor trailers bearing down from behind. With grilles high enough to hit the nearly invisible stern of our tiny boat, a careless bus could end our trip before I ever got a chance to throw up at the start line. Janie was to yell, "Move it, Mommy!" if a truck threatened S4, and I was to switch lanes, carefully of course, to get the boat out of harm's way. My young crew tenderly and cheerfully cared for both sculler and boat mile after mile up the Hudson. I think she welcomed the temporary reversal in roles. Then we got lost in Albany.

By the time we saw the day's last glow glinting off the buildings of Albany, it was almost eight o'clock. I missed the exit for the regatta venue, doubled back, and missed it again. Finally we saw a truck towing a trailerful of eight-man shells, and followed it. Sure enough, it led us off the freeway, wound around until it pulled up under an overpass. We had arrived.

I'd never seen so many boats in one place. Trailers and vans from St. Paul's, Exeter, and community rowing programs from across the Northeast, and cars of every size with boat racks—some jury-rigged and homemade, some sleek aluminum—had all followed a well-worn path from regatta to regatta. There were scores of rowers of all ages, laughing and tossing wrenches to one another as they applied riggers to hulls, swearing at the rigger nuts that jumped out of their hands and found the nearest deep crack in the tarmac; everywhere were wrenches, seats, shoes, sweatshirts thrown carelessly over piles of duffels and mounds of equipment. Everyone knew someone. They greeted each other, comparing notes on the trip and talking about the last regatta.

Well, I knew Jeff Schaeffer, my one friend from the rowing club at home, but he wasn't there, and I knew Mary, the regatta secretary, from my last-minute phone call asking for directions, but she wasn't there either. So I looked for someone in charge and found Scott, a coach in the local community rowing program. Scott knew the ropes. "Just put your boat over there," he said, "and make sure you leave plenty of time in the morning to make the meeting and get your bow number." Then he noticed that my bow had no clip for the plastic card that allows race officials to identify the boats on the course. "Looks like this boat has never been raced." If I'd known more, I would have said that at thirty-eight pounds, it was never meant to be. "Grab me in the morning and we can put your number on with duct tape."

I saw the temporary launch docks, inflated black plastic squares linked into a grid, and thought I was going to be sick. Vaguely I heard Scott saying, "You'll launch from there, then cross the course when the officials tell you it's clear. After that, row way down by those willows, see down there? That's where the two thousand meters start. After they get you going, you have to keep an eye out for that railroad bridge where it gets a little tricky. The course turns there, and you need to line up for the turn, and for your new course. Can't see the finish from here, but you'll know you're there when you see the big orange buoys. You'll be fine." I wouldn't be fine. I would flip at the start or crash into the bridge or die of a heart attack. Scott waved goodbye and turned away. Then he turned back. "Don't worry, I'm going to be in one of the chase boats and I'll make sure you stay on course. Watch for me."

Janie and I took *S4* off the top of the car, tucked it in on its borrowed slings for the night, making sure the oars were securely stowed under the hull. It was almost eight-thirty, twelve hours before race time.

We found a grocery store and bought sandwiches for dinner,

then followed Mary's directions to the motel in downtown Albany. Night had fallen when we pulled into the empty lot. We parked under the green glow of fluorescent lights, startling ourselves with the echo of the car doors in the chill air. My little overnight bag felt insubstantial; I felt insubstantial. We checked in and found our room, ridiculously elated by our own key, our door, our bathroom, as if we had never been in a hotel before. We loved our little Camay soaps and Prell shampoos, far more thrilling than the French stuff at the Ritz-Carlton where I had been with my husband on business trips. This was *our* adventure, Janie's and mine. We watched TV and ate our sandwiches. At ten-thirty I switched off the light. Ten hours to go.

I tossed that night between the stiff motel sheets dreaming of a race, my little girl sleeping fitfully next to me. I dreamed of pain and wild water, of powerful ocean swells rolling down the Hudson, of passing the dark stones of a bridge tower, span impossibly high and arching over my tiny craft. In my dream I was a grown woman, and I was a little girl. In my dream there was no turning back. I woke. If I could survive the waves and the pain—eight excruciating minutes— if I could pass through the bridge and cross the finish, some part of me knew I would never be the same.

It was time.

Mercifully the air was still, the water flat when we arrived at the river. No whitecaps this morning. I found Jeff tightening down the riggers of his blue Van Dusen single. He was wearing stretched-out Lycra rowing shorts and a Cambridge Boat Club racing jersey. "Watch out for this woman from New Hampshire," he said. "She's state champion and she's pretty good. I think she'll give you some trouble." Jeff was quite cheerful, clearly feeling that he was giving me encouraging and useful race information. Give me some trouble? I expected trouble from everyone and everything. The New Hampshire state champion was the least of my challenges.

I checked out the situation. Everyone had an official racing out-fit, a stretchy one-piece suit that looked aerodynamic and showed the rippling muscles of the wearer. Mine consisted of the shorts and T-shirt I used to wear to my daily aerobics class at the Presbyterian church in Locust Valley, plus a Sagamore Rowing Association jer-sey—sized men's extra large because that was all the club secretary had in the wadded-up plastic bag pulled from the recesses of his trunk. I had tucked the jersey into my shorts to keep the tail of it from becoming entangled in the little wheels under my rolling seat (a not uncommon occurrence that quickly brings the boat to a stand-still), making for a bulk that was clearly not at all aerodynamic.

And then there were the boats. The single shells I saw were exquisitely beautiful. *S4* was plucky but outclassed. These were light and stiff, some as light as twenty-eight pounds, ten pounds lighter than *S4*. They tapered to almost nothing in bow and stern. All had lightweight track shoes bolted to the footboards to connect rower to hull, unlike *S4*, which had simple footpads with a velcro strap over the rower's toes to hold the feet in place. These boats were high-modulus carbon, the cutting edge of composite material, though a few were exquisitely wrought of mahogany, stiff and strong, yet with a hull thickness of only a sixteenth of an inch. Step carelessly into such a varnished masterpiece and your foot will crash through, sending a thing of great beauty to the bottom of the river.

I heard the dockmaster calling my race for launching. "Masters Women to the dock, please." There was the fierce-looking woman from New Hampshire. She had blond, cropped hair and wore a sea-soned game face. Lord, I thought, she's just picked up her boat, bal-anced it on her head, then picked up her oars at the same time. I couldn't even get my boat on my head, and I'd never seen this partic-ular maneuver. Down to the dock she went, her fingers barely touch-ing the boat overhead. The other women in my category, Masters Women, followed suit. In the afternoon I would do the novice race for scullers in their first competitive season, but Masters Women, women over twenty-six years old, were racing this morning. One month shy of forty-three, I was undeniably a Masters Woman, and I would race my race.

So I slung *S4* on one hip as usual and walked to the water, and Janie trailed behind me in her overalls, juggling my oars. I approached the edge of the dock, feeling with my toes for the edge as I had been taught, and set the boat in the water, locking the oars in the oarlocks and securing them. Backward. This was not quite as amateur a mistake as it seemed, though oars secured backward render a boat utterly unrowable. Since that morning I have heard of four or five Olympic- and World-class rowers who have done the same on the morning of the big race, corrected the mistake, then gone on to glory, so I was in good company. The trick is to discover it before pushing off from the dock and making a fool of yourself in front of a crowd. I rotated the oarlocks and snugged down their locking gates once more.

The other women pushed off from the dock. I noted they were all doing warm-up exercises—pause drills, little choppy drills, hands-in-tiny-ellipsis drills. The sight of all these professional-looking women metronomically picking the water with short strokes precise as the moves of synchronized swimmers left me weak with intimidation. I didn't know any drills; all I knew was what I'd learned from my few lessons, from watching the birds skimming Lloyd Harbor morning after morning, and from all those books on rowing. All I could do was row. Just row.

So I kissed Janie, lowered myself into *S4*, lashed down my toes with the velcro straps, took up the oar handles in hands callused from all the other mornings on the water, and pushed off, following the Masters Women across the lanes, across the river. But this morning was not like all the other mornings. This was a morning of crossing over. Go, Mommy, go get 'em.

Slowly, I rowed downriver past willows and an old shopping cart. I could see the congregation of boats near the start—the shells in the race before mine being aligned for the flag and the officials' launches milling, waiting for the signal to follow the competitors and guide them if they strayed off course. There were the stake boats— small skiffs moored at the start line, one per lane. Each had an attendant who reached out to align the shell's stern according to instructions from an official onshore, holding it in position until the start signal. I rowed past the start line and circled in the warm-up area. No one talked this morning. Jeff had told me to be sure and warm up— take a series of hard strokes to loosen my muscles, and listen for the starter to announce my race over the megaphone.

"Masters Women to the line, please." I didn't know whether to laugh, or cry, or throw up. My stomach felt as if I were in an elevator heading down. I rowed upriver just past the start line, then backed slowly down to the stake boat in Lane 3, placing *S4*'s stern in the waiting hands of the attendant. This wasn't as easy as it sounds. I did a damned good job, though, because one of the books I'd read talked about how many people train hard to race but forget that they can't race if they don't learn to row backward to the stake boats. In the month before Albany I had taught myself how to back the boat, finishing every session with a few minutes of practice aiming my stern at pieces of flotsam in Lloyd Harbor—a broken chunk of Styrofoam, a fisherman's float adrift, a half-submerged Coke can. By June 8, I had it down cold. (I have learned since that my backing technique, while perfectly effective, is, to this day, dead wrong.)

Finally we were at the line. I'd read about what happens next. An official with a megaphone yells instructions at the stake boats: "Lane 3, out one foot. Lane 6, bring it back a few inches. Lane 2, hold." We sat quietly in our boats while the stake boat attendants shifted our bows into a perfect line. I twisted around, sighting up the lane, orienting my bow to a target landmark in the distance just east of the Albany-side bridge pylon, then looked back past my stern to find a tree or building on which I could take a bearing. If at that stage I'm true in my lane, the landmark behind me becomes the point on which I will focus to stay on course the first half of the race.

The starter began calling out the lineup. I rolled up my tracks to a point of three-quarters compression—legs bent not quite as far as if I were taking a normal stroke—and squared my blades perpendicular to the water where they would lever the boat as soon as I applied pressure. "Lane 1, Cambridge Boat Club. Lane 2, Unaffiliated. Lane 3, Sagamore. Lane 4 . . . " The starter read the club names for all six lanes. Each of us nodded nearly imperceptibly when her name was called. Then there was a pregnant pause.

The air was still, boats were still, birds were still, surely the fish swimming in the dark river below my hull were still and suspended, feathering lightly with their fins. Waiting. The arms reaching out from the stake boats holding my stern were absolutely still, the whole world was still, stopped on its axis for a long moment. Even my heart, which had been banging for days, was still. "ATTENTION . . . GO!" The flag dropped and nothing was still anymore.

An experienced racer jumps off the line by "lifting" her boat with four short, swift strokes, taking care not to rip the water with her blades, coaxing the boat to speed. I didn't do that. It wasn't that I didn't know the theory; I didn't have the technique to execute it. After the start strokes, most racers take ten fast hard strokes—called a *power ten*—before settling into a rhythm and pressure they can maintain for most of the more than two hundred strokes of the race. I tried a power ten, but to apply strength effectively in a shell requires a seasoned technique, so I wallowed, frantic and off balance. I reminded myself—*Row, just row.* So I rowed.

Within thirty strokes, everything was on fire and I was off-course. My hands, arms, and shoulders were aflame from gripping the oars and hauling each stroke that morning in Albany: digging my oars deep into the water, lunging with my back, yanking with my arms rather than pressing with my legs. The hair on my forearms should have looked singed; my arms were ablaze. My lungs were bellows for a heat centering in my chest, legs, and back that seemed about to combust. Oh my God, the pain. How did I get myself into this? When would it be over? Why have I chosen this? As my sister Annie, mother of three teenagers, says with great inflection, *"Duh!* Like being in labor, the reward comes at the end, that's why."

One of the challenges of rowing, in addition to mastering an extraordinarily complex technique, is that you're moving forward at a pretty smart clip, about as fast as a well-trained runner, while facing backward. This makes it hard to see where you're going, and if you fear smashing into a bridge pylon, your fear is magnified by the fact that you can't see the pylon as the gap between you and it rapidly narrows. By the time I'd rowed a thousand meters, I realized I'd lost track of the point on the shore keeping me straight and *S4* was zigging and zagging toward the bridge. The chase boat parked itself behind me. Scott waved his flag to starboard, then to port, then to starboard. My breath tore in my throat and every part of me silently howled. The arches approached and some sixth sense made my back prickle with the weight of the railroad bridge bearing down on my bow. There on starboard was the first buoy marking the entrance to the bridge zone; there was another, behind me now, tugging at its anchor in the wake. The water was flat and gray, sky heavy with clouds. There were no shadows. Out of the corner of my eye I saw the dark bulk of the bridge towering over my back. Scott snapped the flag to starboard; I pulled hard with my right hand. He snapped it vertical; I evened out. I must be there now, I thought, I must be there . . .

Then I slipped through. Easy, easy, the stones of the old bridge so close, the grain and mortar and soot of the stones right there, next to me vivid as my dream, slipping me through to the other side after all the pain and fear. The bridge arched overhead, dark and rusted. It enfolded me, then released me from its embrace as I passed through, my wake a little wrinkled, shining tether holding me to the other side, then fading into the waters of the Hudson, gone.

I came back into the light and heard my daughter's voice drift across the water: "Go Mom, go, go, go!" Scott waved me onto the new course, setting me true for the finish. Almost there.

M_y wrists and forearms no longer burned; they were leaden. I knew this feeling. Years ago, rock climbing, I was halfway up a pitch when I realized there was nowhere to go. I clung indecisive for a minute, then understood that something was happening with my hands. They were simply opening up and letting go. This can't happen, I thought. Concentrate and they will hold. But they didn't hold; they'd had enough and contracting the muscles wasn't a matter of will. I fell, luckily not far. Muscle failure is the body's way of saying, I'm not going to play anymore. At eighteen hundred meters, my forearms and wrists had had enough. I could no longer feather the oars; my wrists wouldn't execute the "roll out, roll in" necessary to turn the blades on each stroke. Two hundred meters to go. All I can do is make my body go through the motions one stroke at a time without feathering, blades dragging across the water.

Out of my chest came organ pipe noises, the sound lathered horses make when they are galloped over miles of prairie. A musical wheeze of extreme exertion, this was a sound I didn't know humans could make. I narrowed on a hundred meters.

And then the chase boat, knowing I was on course for the finish now, tired of waiting for me. Chase boats are supposed to follow the slowest competitor, their function not only to guide but in some sense to mop up the last loose pieces of the race. Perhaps this chase boat had never been challenged by a racer with my breathtaking lack of speed. I had lost sight of the other participants in my race within twenty seconds of the start and all must have long since finished by now. The chase boat passed, leaving a rolling wake behind it, a wake quartering swiftly toward my port side. It arrived and what precarious balance I possessed was overwhelmed. Tossed in the rolling swells, first my port oar caught, then popped out, snapping me to starboard where my left blade buried. My heart rate, already well into red-line, jumped. This is it, I'm going over.

Then I heard a calm voice. "No, not after all I've been through," said an authoritative voice I didn't recognize, had never heard before. This sounded like a warrior, a tough teacher, a firm parent looking a child right in the eye. Issuing from my own head was the cool, decisive tone of someone unquestionably in charge, someone with whom there will be no argument, no but, but . . . I heard it again, clear and strong. "I will not flip this boat, no. Not today. I will finish this race."

I feathered the port oar with a wrist that had told me a hundred meters ago it was done for, and braced while I pulled up the starboard blade. Fifteen strokes to go. There were the orange buoys, right there. There was the chase boat, idling, the other competitors milling, orienting themselves for the row downriver to the dock. Five strokes. There was the bridge far behind me. Two more strokes. Here was the line. Here. I crossed and nothing would ever be the same. I would never be the same. I had finished dead last in the Womens Masters Single race at the Empire State Regatta. Twenty-six months later I would cross a different finish line on a different body of water in a different city to win a World Masters title in the single shell; yet that moment in Albany in 1996 remains the greatest triumph of my life.

Chapter Two

BEING

A FISH

I love to watch my daughter move. Janie
is a teenager now, and sometimes she walks with
an elegant, slouchy, well-oiled grace, pleased with
the way her new jeans ride or the height she
commands with those funny chunky shoes.
She cocks her hip as she takes an
eternity to choose which of the narrow
bracelets on her dresser will best accessorize her
new gray T-shirt. In the morning she gets into my
little car, late again, folding her impossibly long
legs, juggling a bowl of oatmeal with brown
sugar and a backpack that must weigh
sixty pounds. When I pick her up at school
in the afternoon, I watch her break away from her
friends and stride to the car, swinging her hair out
of her eyes. No one could ever mistake her for a
twelve-year-old. She has the tall, narrow

look of adolescent girls, all height and no volume—like the reflection in a funhouse mirror, a look that lasts only a year or two before breasts and hips fill and proportions change. As a mother, I've watched Janie and her friends, watched them watch themselves, watched the surreptitious attention with which they watch others watch them. They are like sixteen-year-olds learning to drive—aware that a hitherto inaccessible source of power is suddenly at their command. Elated, self-conscious, they control it in fits and starts, popping the clutch, racing the engine, slamming on the brakes. Their sexuality is exciting to them, but the elemental energy released at the touch of the accelerator is unnerving.

In August, my daughter asked me if she could join the community crew program here in Boston this fall. Now it is September and last week, rowing upstream in my single in the late afternoon, I saw Janie in the bow seat of an eight-man shell, my child a lovely, willowy creature, blond hair pulled tight in a knot, a teenager long out of the yellow overalls she wore in Albany. She didn't see me. She had told me I have to stay away: "Don't you dare act like you know me." So when our boats passed just downstream of the North Beacon Street Bridge, I gave no sign that we were connected, just one boat passing another. How beautiful she looked, rhythmically feathering the heavy oar, suspending her narrow back from long, slender arms as she drove through the stroke, thighs pressed down as the blade released the water. She was focused on her task and didn't see me. Later, I asked her about her workout. What did you like best? "I love how the oar goes *thunk ssshhh*," she said, stroking the air with her hands, describing the feathering of the oar when it is free of the water, the skimming arc it makes as it reaches back to enter once again. "I like how it feels in my hands. I like how it sounds."

When I was Janie's age, I was a fish. I loved to swim, loved the feel of water on my body, my hands working instinctually, like the fins of a trout, propelling me to the deep end, and when I raced, propelling me to the finish. I was comfortable in the water, comfortable with my body and the way it felt, pleased with how it looked. The resistance of the water was smooth and sure on my fingers, the twist and torque of my body as I swam the hundred-meter freestyle a pleasing engagement with a medium both elusive and resistant. Rhythmically stroking down the black lines on the bottom of the pool, burying my head under the water and throwing my arm forward to catch it with my fingertips, I was never sure if I was holding the water or it was holding me.

I loved to race. Sprinting allowed me to feel the explosion of all the will in my hundred-and-five-pound, five-foot-five frame. Butterfly, freestyle, or backstroke—it was the intensity of racing that was exciting. In competition I could find a new level of speed, feel a joyful fierceness in pitting myself against my competitors. At thirteen, I loved the intensity of the battle and the sensuality of sport. Water and speed were passionately mixed for me in a current of joy and welling of authority. This was my medium, my arena—the chlorinated water of a twenty-five-yard cement pool in Boulder, Colorado.

Thirteen was my last year on swim team. Everything changed when I was thirteen. Everything. The body that played in the woods and waded up the creek after school every day was changing. I grew four inches in one year and, just like my friends, asked my parents for a garter belt and nylons (shade "suntan") for Christmas. All of us had trepidation and excitement about our new bodies. I can hear the same now in my own daughter's voice when she asks me if the slinky shirt looks better than the loose one. We worried about what the Kotex pamphlet on menstruation our gym teacher handed out called "Becoming a Woman." Getting a period was proof one had reached the glory of womanhood; it also seemed scary and icky. One day the school nurse called a special meeting for all the girls. We saw a film about the ripening of the egg, the sponginess of the uterine walls, the sloughing of the cells. A knowledge of all that, and of the physical acts we would experience someday, acts of which we now had a pretty graphic notion, seemed scary and icky too. One day in the locker room a girl who had already "become a woman" showed us her sanitary pad. There it was. We looked at the blood and looked at each other. This was not theory, this was real, and in considerable contrast to the pink and powdery-smelling Kotex pamphlet with the picture of a smiling girl in a sweater set.

When I was growing up, my sister Caroline had the corner on femininity. Two years older than me, Caroline seemed hugely glamorous. Caroline *was* hugely glamorous. She knew how to do things with Vaseline I'd never dreamed of. The gleam of her lips and the highlights under her brows, just like real makeup, dazzled me. I had spent most after-school hours building forts and damming the creek with sticks, but as I approached thirteen I found myself in the bathroom gazing at my face in the mirror and examining Caroline's mysterious nostrums—Dippity Do to form her hair in a perfect flip, purple scruffing mud to free her complexion of blemish-producing bacteria, cotton balls and astringent in tall pink bottles to liberate her forehead of dulling grease. Caroline's mysterious pharmacopeia of beauty products posed an increasingly irresistible allure. Part of me longed to buff and tweeze, the other to leap back into the water, a slippery shining fish. The bumpy road toward womanhood in early adolescence was confusing and exciting. It also turned out to be perilous.

When I was thirteen, a man in his fifties who had been a loving presence in my life for seven years, a rancher who let me help him fix the gate and herd the horses, who taught me how to tighten a girth and drive a car (long before I could ever get a license), who for years had tucked me in with a goodnight kiss every night I slept on the hard bunk in the Lodge during weekend visits, started putting his tongue in my mouth and his hand on my small, new breasts. Unlike my father, a man for whom daughters were an alien species to be viewed warily, this man didn't mind girls at all. On autumn weekends he drove my friends and me up the mountain to his ranch, a summer and autumn weekend camp for children, to ride horses and build campfires.

As I turned eleven, then twelve, I was delighted by the rancher's increasing willingness to let me hang out with him and do special jobs while my friends braided lariats up on the big porch. He let me help him fix the hinge on the barn door, the broken strand in the barbed-wire fence. I held the drill, the pliers and the screwdrivers, and handed them to him one by one as he asked for them. I remember the look of his hands as he twisted the wire. I was always willing to get up at dawn to go out in the car with him, just the two of us, to round up the horses which had been trained to lope to the barn for hay at the sound of the car horn. He told me to sit close and hold the steering wheel, honking the horn as we careened over the bumpy pasture. He told me that at this rate I would soon qualify as a "wrangler," an honor usually reserved for much older campers.

I was important; I was useful. In the evenings he would build a fire in the big stone fireplace of the Lodge and hold me close on his lap. I remember the roughness of his whiskers and the flicker of the firelight on the unpeeled logs and dark windows of the big room. Under my hand I could feel the softness of his plaid flannel shirt and his heart beating. "Pretty soon you'll be too big for my lap," he said one night, holding me closer. Here was a fatherly man who liked to spend time with me, a man who wanted to hold me safe and dear.

I was starved for a father who liked me, who liked to be with me. While my own father has become very loving and attentive to me and my sisters as adults, in those days he seemed resentful of us, particularly of our inconvenient and unavoidable femaleness. Being together in an easy, intimate, relaxed way was not part of our experience of each other in my childhood, so to sit on the rancher's lap, to ride next to him in the front seat of his old white Chevy station wagon, was food and drink to me. I grew full and happy on his attention and interest. I loved him.

As an adult, I look back and think what a powerfully affirming influence this man could have been if he had been able to control himself. In him I could have had a father who demonstrated with his words and his attention my likeability and value. A father who could have told me fondly, "What a young lady you're getting to be," and thrilled me with his recognition of my new femininity, while putting increasing and appropriate physical distance between us. The year I became a teenager he was everything my father wasn't, and, unfortunately, more.

There are no lurid details. There was no penetration, no body fluids, no frightening first encounters with stiff flesh. The violation lay not in the degree of what he did, which was mild in comparison to what other women have told me of their experiences, but in my unequivocal knowledge that what was happening felt very, very wrong and very, very bad. I yearned to round up the horses with him, but rounding up the horses began to involve a hand on my thigh to steady me, a kiss to reward me. I didn't know what to do about his hard wet tongue and callused hands. There were nights when I lay in the dark on my bunk and he came in to say goodnight, his breath close. I remember his smells—his pipe tobacco, his hair tonic. Remember mine—the mothball smell of my cloth sleeping bag from Sears and the sweetness of my lotion, "Bluegrass," a castoff from my grandmother's travel case. No one must know what he did because I would be taken away from him; but I wanted him to stop.

I was frozen with confusion and panic. The confident internal voice that had always guided me was choked in my throat by a lump so large I felt I could hardly breathe. I knew right from wrong, and this was wrong, but I was powerless to make a decision or take any action. I endured his tongue and his hands with a frozen, silent paralysis, a voice inside pleading, "Run, run, run!" But there was no run, run, running, and finally I stopped listening. The voice inside me became mute; there was no answer, no action. Only numbness.

Then, on a spring afternoon as we were getting ready to drive from his house in Boulder to the ranch to feed the horses, his wife walked into the kitchen just as he was kissing me. I saw over his shoulder that she had seen. She waited until he picked up a box of groceries and walked out the back door, waited until his footsteps sounded on the back steps, then she cried my name. I couldn't move. She crossed the kitchen and took my shoulders in her hands, holding them tightly. The face I saw was urgent and frantic, not angry. She was afraid. Looking back now, I know she must have caught him touching other young girls, and I remember that she always slept in her own cabin down the road, almost out of sight. "Don't let him ever touch you again. Please, Sara. Never again. Don't let him touch you and don't tell anyone. Never. Never." It was as much her fear as her words that made the wrongness of it real. I felt struck by a blow. My ears roared and my vision darkened. I thought I might fall, or dissolve, or simply end.

That's all. She didn't tell me what to do next, didn't offer to drive me home. When you break an arm or a leg, sometimes you know how terrible your injury is not so much from the pain as from the bizarre symptoms of shock—the numbness, shaking hands, inability to breathe. I knew something inside me felt permanently damaged—a nerve cut, a bone shattered. To spend another moment near him was inconceivable; yet I made myself walk out the back door and down the steps to where he was leaning against the car, watching me and waiting. I made myself look at him and say I couldn't go to the ranch after all, that I had to get home to do my homework. Then I turned and walked up the street, walked home. I was thirteen years old.

I never saw him again. His wife called me at school a few days later, getting me out of English class to come to the phone in the office of the junior high where I was in eighth grade. She wanted to make sure I hadn't told my parents and made me promise again that I would never tell anyone. Never. Never. I kept my promise until I was in my late twenties, when I made the terrible mistake of telling my soon-to-be husband in a tender moment since full disclosure seemed a measure of love. I asked my parents if I could go away to boarding school that fall—even being in the same town as him felt unbearable—and so within a few months was bereft of both the surrogate father from whom I had torn myself and the mother whose love and shelter I desperately needed. When I was in my late twenties, I heard he died.

All these years later, when I think of him at all, I think unaccountably of a night months before the last time I saw him, a night when he walked into the Girls' Bathroom dripping blood from a palm he'd cut to the bone mending bridles with a utility knife. The other girls and I in our Lanz flannel nighties were breathless with horror and excitement. There was something deliciously dangerous about his invasion of our female territory and bedtime rituals—the curlers and sanitary pads. He dripped blood on our floor and filled our sink with bloody water. He didn't wince. He didn't cry. He was so brave.

I could weep.

I've read recently that as many as one in three women experience sexual abuse as children. What happens to those women? What happened to me was that I felt a terrible longing and shame, and an aching sense of loss. I had lost a father I loved, and the self-inflicted surgical excision of him—the turning and walking away—did nothing to mitigate my need to be loved and accepted. Yet my longings were imbued with the shame of what had happened and the certainty that it was my fault, a certainty that, because I never told anyone, became powerfully etched.

Less clear to me, but ultimately far more destructive, was the loss of my own sense of sureness and goodness—my "rightness" in the world. There's a perception that many women who suffer what I did are crippled in relationships because of a loss of trust in men. For me, and I suspect for other women as well, the "nerve cut, bone shattered" is something far greater: the loss of trust in self. The part of me that had always charged forward confidently was stilled, the voice that spoke my feelings became tentative and muffled, the part of me that trusted that voice unsure.

And so it was that I gained a lasting legacy of uncertainty about my heart, which had betrayed me in its need for this man's love, and my body, which, in its metamorphosis from child to woman, had transformed him from father to lover, had "made him lose control." The sweetness and excitement of adolescence, of emerging into life as an individual and as a young woman, were cut short. I look back on a photograph taken that spring at the ranch of me holding the halter rope of a raw new colt and see a girl with ridiculously long skinny legs, ankles that look like they couldn't support a bird, and high pointy little breasts, pushed into shallow cones by a "training bra"—so thrilling to a thirteen-year-old. Both girl and foal look shaky, tentative.

The gawky body, so fierce and graceful in the water, so mysteriously and increasingly female, became an instrument of betrayal and sorrow. As I continued to grow, the mirror accused me daily of becoming more and more the girl whose femininity corrupted the love she needed most. How could I allow myself to revel in this tall frame with its bosom and hips? Confusion and shame sapped my power where before I had stroked, twisting and aggressive through fifty meters, through seventy-five. The joy of riding a horse bareback down the back pasture became muted. It was as if the exuberance—the sheer pleasure in how my body looked, in inhabiting myself—were submerged, a deep underground current still powerful and coursing but invisible, inaudible, unsuited to the light of day. My desire to propel myself—into love, off the start block into the pool, across the creek—was tainted and dangerous.

Even my voice in the world became dim. I was less able to *say* my mind because I was less able to *know* my mind. I no longer trusted my own senses, no longer had a sure sense of who I was, what I felt, how I existed in relation to others. Some of these issues plague every adolescent, but because of what had happened to me, they cut short for me the unfolding of my new womanhood. My race was over before it had begun.

I used to think I married the man I did because of a need to punish myself. I no longer think so. I married him because I couldn't hear and understand the voice of my intuition. I met him when I was in my late twenties, he in his late thirties. He was bright yet also seemed brittle. So, while I was dazzled by his brains, the woman in me responded to his vulnerability.

During our quick courtship, I could hear a voice inside me trying to tell me something when I noticed the condescending and dismissive tone he used with his mother on the phone. Or when he talked about how women get what they want by being "terrorists," manipulators who leverage against a man's desire. Or when he spoke with bitterness of his first wife, who had left him three years before. But if my heart's voice was urgent, it was also distant, indistinct, as if I were calmly paddling toward the lip of a dam while someone was calling to me with a desperate warning from the far shore, just out of earshot.

Here standing in front of me, speaking clearly in a beautiful voice, was a man in a handsome blue suit and a face full of longing. A man who said he wanted me, needed me, that I was the one. A man clever, funny, wanting to build a family and an empire together. I married him because I couldn't hear the voice that was screaming, "*Stop! Look! Listen!*"

Soon I found I had married a man who desired me but who seemed viscerally afraid that I, that any woman, would leave him. If some part of him needed to control, controlling me was easy: I would never get away as long as he could convince me that as a woman I was, by definition, both flawed and deeply in his debt, for in the magnitude of his love, he would care for me in spite of my shortcomings. It was child's play. His fear of femininity, reflected in what he said, how he spoke, meshed with my own. In awful irony, the need I sensed in him kept me safe from my own ambivalence about releasing the powerful physical passions still very much present under what soon became an excruciatingly conventional exterior.

Yet as I passed thirty-five, then forty, I found that beneath the pearl earrings and Talbot's dresses, the story of my loss, and the possibility of redemption, still expressed itself in my inner life like a quiet heartbeat. In the rhythms of my nightly dreams and in the books I read to my children at bedtime were recurring tales of expulsion from the Garden and the hope of attaining, if not a state of original innocence, at least an ability to express the welling of passionate energy, scribe the lilt and line of grace. Of finding in adult life my own version of the passion I had seen in my mother, swaying on the padded piano bench to her fugues and toccatas every afternoon when I was a child.

As the mother of three small children, I rarely found the time to read "grown-up" literature, but the dreamlike quality of the children's stories I read nightly by the light of the cowboy lamp next to my son's bed spoke, if not to my intellectual, certainly to my emotional needs.

In reading these stories, I rediscovered many that echoed my own stifled longing: stories of a fall from grace; of exile from a natural rhythmic, expressive state; of the misery of having been severed from one's deepest source of vitality and wisdom. I yearned for each character to culminate her odyssey through the landscape of sorrow and loss by arriving, finally, in a kingdom where she finds and reclaims her goodness.

I sometimes found myself weeping over *The Little House* or *The Secret Garden*. But *The Little Mermaid* (not the Disney movie, which I have not seen, but the Hans Christian Andersen story) captivated me. My heart broke as a child, and broke again as a woman, over the girl who, in her need for love, turns away from her own kingdom, the watery home in which she experiences the joy of her powerful tail and the beauty of her hair fanned out in the current, and trades her birthright for legs.

Mute as she was, the Little Mermaid spoke to me again and again. Her haunting little face peered at me in dreams, scales flashed through the no-man's-land between sleeping and waking. When I swam in the ocean on summer mornings, I sometimes imagined she might rise next to me, stroking up from the deep with her undulating tail. I remembered from the story her watery palace, with its mussel-shell roof rhythmically opening and closing in the current, fishes darting in and out through the amber windows. Remembered her looking up at night through the dark water from her sea-floor palace to the world of men.

But how many haunting little faces there are in the waves—the face of every young woman who, in her relationship with a man, even a Prince, has relinquished the authority of her voice and body, abdicated the power of her own instinct and experience. For her, for the Little Mermaid, and for me, "Becoming a Woman" meant a bloody and apparently irreversible loss of sovereignty over our selfhood.

The Little Mermaid's story seems both ancient and oddly contemporary. Week after week in her watery kingdom she pines for her Prince, ignoring her garden and moping around the castle, desperate to trade her tail, source of her identity and mobility, for legs. Finally she strikes a bargain with a loathsome witch who requires that she give up her beautiful voice, "far finer than that of any human being," to gain the coveted legs that will render her suitable for the human Prince. In surely one of the most wrenching and bloody episodes ever illuminated by a child's bedside lamp, the witch cuts out the mermaid's tongue in one swift stroke, payment for a magic elixir. In an instant she loses her shimmering iridescent tail and her confident, musical voice, replaced by legs that feel with each step as if she is walking on knives.

The rest is grindingly tragic. She leaves her sea kingdom forever, robbed of the ability to speak her heart, rendered impotent by the loss of her tail, tormented by the excruciating pain necessary to pursue the relationship. Her mermaid sisters weep and tear their hair at her folly. They appear in chorus, begging her to reconsider and offering her the possibility of regaining her tail and sea kingdom inheritance; but the Little Mermaid won't listen. The Prince is ultimately unattainable, and she dies.

Recently, I reread the original tale and was discomfited to find in it considerable drivel about rosy lips and smiling, dark-lashed sapphire eyes—like the lissome heroine of a Barbara Taylor Bradford blockbuster—and an ending full of cloying sentimentality about sweet immortal souls and the necessity to "give joy" and not be "naughty and wicked" in order to advance one's place in the queue at the heavenly gates. But the story I hold in my heart is one of an adolescent girl like me, whose longing to be loved and seduction by a man's need for her leads to the loss of a joyful kingdom to which she is perfectly adapted and in which she enjoys a sense of potency. This is the Little Mermaid I remember. In the recesses of my heart, "far out in the ocean where the water is blue as the petals of the most beautiful corn-flower and clear as the purest glass," all I've ever wanted—for her and for me—is to reclaim our voices and our shining powerful tails, fan our hair in the current. Almost thirty years after my thirteenth birthday, driving along a salty harbor in the late afternoon, I discovered in the image of a single, shining sliver of a boat that, for me, it was not too late.

Chapter Three

MINE IS

TO SERVE

Although the rebirth I found in the
single shell on the race course in Albany was a
long time coming, those years were not without
compensation. I was thirty-one when Janie was
born in January 1985. The summer before,
I had bought a banged-up white rocking
chair at a garage sale. It had good long rockers,
a deep seat, and a pair of arms flared slightly and
of a perfect height to support the elbow in which
my baby's head would rest. When Janie was a
newborn, we rocked hour after hour. She
nursed herself to sleep; I watched her eyes
moving under her lids as she dreamed what I always called her "dreams of bunnies and nipples."
I loved how small and snug her room was, with
its angled ceiling and paned window looking
over the pond. I had put the rocker next

to the window so I could see the shadows of the trees and flurry of snow on the ice during the day.

Watching the flushed face of my baby greet me from her crib was a miracle. When I was seventeen, it had emerged that I was a DES daughter, one of thousands of women born in the fifties whose mothers had been given what turned out to be a dangerous hormone, diethylstilbestrol, or DES, thought at the time to prevent miscarriages, during their pregnancies. In the seventies, many of us began to discover that though our sexual function was unimpaired, our ability to conceive and bear children was.

All of us feared we might never be able to have a child. Our wombs were described by gynecologists as "precancerous," or "anomalous," or, in the words of one particularly insensitive, and as it turned out inaccurate doctor, "infantile," a verdict devastating to the ears of a teenage girl. Here was confirmation that not only was my femininity a source of sorrow and guilt, but the bleakness of those feelings was physically manifest in the possibility of actual barrenness. For years I felt that my stillborn womanhood was reflected in the very center and most feminine part of my body.

After I married in my late twenties, my friends got pregnant, grew large, went to Lamaze training, wore maternity leggings to exercise classes. I finally conceived after three years of tests and pills, lost the baby after four months, conceived again, again lost the baby. Believing I was never to have a child was confirmation of everything I knew and feared about myself. Then I conceived Janie, and after a frightening round of mid-pregnancy surgery and seven months of bed rest, she was placed in my arms. She weighed nearly nine pounds.

Janie gets very impatient with me when I go on about the wonder of her tiny fingers and toes when she was born, but they were a source of delirious excitement to me. Here at last was fulfillment as a woman—in the child of my body. I relished making corduroy jumpers at my sewing machine with Janie crowing at me from her nearby playpen, found happiness folding laundry in the sunny little living room on a late autumn afternoon with Phil Donohue interviewing a movie star on TV and Janie crawling through the pile of clean clothes. I remember one afternoon seeing her little fingers appear on the arm of the chintz sofa next to me: she'd pulled herself up for the first time. I had waited for all this so long.

Often in the middle of the night her cry called me to her warm little room under the eaves. One night, there was a full moon and a cracking cold. The moon hung over the oaks on the far hillside and the pond glowed white with ice and old snow. Winter would be over in a few weeks, but this was a late February night of the deepest chill. I picked up my daughter, warm and damp from her flannel sheet, and settled the two of us into the rocker, brushing her hair back and caressing the back of her head as I held her close. As we began to rock, lulled in the soothing groove of a beat, her crying quieted and she began to nurse. Nothing can be better than this, I thought. The radiator clicked and ticked as the furnace cycled on, the chair giving a little squeak with every rock, a comforting rhythm on a frozen winter night.

Rhythm is what being a mother is all about. A woman with young children must welcome the rhythm of daily ritual and exist "in the process," for she would go wild if she approached child-rearing as a goal-oriented activity. For one thing, nothing ever gets finished— the laundry basket makes it only halfway up the stairs because the baby has pulled over a lamp in the living room; the milk is still dripping off the edge of the table because the three-year-old is trying to pry the childproof caps off the electrical outlets with a fork. Even the groceries sometimes take two hours to get from the car to the refrigerator—the baby in the car seat wakes and cries, just as the phone rings in the kitchen, just as the plumber arrives to rout the toilet the toddler threw the bear into yesterday.

One day when my children were small, I read an article by a noted psychologist who stated that an emotionally healthy adult is one who has developed his or her (mostly his, I concluded) full capacity to Work, Love, and Play, and balances the three in a skillful juggling act. I laughed. Most mothers don't have the luxury of such juggling—or reading or meditation or anything but doing the breakfast dishes, picking up toys, and trying to get your child to hold still long enough to put her shoes on and wishing you could somehow lock them on her feet. When your children are young, they *are* your work, *are* your loves, and there *is* no time to play. Period. A mother, particularly a full-time mother (as I and many of my friends were, in a social environment on the North Shore of Long Island that was a throwback to the fifties), is plunged into an endless series of repetitive cycles. It begins the moment her baby is put in her arms on the steps of North Shore Hospital and she vainly tries to fit her into the baby seat for the first time, wondering how to get the crotch strap through the precious one-piece gown bought for the triumphant homecoming. Baby cries all the way home; exhausted mother holds fussy baby, walking with the bouncy baby-soothing step she will come to know so well, feeds baby, baby goes to sleep, and so on and so on. The rhythm of her step, of the baby's hunger, of the milestones—roll over at four months, sit at six, crawl at nine, walk at a year—are all part of a larger cycle of passing years and siblings' births.

I remember reading an article in the *New York Times Magazine* in which the author interviewed scores of women, many of them with young children, who intimated they would cut their wrists if they had to give up their jobs, no matter how menial, and stay home with toddlers. A friend of mine, a courtroom lawyer, told me with a laugh she would go berserk. To be a happy mother at home takes a special appreciation for the subtle, non-remunerative, day-to-day rewards of parenting, and a tolerance for motherhood's endless, thankless repetitive labor in lieu of a career's year-end bonus, trips to nice hotels, and opportunity for grown-up talk.

Yet I was a happy mother at home in those earliest years. I was filled with contentment from the satisfactions and security of routine and those sticky little hands in mine. I remember the mystery of my baby's ability to fall asleep for a morning nap at exactly 9:07 day after day, in strict adherence to some internal clock. I loved scraping puréed carrots off a little chin with a lamby spoon, found satisfaction in folding in a neat pile the cloth diapers fresh out of the dryer. It was all so comforting after the years of fearing I would never cup the back of a child's head in my hand.

Sometimes I think I perfected the rhythm of the rowing stroke that so moves me in the process of being a mother. I have an appreciation for doing the same thing over and over and over—thousands of times—with only infinitesimal variation. Rhythm would come to imbue my life on the river as it imbued my life as a mother, even imbued my home with its cycles of taking off the old wooden storms, putting them back on six months later, putting the garden to bed in the fall, tilling it in the spring. Like many other women, I built an empire of mortgages, station wagons on endless daily circuits, baby seats migrating to the cellar, mountains of little socks, and later, larger soccer socks traveling up and down the basement stairs in the laundry hamper; caches of old Christmas cards with the pictures of children one year older, then another—children who have also grown out of little overalls and are well on their way to having voices that crack and Nikes the size of small dinghies.

My reward was in the comfort of the rhythm itself, and the satisfaction of checking on my children every night and seeing their calm, full faces in sleep. Never had I been so useful and loved; never was my willingness to subsume myself in the lives of my children (and exist on five hours of sleep a night) so valued and important as when they were young and I was dedicated solely to their care. I experienced the cadences of motherhood as a blessing, the opportunity to nurture the fulfillment of a basic yearning and the allaying of a deep fear.

Expression of self? Freedom to explore an interest or passion? Joy in the body? These were subjects of fleeting daydreams for me and, I suspect, for many other women with small children. Most of us were far too tired by the time the dishes were done, the kitchen floor swept, the stories read, and the kisses dispensed to do anything but fall into bed with a book of which we would read maybe four pages. (For a few years I didn't even try to read books. I always owed a fine on them by the time I got to the third chapter.) Janie was followed by a son, John, when she was three, and another son, William, when she was six. Thoughts of personal freedom and expression seemed beside the point when I was changing diapers for nearly a decade. As wife to a man who worked long days, traveled frequently, and had, early on, expressed to me his policy of non-participation in parenting, I handled all the daily needs of three small children. When the baby got croup and couldn't breathe, I was the one who rushed him to the hospital. I was the one at teacher conferences, at school plays, doing volunteer work at the camp and at school. When I had difficulty quieting a baby crying in the night, I remember my husband shouting angrily from our bed, telling me to make the baby be quiet, he had to go to work in the morning and earn a living.

Even if I'd found the time, an interest out of the tight orbit of our Beach Club, or our Episcopal church, or our exclusive nursery school was out of the question. My husband had communicated to me strong feelings that I should associate only with people who had been proposed and seconded in life. One brief friendship with a woman outside this circle he quashed because, even though she'd gone to Oxford, her husband owned a shop in town. Passions of my own other than making cunning eucalyptus topiaries for our fireplace mantel were not an option. Travel was not an option, not only because getting child care was difficult, but primarily because my husband made it clear I was to stay where I belonged—at home, tending what in public he called "his children" and at home sometimes called "your science experiments," a reference to my reproductive shortcomings and all the medical intervention that had been necessary to overcome them. While the confinement in which I found myself was due in part to my job as full-time mother, it was a confinement that I came to realize was far greater than that of other women in my position. But the troubling aspects of my marriage were generally concealed under a blanket explanation—Motherhood—and for the most part I was too exhausted and too afraid to lift the corner and face what lay in the dark.

Thoughts of time for myself rarely crossed my mind. One of the few times I got to take an airplane trip by myself was the result of a rare moment of defiance. One November I arranged for the baby-sitter and told my husband I was going in two months time to visit my parents for a week. Then I bore the consequences—weeks of sarcasm about my selfishness, sullen silences. Ironically, I discovered in my first moments of freedom at La Guardia that my ability to function as a competent adult in the world had atrophied after years of marriage, like a damaged wing that had been bound tightly for too long. My journey through the check-in line was a comedy of dropped tickets and lipsticks. I forgot to put my purse on the conveyor as I went through security, forgot my flight number almost as soon as I read it on the overhead monitor, sat patiently, ticket in hand, at the wrong gate. As a nurturer, I had grown fully fleshed; as an individual, however, I felt shrunken and helpless. Nearly invisible to myself.

Then my children got a little older. As the years paraded by, my routine revolved less around diapers and mashed yellow vegetables and more around shuttling children to various play dates and sports activities. In summer, day after day, I would arrive at the Beach Club, where all the children splashed in the pool and all the mothers sat in the shade near the swing set, wrapped in terry cover-ups and talking the day's news. In the winter, day after day, I would arrive with the children after school at the skating rink, where all the children circled in the waning afternoon light, their breath billowing and mittens stiff with ice, and all the mothers sat at Formica tables in the warming hut, drinking coffee and talking the day's news. Day after day the children

Mine Is to Serve

53

twisted and spun—jumping into the pool, speeding on the rink. Day after day the mothers waited patiently, talking and watching.

One day at the rink I looked at the children, looked at the mothers as we sat there in our wool slacks, pleated and ample in the hips. I saw the vapor of the children's breath in gusts as they sped, saw the steam of the coffee cups in our warm spot by the big glass window, and realized that for us, speeding on the ice or leaping off the diving board or simply jumping for joy was inconceivable. It was as if we had undergone a metamorphosis that rendered such activity not just unseemly but physically impossible. Suddenly we all seemed to have accepted a destiny dictating that from here to the grave, our lot as adults was to dedicate ourselves to watching the children engage in life and accept that our own time to perform as individuals, to jump and speed and twist, was past. It wasn't that the sitting and watching was lazy—we deserved the camaraderie of a cup of coffee and conversation—but the air of being terminally settled in body and soul, like an airliner locked in a long sloping descent pattern to the inevitable final destination, stirred some tiny, long-forgotten voice. It said: "I'm still here. Wake up. Arise."

There was about the other mothers and me a sense that the mission of our bodies—to bear children—was complete, and that their primary purpose was to move us from soccer game to grocery store. It wasn't that we ignored our bodies; most of us went to exercise classes once or twice a week. When I went to the gym, however, there were always one or two women who parked on curbs and in handicap zones so they didn't have to walk across the large parking lot to aerobics class. I always laughed at the irony of it, but now I began to see a pattern of women who no longer seemed to associate physicality with expression or gratification. (And I sometimes wonder if my observation of them heading toward their long goodnight of the body somehow sounded an alarm that woke me from mine.) For them, the gym was where you exercise to be a strong service unit for your children, a physically pleasing service unit for your husband, a shapely service unit on which to hang clothes suitable to your husband's rank. Walking—what's that about?

Sometimes I suspect that the change rowing brought to my body deeply frightened my husband. I had been large and soft, moving with the lassitude that comes of not enough sleep and more than enough consumption of leftovers. Suddenly one summer I became lean, as my husband said, "stringy, sort of gristly." Suddenly my body felt hot and good and alive for the first time in many years. Was it necessary to sacrifice body and spirit for marriage and parenthood, as if one couldn't be a good mother without giving up vigorous engagement with life? As if one couldn't be a good wife without giving up everything of one's own? I'm not being rhetorical. Many women will be taken aback, even disgusted with me that I really didn't know. But I really *didn't* know. While a loss of self affects many stay-at-home mothers to some degree, the nature of my marriage began to force it into stark relief for me.

Nothing in my life was mine. Though we had a large house and my husband had a study, the children their own bedrooms, I didn't even have my own closet. I had no activity that was mine. Everything revolved around the children's activities, maintenance of the house, the social engagements it was my job as wife to make. My husband indicated that for me to have an extracurricular focus he didn't share was somehow unnatural. Activities like gardening or home decoration were fine because they were directly related to nurturing. Tennis was fine, too—it furthered social connections. Buying antiques and expensive English fabric was okay because they reflected his success. Not even my body was my own: my husband entered it without even a knock on the door every morning from six-thirty to quarter to seven, when I woke the children for school. He overwhelmed me with his conviction that a good wife *wants* to be always sexually available, *wants* to have the same friends as her husband, *wants* to have the same interests. For a woman to want or need anything else was dysfunction or immaturity or both.

How could I have accepted the notion that a real woman needs no other satisfaction than the service of husband and children, should limit her aspirations to wishing fervently for her husband's promotion because of the resultant improvement in housing assignment? Over the years the distant voice pleading with me, "Can't you see? Can't you stand up for yourself before it's too late?" was drowned out by the cacophony of the dinner hour and my own fears. If voices sometimes called urgently from my dreams, I woke at dawn, put on my L. L. Bean slippers, and went downstairs to make the pancakes. In wifehood I had found fulfillment of my desire to have children; but in it, too, I had found a skillful and determined keeper. While I don't suggest my husband played on my longing to be a healthy, normal woman in a calculating way, certainly in his knowledge of both the rancher and the DES, he was not unaware of my anxiety about it. Early in our marriage, when he convinced me that a good woman wants nothing more than the gratification of her mate, I had reached out my bare white arms for him to slip on the cuffs, like a wedding ring at the altar.

One winter day, when my youngest son was three, I picked up the kids at school to take them to the ice rink as usual. I tightened the laces of their skates, sent them off to lessons and endless circles, and opened the bag I had assembled that afternoon. I pulled out the beat-up white plastic figure skates I'd bought the day before at the local thrift shop, and Janie's Rollerblade pads—a set for my knees, my elbows, and my wrists. To the surprise of the other mothers, I put on my armor, cinched up the skates, and went out on the ice.

In Colorado we skied in winter, rarely skated, so I didn't approach the rink with any skill other than the tentative shuffle of all beginners. But I had arranged to have a lesson and I was going to learn. In the course of the next three months I raced to the ice rink every morning after the children were in school. I practiced, took notes, took my twenty-minute lesson once a week, dreamed of skating—not the spangly costumes and the hokey dance tunes, but the pure cutting curves of blade and ice. In the afternoons I was on the ice with the children, and when I fell, which was often, they gathered around me in astonishment, as if a mighty tree had toppled in their midst. They had never seen an adult go down, and after they got over the shock of it, they were amused and solicitous. I learned to do crossovers, three-turns, rudimentary spins. Learned to skate backward fast enough that I could lean into the circle and feel a little dot of scalp exposed to the winter air as my hair blew forward into my face. Day after day I stroked to the rhythm of the music on the loud-speakers, feeling the pressure on my edges as I banked into a turn.

One afternoon, after weeks of lying awake in bed next to my sleeping husband and playing the move over and over in my head, I jumped. Both blades left the ice and I was aloft, turning, landing just right on one foot and carving a long curve as I sped backward, one leg in an arabesque, both arms outstretched. The mothers in the warming hut were blown away. The children on the ice were blown away. I was blown away. I could fly. All it took was practice and the courage to make the leap.

That summer, I started swimming in the Sound for the first time with my friend Marion Ahmed, a powerful former competitive swim-mer. Each morning after we dropped off our kids in day camp, we went to the end of the dock in our Speedos and goggles. The first day, Marion warned me to take off my wedding ring and watch, which were shiny as lures and might attract sharks or bluefish. I remember how dark and opaque the water of the harbor was. We shivered on the dock, pressed our goggles to our faces, and leaped. Our course took us a half mile past the umbrella tables where the mothers were having coffee, past the dock with the big motorboat, outside the island of rocks where the cormorants ruled, and finally down to the submerged finger of rock where we turned and stood for a moment on the rocks, the water up to our thighs. Often I imagined us to be two strong sea mammals, warmed by our layer of fat from childbearing, stroking with a synchronized rhythm through the dark water of a sea kingdom, jellyfish brushing our fingers with a ghostly touch. Sometimes my body remembered the long-ago feel of water against my fingers, of levering myself against its pressure and slipping through like a fish; sometimes on cloudy days the thrilling darkness and depth below was so scary I closed my eyes behind the goggles on every stroke, not even allowing myself to imagine what lurked down there. And sometimes, when the sun shot light through the water in shafts, I strained to see her, the one with the iridescent tail.

One afternoon in March 1995, the winter before I saw a single shell for the first time, I stood on a frozen river. The ice was thick and opaque, hard as rock, and wind blew flurries of snow across the surface. Yet I could hear it groan like a living thing, could see the deep cracks where it had adjusted and fractured day after day according to the pressures of the long winter's chill. It cracked with a loud report as a fissure worked itself free. But there was another noise. I could hear either with my ears or in my heart, I couldn't tell which, the rumble of water, thousands and thousands, millions of gallons, an ocean of submerged energy moving inexorably underneath me, waiting for spring to surface.

Would I live out my days in pleated wool slacks, abandon myself to a lifetime dedicated solely to serving and observing, fixed, frozen, contained? Or would I have the chance to uncover a purpose that would allow me to encompass motherhood and a passionate *me* so long submerged I no longer knew what she looked like? In the spring of my forty-second year, I found the answer—past the stone fence, over the rise with the gray shuttered house, at the bottom of the long hill as it eases into salt marsh. Found it where the osprey whistles and the sea grass grows.

Chapter Four

FALLING

IN LOVE

In April 1995, when my children
were ten, seven, and four, I drove the
harbor road one late afternoon. I was in a
hurry—the line at the grocery store
had taken forever, and I needed to
get the boys dropped off for a
play date at a friend's house on Lloyd
Neck and get back before the post office
closed. I was distracted, thinking about the
leak around the upstairs window I thought
I'd fixed with roofing tar. The kids were
cranky and anxious to get to their
friend Michael's house before
Power Rangers came on.

We wound over the top of the hill
and down the long descent to the harbor. I opened
my window a crack to smell the salt and spring as

we approached the tidal flats of the causeway linking Lloyd Neck to the mainland, Lloyd Harbor on one side, Cold Spring Harbor and Oyster Bay on the other. The sun was low over the water, and one early sailboat was on a long reach from Centre Island into the cove. I rounded the end of the causeway and started down the mile of shoreline before the road to Michael's house took us into the hills. Across the narrow harbor I could see the boathouse of the local high school crew program, one door open, one pair of shoes on the dock. Other afternoons I had seen the high school crews walking their eight-man boats down the ramp, the dock on those days littered with sneakers and oars. I remember thinking how lucky they were; their parents had checked the box marked "Crew" and here they were, spending their afternoons on this sparkling harbor. Province of the young, the graceful long boats. Too late by more than twenty years for me—I missed my chance. I drove on. Then, in the moment separating what has been from what will be, I fell in love.

Working its way up the shoreline was a tiny sliver of a boat, a single shell impossibly narrow, a shining white arrow moving in the late sun with liquid smoothness and divine grace. One rower, I'll never know who, one boat so gorgeous, so lyrical, so piercing that I pulled over onto the shoulder and stopped the car, my heart pounding. The boat moved steadily up the far shore along the sedge grasses with a quiet, measured rhythm, narrow bow riding up with an infinitesimal breath on every stroke, riding up, then cutting into the surface of the cold green water of the harbor with the stroke's subsidence, its bow wake nothing more than a shimmering crease, a neat V, like geese flying south over the harbor in a chill autumn sky. The sculler's blades, white and forest green, traveled in a graceful arc as they swung forward again and again to meet the water like a prayer—infinitely patient, infinitely repetitive—flashing in the late sun as they rolled to square just before dropping silently to incise the surface and embrace the water. With each stroke, the sculler's body swung with the rhythm of chant and breath. Over and over. It was all here before me—the rhythm of a heart, of a wingbeat, of a body in love, of a breast filling and a child nursing, of the Little Mermaid's mussel-shell roof opening and closing.

In the quiet thrust of the boat, the sweet swing of the sculler, I saw everything I wanted to be, everything I always had been beneath the sensible dresses and the sorrow. Found in that moment the mission of these hands, this body, this heart.

How did it happen that I found love in an image I'd passed a hundred times without another look? Why was I stopped in my tracks, heart in my throat, this day? Why this moment? Who was I now that I hadn't been a week before? Why was my heart ready to embrace this vision utterly, finally, in an instant? It was as if driving the harbor road with the children bickering and the radio blasting I was suddenly face to face with an image so beloved and familiar, yet so long lost that over the years I'd almost convinced myself it had never existed at all. A face rising from the cold green water and calling to me: "Remember who you are, remember. You have another chance. Come with me, come with me now . . . "

My children sometimes pore over a book that consists of page after page of apparently random patterns in which, if you look at them just right, you will discover detailed three-dimensional images. You look and look, vainly seeking the promised picture. Finally you give up, accepting that the page holds nothing but chaos. In the moment just before you turn away to find an amusement more immediately gratifying, the scene comes vividly into view and you don't understand how it could have eluded you for so long. I had driven the shore road that hour of the afternoon countless times and all I'd thought about on those days was that the water was pretty and I was in a hurry.

There are myriad stories of people who were feeding the cows or riding the subway and suddenly saw the Virgin Mary in a bale of hay or a matrix of grimy wall tiles. Out of the material of everyday life suddenly springs a glimpse of another, vastly richer dimension that brings the wheeling momentum of your existence to a standstill, your astonished reverence arresting you only long enough to take a breath before you shape the rest of your life according to what you have witnessed.

The likelihood of my falling in love with a transcendent vision on an afternoon distinguished by long lines at the grocery store and spilled grape juice that had seeped under the kitchen radiator before I could catch it with a ragged sponge was as remote as my suddenly seeing the face of Jesus in my laundry hamper. To find my heart's desire while speeding down the shore road was to find, out of a nothing, a *something* so monumental and so defining that my life shifted in its orbit.

I was no longer simply swept along toward the inevitable end of the long march of days and years, drifting, just along for the ride. Now my desire might propel me toward a destiny. The power of the harbor would become my power, temporal current a context in which I might move strong and clean, flexing and testing my fiber—the strength of my courage, the depth of my capacity to feel. Suddenly I felt engaged where I had been adrift, alert where I had been lulled by habit.

When I was in high school, my mother used to tell me something her mother had told her. "When you get to Heaven," she said, "and God looks in His big book under your name, He will see a list of the talents He gave you. He's going to look you in the eye and ask how you used them. You better be ready to tell Him." Whenever she told this story, I felt tired and guilty, as if life were one long oppressive all-nighter before the term paper was due, and here I was still vainly casting around for a topic. Year after year in young adulthood I would occasionally think of my mother's admonition and year after year I would wonder when God was going to shake me by the shoulders and say, "Here's your assignment. Get going!" I read *What Color Is Your Parachute?* in most of its editions. The last copy in my bookcase is from 1984, just before Janie was born.

In the years since, my "special gifts" were expressed in the ability to whip up three dozen cupcakes in just over an hour. But now suddenly at the age of forty-two, after decades of halfhearted searching, after not seeing the pattern in the page year after year, my topic simply presented itself to me in the form of a white boat on a riffled harbor. Though the hour was late, the pencil was sharp. As it turned out, there was still time to produce a heck of a paper.

I *recognized* myself as a sculler, didn't have to wish it or imagine it, knew instantly and without question who and what I was, like the Ugly Duckling who, having spent his life going from pond to pond trying unsuccessfully to quack and waddle, suddenly and with profound relief finds his flock and realizes he has undergone a lifetime of going through the motions of an existence designed for someone else.

I suppose ultimately he could have figured it out: white feathers, black beak, long snaky neck, looks like a swan, flies like a swan, trumpets like a swan. And ultimately I could have figured out, too, that my habitat was the surface of a gleaming harbor—I had loved always the cadence of a stroke and the feel of water's resistance against my hand.

But a calling doesn't come in the form of a checklist. It is heralded by an experience, a transforming moment that reveals a template for the exercise of one's "special gifts." I feel unutterably blessed to have been given such an experience—one for which many people wait in vain all their lives. Because suddenly, on a late spring afternoon in my forty-second year, I knew beyond doubt that I was destined, and had always been destined, to feel all the rhythms of life and sing them with every stroke.

Chapter Five

BATHED IN THE

SALTY WATERS

So, in the spring of 1995, a few weeks
after that gleaming vision on the harbor, I
started where we all start—immersed in warm,
dark, salty water. If the Albany race in June 1996
was a frightening and joyous rebirth, the summer preceding it consisted of constant
contact with the waters of my beloved
home harbor. Narrow, shallow, protected,
Lloyd Harbor on the North Shore of Long
Island was the enveloping womb where in the
predawn hours I could fumble alone through the
first frustrating months of trying to balance a
ten-inch-wide boat, overturning again and
again, the lap of the waves a muffled
heartbeat keeping me company. How
thrilling that first year was. Each weekday
I would awaken before dawn and rise from the

big bed and my sleeping husband to slip down to my station wagon in the chill of early morning. The steering wheel was cold, seat was cold, windshield was cold and misted. My car smelled like the Happy Meal french fries that littered the recesses under its seats, even in the dense, cool air. Each morning I put on the defroster and coasted down the driveway, engine idle and headlights off so as not to wake my children or their father. Then I drove up West Neck Road, went right on School Lane, and left down the potholed road through the woods toward the harbor, still no sign of light in the sky.

Parking in the muddy lot, my headlights beamed across the long field starred with dew. I shivered with cold and the anticipation of locking up my car, walking across the dark wet field, through the stand of oaks—leaves brushing my face in the dark—feeling my way over their gnarled roots, sneakers now soaking. Each morning I sensed the bulk of the old frame boathouse, smelled the proximity of the water and the faint sweetness of the bridal veil spirea, a remnant of an old estate hedge. When I approached the steps leading up to the dock, the motion sensor lights under the eaves of the boathouse snapped on with a glare. They harshly illuminated everything just long enough for me to roll the thundering wooden doors ajar, take oars and boat down the narrow ramp to the landing float, and rig the boat, oars in oarlocks, ready for me to settle into my seat and push off into the harbor at the first sign of light. Then, suddenly, the lights snapped off and all was dark again.

In the inky dawn I sat and waited on the dock in silence, knees drawn up to my chest, ears pricked, eyes readjusting to the dark—just me, the boat by my side, the water, and the distant ruby lights of the four Eaton's Neck power stacks, like a totemic altar glimmering far across the larger harbor of which Lloyd Harbor was a sheltered cove.

In my new life in Boston I go out in the dark all the time, one of a handful of early scullers up and down the Charles River, wearing flashing red warning lights like flickering fireflies, scuttling under bridges, sliding past docks. But in my first year I was afraid to go out on the water in darkness all by myself, so I waited in the dense quiet for a few more minutes, my little boat next to me like loyal Toto. Waited for the first gray on the margins of the sky and our adventure to begin. It was deeply exciting to be by myself. In my life as a wife and mother I almost never experienced solitude. Now, for a few precious minutes, I was free of the marital bed, free of the fetters of shore. Free as a bird or a fish.

No one came to the dock this early; it was all mine every morning, the moldering boathouse my tiny dilapidated kingdom to which I had the key on a green lanyard around my neck, a kingdom smelling of varnish and gas cans, littered with discarded water bottles. No one paid any attention to me or my quest that summer; no one was there to see it. All the world slumbered contentedly under comforters, bedside clocks glowing and automatic coffeemakers still an hour from filling each household with morning smells. But I was vibrating with anticipation. I was awake, and I had never been more alive.

When I think of that summer of 1995, I am reminded of the sweetness and magic, years earlier, when I felt my first baby quicken, a flutter of life so tiny and incidental I thought this feeling, delicate as the movement of a butterfly wing, must be my imagination. That first summer on the harbor I floated in my safe, secret place, day after day stirring to the rhythm of the tides and the breaking dawn. There I would learn to balance and to use my blades as I had used my hands in that long-ago race when I was thirteen. Learn how to stay upright by overturning again and again—to become mindful of my craft and the position of my body. I learned to use my legs and my back not just to lift a baby into a car seat and a load of groceries into the trunk, but to move a shell through the dark, salty waters with a driving stroke that sent the boat like an arrow, and left a wake like a scar, healing itself with every second.

That summer, the dawn hours, not bedtime by the cowboy lamp, were the story hours for me. That's when the fables I read to my children at night came to life, when my own story came to life. Stories about the orphan Arthur whose fate it was to lead a kingdom, and his teacher Merlin whose cave, like Lloyd Harbor, was tucked away, hidden from the larger world, accessible only by a narrow opening. In that secret place Arthur learned to wield more than arrow and sword; he learned to draw on the mysterious powers at Merlin's command, the talking birds, the potent herbal elixirs, learned to use the energy of the natural world and make it his own. Like Arthur, I was granted my season to prepare my body, hone my skill, sharpen my mind before going forth, armed with a meager boat and an eleven-year-old child, to the mighty Hudson and the first of many battles.

Of course, I was no epic hero. In my suburban aerobics-class Lycra and short, sensible-mom hair, I was hardly heir apparent to an empire as I quivered there on the dock in the dark. I was no wiry, downy-faced Prince readying himself to reclaim his kingdom. And yet, while I didn't have the youth or the gender, I was readying myself to claim stewardship of a lost land. I too had been exiled from a kingdom in which I could express whatever vitality and courage were my birthright, a kingdom in which the time to claim dominion had come and, I thought, gone forever.

Yet what I had seen on the harbor that day in April told me I might still pull the sword from the stone. I may have been a forty-two-year-old housewife, but I was as fresh and ardent in my pursuit of mastery as Arthur; just as willing to endure privation, just as willing to make mistakes and risk looking the fool. I practiced day after day—soft hands bloody from blisters and nail cuts, arms bruised yellow and black from clambering back into the overturned boat—to ready myself for the task ahead, for the time when my hands would be tough and callused, my boat steady, my heart afire.

The harbor was Merlin's cave. Who was to be my Merlin? The boat was my weapon. Who was to be the inscrutable Master, teaching me to be canny and making me strong, twitching a jaw muscle with approval when I made a particularly good stroke? I had chosen the single shell and, right from the beginning, the single shell experience was, for me, the loneliest pursuit—a solitude in turns brutal and blessed. I had no Merlin. I did, however, meet a man who pointed me on the path. His name is Jim Long.

I met Jim Long at six o'clock one evening in late May 1995, at the big dank cement boathouse in the town of Huntington, three miles across the open water from Lloyd Harbor and Sagamore Rowing Club's run-down old structure. He was sweeping duck droppings off the dock with a push broom and infinite patience—five strokes, dip the broom in the sea, five more strokes. Jim was coach for the Huntington Park and Recreation Department crew class that was given every few weeks in the summer for two hours a night in heavy eight-man boats.

Back in April after I drove the harbor road, I called my friend Tom Thompson, who had mentioned once that he helped run a rowing club. He was happy to hear from me and excited that I wanted to row. He told me I could join the club if I took the local Park and Recreation class. Though I'd said I wanted to row a single, he told me that rowing an eight would give me basic instruction in terminology, boat handling, and the rudiments of the rowing stroke.

This kind of rowing is called *sweep rowing* and involves up to eight rowers, each of whom has one large oar twelve feet long and weighing almost six pounds. The kind of rowing I wanted to learn was called *sculling*, and involves up to four scullers, each of whom has two smaller oars, though not much smaller—a sculling "blade" is nearly ten feet long and weighs close to three pounds. (The single scull, or single, involves one rower, the double scull, or double, two, and the quadruple scull, or quad, four.) After taking the two-week class, an investment of seventy-five dollars, I was to pay one hundred fifty dollars for my yearly membership dues and get my free one-hour introduction to a training single—a shell wider, heavier, and more stable than a racing single—from a club volunteer. At that point I would be given a key to the boathouse and the right to use the facilities and the club boats any time of the day. So I signed up for the class; arranged for the thirteen-year-old daughter of a neighbor to watch the kids, to whom I had already dished out macaroni and cheese; and appeared at the dock promptly at six.

There is nothing glamorous or mysterious about Jim Long. Other coaches radiated charisma. Not Jim. Other coaches were the undisputed power elite in the boathouse; Jim stuck quietly to his business, getting down to the boathouse fifteen minutes early so that he could sweep the droppings off the dock and the sand out of the boat bays, something I never saw any other coach do. A former member of the Catholic order of teaching brethren, the Marist Brothers, Jim loves rowing with all his heart and brings to his mission a quiet fervor that has swept a host of souls into the congregation of passionate rowers. In the years since the first evening we met, I've known many men Jim's age who became oarsmen at Harvard or Penn and rowed for legendary coaches. Jim started rowing at Marist College in Poughkeepsie, New York, in the early sixties. "Someone donated an old boat," he said, "and a local coach, not from the monastery, gave us one lesson. We were all Brothers and had never heard such blue language. . . . After that afternoon, the rest was up to us." For thirty years Jim had taken all the raw recruits of disparate personalities and ages, and in two weeks, shaped them into a crew pulling in unison to a common purpose. If this isn't God's work, I don't know what is. Jim has never gotten any tributes at the U.S. Rowing Foundation's annual dinner in New York. He hasn't needed them; missionary work is its own reward.

Those ten days in late May, the only days I was ever to row in "sweeps," I loved Jim's matter-of-fact coaching style. He didn't display a hint of the prima donna, didn't raise his voice, didn't sound remotely panicked. Ever. In fact, if you didn't know any better, you might think he was just a little sleepy. I found his demeanor reassuring. He was so calm it seemed inconceivable that anything alarming would dare to happen. When it looked like we were about to run the riggers, the spiky aluminum framework on which the oarlocks are mounted, smack into the boathouse door and tear the bolts out of the fiberglass hull, he would issue a lazy, "Watch your riggers, kids." If we were rowing down the channel to the yacht basin at what was, for us, top speed and suddenly the boat tipped so precariously we yelped in panic, Jim would say with infinite patience, "Careful of the balance now." He had seen it all, done it all, and nothing was going to raise his blood pressure except boathouse politics, which irritated him like a nasty splinter.

My Park and Recreation class turned out to be a hodgepodge of adults whose participation was sparked by a range of motivations. A couple of women in their twenties liked water sports but, more important, liked the prospect of connecting with broad-shouldered guys with whom they hoped to slake their thirst at CoCo's waterside bar after each arduous workout. They soon discovered a paucity of prospects, but were still game to row. A pleasant fiftysomething executive from a mammoth toy company regaled us with stories of the next Big Thing. I don't know that he ever took up an oar again, but he pulled hard the two weeks I knew him. A sporty married couple in their thirties were looking for an activity they could share. I was impressed with the size of her quadriceps and her voice, both of which dwarfed his. Two graduates from one of the 1994 classes filled two more seats. One was a youthful grandmother with a beatific smile who liked being out on the harbor in the evening. The other was Keith, a young man who clearly enjoyed being the old hand. We liked having Keith stroke the boat because, compared to us, he was vastly experienced and gave us a pleasing sense of security. He set the pace from his seat in the stern and we followed like lemmings, happy to throw our lot with someone who knew what he was doing. And there was me—the mommy.

Each evening, a laconic Jim would gather us to carry the oars down to the dock. Then there was the moment when we all stood in the boat bay eyeing our vessel. The shells Sagamore Rowing Association allowed the Park and Recreation Department to use had seen a lot of action. A high-performance eight-man shell is light and stiff, with the best weighing in at two hundred pounds fully equipped. An eight has eight rolling seats on tracks, eight pairs of track shoes bolted to adjustable footboards, and eight riggers holding the oarlocks at a precise distance and angle from the hull of the shell. Such a boat is stiff enough that if you lift the bow and stern off the rack, the remainder of the sixty-foot-long, two-foot-wide shell rises at the same instant like a very long, very stiff spear. The boat we used was probably fifty pounds overweight from water that had seeped through various puncture wounds to the honeycomb core, and when you lifted the bow and stern, you got the sense that you needed to send an e-mail to the rest of the boat to get it up and going. But Jim organized us into an efficient machine to hoist this aged colossus. Each evening he would drawl the commands, *Hands on. Overhead. To shoulders. Walk!* And off we would go, a well-oiled team, a gathering of warriors bearing our spongy old battleship past the fishermen with their coolers of beer and bags of Doritos. One day I looked inside the bow port and found an old ID plaque which read "Columbia University." I had a vision of the old dear having started its career as a hot Ivy League varsity boat, making its way down through the ranks of the Freshman and Novice crews, down through various high school programs, and finally to the damp boat bays of Huntington and the hands of housewives.

The next trick was to get the boat into the water without tearing off the skeg, a fin about the size of a tea saucer mounted on the underside of the hull. Once afloat, we placed oars in oarlocks, tossed our shoes on the dock, stowed water bottles, and got ready to push off at the command: "On three—one, two, THREE!" Off we went, up toward the half-sunken barge which, at high tide, was a submerged hull-ripper, threading our way through the moorings and around the channel marker. We generally had some local ninth grader as coxswain, the "boat boss," who sits in a special molded seat embedded in the stern (or, these days, bow) of the shell. The cox has a megaphone or microphone system through which to yell commands at the crew; like *Weigh enough!* the rowing command for Stop Rowing Now, and *Hold water!* meaning Square Your Blades to Arrest the Forward Motion of This Boat Before We Do Some Real Damage, useful when we were about to ram someone's dock or collide with a hapless dinghy wandering into the path of our juggernaut. One day we were passed by a solitary sculler, a young man with long hair tightly bound in a ponytail and a red bandana wrapped around his head, Eakins-style. How could one guy go faster than eight of us? He seemed wonderfully renegade to me with his bandana, his finesse, and his frisky little boat—a Lone Ranger.

One evening early on we were treated to a short video about safety. It seemed that rowing was perilous as well as fun. We learned about the danger of freezing to death in icy water; rowers who had capsized, then struck out for shore only to drown, stricken by hypothermia. "Never, never leave the boat!" Jim told us with more animation than he'd ever displayed before or since. "And *always* get off the water if there is lightning!" He didn't bother to go into the ill-advisedness of rowing by oneself in the dark; after all, no one with any sense would venture into a single shell anyway.

After four or five days of rowing up and down the channel, we were darned pleased with ourselves. We knew the lingo; we knew the theory of the stroke—the *drive, release, recovery,* and *catch*. We'd started to be able to lounge around the dock before class and talk technique and stroke ratings—the number of strokes per minute. After ten days, we graduated.

On the last night, Jim followed us in his coaching launch as we rowed slowly down the channel toward our destination. Officially, the goal was to row to the end of the channel and back. Unofficially, we were all aware that our course took us in close proximity to CoCo's, whose terrace overhung the water and was filled with Friday night revelers just getting into the swing of weekend recreation. I knew, we all knew, we wanted to row past CoCo's looking buff and acting like we wouldn't be caught dead doing something as useless as lounging over a railing drinking a margarita.

What a satisfying graduation it was. The crowds at CoCo's moved toward the railing in a tidal surge. If the terrace had been a ferry, it would have capsized in an instant. We executed what we considered to be a flawless row-by with a powerful, steady cadence: grandmother, sporty couple, steely Keith, toy magnate, administrative assistants, mommy. The crowds called down to us, some raising their glasses, some clapping in rhythm, some yelling: "Stroke, stroke, stroke!" and: "Hey, you guys going to that race in England, you know, Henley or something?" We tried not to crack a smile. Back at the boathouse we stowed the oars in their upright racks and gathered up sweatshirts and water bottles. We got ready to disband, asking one another, "Are you going to do the class again?" "You going to join the club?" "Going to come back next year?" When asked, all I said was, "I'm going into the single."

The single. I'd spent enough hours on the dock by then that there had been ample opportunity to talk to rowers more experienced than our ragged crew. Four-man boats and eights went in and out of the boathouse with some frequency, and the rowers who came off the water were usually game to share the lore with the uninitiated like me. There was no question in my mind that the single was my boat; I had no interest in the group dynamics and team mentality of the eight, so when I asked questions on the dock in the last light of every evening, they were focused. "Oh no, you don't want to do that," one rower told me when I mentioned my intention. "The single is *way* difficult. Takes years just to learn how to row the damned boat." "Are you kidding?" said another. "You have to be a fool or a masochist to row singles." So I talked to someone who had coached. He looked me over.

"Well, the problem is the balance and the technical difficulty. I think you would really be much happier in an eight . . . "

The more I heard, the more waterfront intelligence became a sweeping consensus: single scullers are considered slightly, or not so slightly, antisocial and obsessive, a tribe populated by almost exclusively male or proto-male loners and visionaries who relish the difficulty of balancing the boat. They thrive on solitude and show little moderation in anything, but most particularly in their attempt to achieve the perfect stroke. Sounded good to me.

Although as soon as I went into the single I didn't have much contact with other rowers for nearly a year, the prevailing boathouse attitude about scullers was confirmed for me fifteen months later at the end of 1996, when I attended the Masters Nationals. Early on the second morning of competition, I was walking on the sidewalk parallel to the course where dozens of rowers milled about carrying oars and athletic bags. I had bananas and juice boxes for my children in a canvas book bag bearing the logo of the investment firm my husband worked for. A man started to pass me, glanced at my bag, and asked how long I'd been with the firm. "I'm not with the firm," I said. "Oh, what firm are you with?" "I'm a stay-at-home mother," I said. "So you must be here rooting for your husband?" "No, I'm here racing the single." He was nonplussed, but attempted to recover. "It's just that . . . well, I've never met a mother who rows a single." I think what he meant was that he'd never met a masters woman single sculler who wasn't a former Olympic medalist, a litigating attorney, a surgeon, or a partner in a big investment firm—all definitely "proto-male" activities.

When I got home, I told my friend Jeff Schaeffer about the exchange. He laughed. "Haven't you noticed you're the only housewife out there? The single intimidates everyone. Men do it because men will do anything. Besides, they always think they're better than they are, and women are just the opposite. Most women won't even try the single, almost none will race it!"

But the truth was that I wasn't rowing the single because I had an extra dollop of testosterone or was particularly brave. There wasn't a scrap of hubris next to the juice boxes in my canvas bag. I was simply following the instructions of my heart, and had to tell the nagging voices reminding me of my fear and technical insufficiency to pipe down, or, as I tell my kids when they whine, "Just shush 'til I get this done, sweetie."

Ironically, it worked to my benefit that, in the rowing world, I remained for nearly two years a total rube, hopelessly isolated from the competitive rowing community and the vigorous rowing grapevine. Rowing a single by myself, I had no interaction with other women rowers who, I figured (pretty much incorrectly), were also alone on their own dark home harbors doing what I was. I was out in the hinterland, thrashing in the darkness and poring over my tired, waterlogged information sheets, sent free of charge from U.S. Rowing in Indianapolis. Sure it was scary, sure it was hard, sure the waves sometimes rolled over my bow and slammed into my back. But I thought that's what sculling was supposed to be.

So one evening about a week after I finished the Park and Recreation class, I sat down at the kitchen table and wrote a check for a hundred fifty dollars, gave Alicja, my neighbor's daughter, last instructions for homework and baths, and headed down the road to the boathouse on Lloyd Harbor for the first time.

Sagamore Rowing Club at that time was located on an old Long Island estate that had been transformed into the campus of a tiny, now defunct college. Administration buildings were abandoned and weedy, dorms had the empty beat-up look of the week after graduation. The clubhouse was a simple wood frame structure, built to house the boats of the estate owner, and converted some years ago by a crew of high school kids and older club members to accommodate racing shells. The club leased it yearly for a nominal fee. From its dock you could look up the water a mile west to the causeway sepa-

rating Lloyd Harbor from Cold Spring Harbor, and down a mile to
the east where the protected harbor met the deeper, bluer, open space
of Huntington Harbor. To the north, a shore road traced the bound-
ary of Lloyd Neck only a quarter mile away. Late in the afternoon
the sun shone straight down the harbor, lighting the grasses of the
shore and the egrets feeding in the shallows. I had made an appoint-
ment with Rich McLaughlin, the club volunteer who gave each new
member a free one-hour lesson in a training single. But I was early, so
I took a look around.

I rolled the heavy, barnlike doors aside to see shells lined up neatly
on long racks, hulls glowing in the light through windows coated
with eons of dust. Oars stood vertically, green and white blades
upright. The smell of old hoses, gasoline, and a certain attic scent of
dry rot pervaded everything. Coiled hoses, gas cans, old kapok life
jackets were thrown in corners to molder. There was a beat-up stand
for the log—a salt-water-warped ledger in which each rower signed
out every time he or she went out on the water, and signed in on
returning. The utility drawer of the stand was half-open and contained bits of seat pad, assorted bolts and wing nuts, old regatta entry
forms, a box of Band-Aids, athletic tape, a couple of worn oar grips,
an empty tube of superglue, and a piece of petrified gum. The base
of the stand was overflowing with old rowing shoes that had gone
their last two thousand meters, rotted from hundreds of hours of
adolescent feet sweating in them. Weeks after this evening someone
pointed out to me a row of tiny blue eggs, each hardly bigger than a
black bean, decorating the nearby dusty windowsill. When the high
school crew was getting ready for the first practice of the year, the
bowman had had the foresight to reach his hand inside his disintegrating shoes before shoving his feet into them for the first time—
and came out with a clutch of eggs. Some little gray boathouse bird
had decided to raise a family in the shoe's inverted toe.

A simple wooden stair led to the second floor and the "Training
Room," decorated nicely with a ratty green carpet encrusted with
long-hardened detritus. There were four "ergs," rowing simulators

universally used in the rowing world for strength and endurance training. Against the wall were two weight benches with both hand weights
and a homemade barbell—two rusty coffee cans filled with cement
at the ends of a three-foot galvanized pipe. The walls were covered by
old regatta posters and charts of the erg scores of both current crews
and kids who must have graduated from college and launched careers
by now, and an enlarged photograph of a young man who'd been on
the high school crew and had died tragically. A picnic bench held an
ancient sound system that offered accommodation to the rarified
ranks of those who still favored eight-track. It was a place where you
knew nothing had ever, ever gotten thrown away—a place with a
pleasing sense of accretion, an almost archeological quality. I
breathed it all in. Then I heard footsteps downstairs. The evening
scullers had arrived.

Downstairs, I found one young woman in a black one-piece
stretchy suit, and two men, all getting ready to go out in single shells.
Peering at the log was a stocky, sandy-haired man who turned out to
be Rich McLaughlin. I introduced myself, and we got right to business. I pulled out my check and paid my dues, got the official tour,
and was briefed on club policies and protocols, which had mostly to
do with not breaking equipment, keeping it rinsed and wiped clean
of salt water before putting it away, and locking up the boathouse
after I was done. Then Rich pointed to a boat named *Chelsea*, a type
of shell he called a recreational single because it was both wider and
more stable than a racing single. This was to be my first boat. I was
to row the *Chelsea* for a few days or weeks until I could demonstrate
a proficiency that would entitle me to take out a much narrower boat;
in fact, an unbelievably narrow boat.

Finally, he led me to a tall boat rack. "This is a racing single," he
said. "When you're ready, this will be your boat." The letters on the
bow said *S4*. No dedications to rowers past, no tributes to sculling
ancestors. Without hesitation I gently lay my hand on *S4*'s tiny, fragile hull near the bow, feeling the smoothness under my fingers, the
curve of the hull at that point no larger than a thigh, long and pale.

How many times since have I rested my hand on sturdy *S4*, which would be my companion for nearly two years? Rested it just like this moment—after a long meditative row, after an intense practice, after a race, after rowing through a storm, after rowing in a dark predawn.

Rich helped me choose oars from the racks nearby, nice heavy ones for beginners, walking them down to the end of the dock. I discovered a week later why the oars have to go out first, the boat last—put your boat in the water first and the wind blows it away down the harbor while you're running up the ramp to fetch your oars. We returned to the boat bays and Rich showed me the proper two-person method of carrying a boat, bow or stern resting in the crook of an arm, eyes alert and watchful of the sharp metal riggers that seemed magnetically drawn to the vulnerable hulls of nearby shells. We walked in step down the dock with the *Chelsea* and placed it carefully in the water.

Rich showed me how to open the tops of the oarlocks—the gates—by putting my knee on the edge of the dock and leaning precariously over the boat. Then we put the oars in the oarlocks, their flanges (called *collars* or *buttons*) snug on the inboard side of the open oarlocks to prevent the oar from slipping through. The oarlocks themselves, by necessity, trailed aft of the oarlock pin, the fulcrum on which the whole machinery of body, hardware, and carbon levers. The orientation of the oarlock to the pin was a fine but important point I forgot time and time again that first summer (giving me additional opportunity to swim). Finally we tightened down the nuts on the gates that secured the oars in the oarlocks—again, just a twist of the fingers that, forgotten, lands you in the harbor before you can say, "I'd rather be home asleep." The boat was rigged. It was time to jump in and row at last.

I stood looking at the *Chelsea* floating there calmly, waiting for me to step in and row away confidently. It was like the first time I ordered a lobster and a scary, spiky thing was presented to me on a large white plate. Here was something exciting, exotic. But how to get into it? The boat beckoned and I was very hungry, but everything about it was either impossibly delicate or incomprehensibly shaped. The seat looked like an artifact, a sort of flattened bony pelvic girdle rolling on little wheels in a track bolted to a deck so small my ample hips were barely going to fit inside the gunwales. In the narrower racing single, both men's and women's hips simply hang out over the water. The riggers with their profusion of aluminum tubes and upright oarlock pins stuck out just where I needed to put myself to shift my weight into the boat. As far as actually stepping in, I had been admonished to place my foot on the one and only reinforced spot on the deck. Place my foot elsewhere and foot and leg would go through the delicate hull and send me and vessel into the mud and seaweed at the bottom of Lloyd Harbor. The cockpit was so small it could be swamped to the gunwales with about six gallons of water, and compared to a racing single, this was a battleship. Thus, like that inconvenient business of learning how to row backward before I could race, I had to learn the choreography of getting into the boat before I could take a stroke.

Getting into a shell and pushing off from the dock is a complex and perilous maneuver executed in view of various milling bystanders most of whom have been through this rite of passage and are watching with empathy and amusement. Since that day I have watched a few children and many more adults go through the same first day experience, and this is what I've observed.

Children embrace the adventure, jumping into a single and starting to row with effortless grace within minutes. They have no fear of the boat, no fear of contact with the water, but especially no fear of losing control and looking like an idiot. Adults, on the other hand, eye the boat with trepidation before they ever walk out on the dock. As soon as they take off their shoes and approach it, they begin imagining the dreadful possibilities. First is the terror of placing themselves into the shell without puncturing it and sending it to the bottom. Then there's the looming ignominy of flipping at the dock, a likely event that neophytes regularly experience. (Tipping into Lloyd Harbor is a shock, but it could be worse—a friend of mine who coaches in Texas likes to mention casually to her novice rowers that she hasn't seen a water moccasin in a couple of days.)

Let's say you've successfully settled yourself on your little rolling seat without mishap, but forget to check that your outboard blade, the one that's in the water and away from the dock, is horizontal and braced on the water's surface—feathered, not vertical, and slicing a neat path to the bottom—squared. It's vertical, you notice, as you find yourself in an unstoppable roll into the drink. As you vainly try to save yourself, you ask two questions: Is everyone laughing? And will I be able to get my feet detached from the boat or will I hang upside down in the water until my lungs fill and my dreams of having all my children in school full time so I can read a whole book disappear in a trickle of bubbles?

Then let's say you get back into the boat successfully and push off from the dock, severing your one link to shore. What a child feels as intriguing tippiness, you experience as horrifying instability, exactly what you have spent your adulthood doing your damnedest to avoid. There you are in a ten-inch-wide boat, trembling desperately to balance. Someone waves goodbye, a friendly encouraging face. You wave back with a brave smile, forgetting the cardinal rule of sculling: *Never let go of either oar handle* (at least until you know enough to hold both in one hand). Again you find yourself in that slow, unstoppable roll to port or starboard. You are again upside down underwater and sensing confirmation of everything you had concluded about adult life: that to let go is to lose your grip, to lose your grip is to lose control, and to lose control means that not only are you no longer captain of your own fate; you are little more than flotsam littering the pristine harbor. So what a child experiences as an afternoon of boating fun punctuated by refreshing dips, you experience to be a cruel reminder of everything you knew about surviving in an unpredictable world. All this before you take a single stroke. Already you have been exposed to the exquisitely metaphorical quality of rowing.

Now it's time to row. Rowing is fun. It's just that to make the boat go, you have to deal with a combination of body and equipment that comprises a mechanical system of articulated levers and angles operating on two axes in an alien medium. The oar shafts are levers on one end of which are blades, which pry the boat past the water, and on the other is the power source—you. The oarlock is the fulcrum. The arms, bending at elbow and shoulder, draw the oar handles in two horizontal arcs that, because of the boat's narrow beam, overlap as the oars pass perpendicular to the boat. As the handles intersect in the airspace over your legs, your hands stack left over right (and when you miscalculate, the fingernails of your left hand neatly rip the skin on the knuckles of your right, something you don't notice until the blood starts dripping onto your knees). Your body swings on a vertical axis hinged at the hips, and the legs, the primary source of horsepower for the whole machine, extend and compress over and over, stroke by stroke, horizontally, just as if you were jumping vertically from a squatting position over and over. And over.

Everything moves, oscillates, contracts, and expands at once and at different rates. At the start of the stroke you must place your blades into the water at exactly the right depth, exactly the right place, exactly the right time, and at exactly the right angle. This is the *catch*. As you draw them through the water, you must maintain the optimum depth, tops of blades just at the surface, as you apply considerable pressure, knowing that any careless movement of a hand is magnified tenfold in the behavior of the blade nine feet away. This is the *drive*. When you have removed them from the water with the same degree of care with which you placed them there, a maneuver called the *finish*, or *release*, the oar blades must be feathered parallel to the surface of the water with a quick, subtle "rolling out" of the fingers and a slight cock of the wrist, and carried approximately four inches above the water in a sweeping arc, called the *recovery*. (And remember, the sculler, unlike the sweep rower, manages two blades, not one.) The recovery is as technically difficult as the drive because if you're too eager to roll your seat down the tracks for the next catch—known as "rushing the slide"—the mass of your hundred-thirty-pound body speeding aft and slamming to a stop will nearly bring the boat, which weighs a fraction of your own weight, to a standstill.

You will need a recovery after all these hair-raising precision moves executed from a platform with all the lateral stability of a small log. Someday, when you get very, very good, you will execute a stroke and you will hear a miraculous nothing—no blade slapping and skidding across the water on the recovery. Some people notice this after about a year of hard work; some notice it after three or four years; some never. I have a friend who has coached scullers for over thirty years. "There's no way around it," he says. "It takes at least five years to get good. Really good."

I made every mistake and arrived home salty and sodden day after day that first week, surviving this stage because my desire to scull was greater than my fear of, well, anything. Nothing could stop me. But many of those to whom sculling looks from a distance like a pleasant, gentle recreation on a lovely harbor pack it in after the first discouraging day.

That first night I did learn to get into the *Chelsea*, and flipped. Did learn to push off from the dock, and flipped. Did wave to a friendly face, and flipped. Did hear Rich's prime dictum, *Never let go of either oar handle*, promptly forgot it, and flipped. That week I flipped at the dock, flipped trying to turn around, flipped trying to pull my blades out at the end of a stroke, flipped trying to land the boat forward, flipped trying to land the boat backward. Rich yelled instructions from shore through cupped hands: "Hang on to your oars with your fingers, not your palms, and put your thumbs at the ends." "Don't lay back so far." "Let 'em [the blades] rest on the water for stability." "Don't let your elbows get behind you."

I could make the boat move, barely, my body shaking with the effort to balance, blades behaving with maddening independence. Every time I had one under control, I realized with a rush of fear that the other was squared and that I was about to go over. It was like rubbing my belly and patting my head while riding a unicycle. How did anyone ever get the hang of it? But after a few days and many unpredictable swims, I could row down the harbor, blades awkwardly feathering and slapping the water, and execute a cautious turn at the end, having flipped twice trying to turn on earlier nights. Finally I could bring *Chelsea* back into the dock without banging the bow or getting dunked. Then one evening Rich pointed to the racing single, *S4*. "Why don't you try this boat tonight?"

I had a fantasy that I would gently lift *S4* off the rack and swing it up on top of my head as I had seen other scullers do, balancing it effortlessly, both hands loosely gripping a rigger, bow leading me out from the boathouse and into my new life as a single sculler. I took a deep breath and placed my hands on the gunwales, swinging it up. No, not swinging it up. I tried again. Still no swing; in fact, I couldn't get it above my shoulders. After three tries, I realized *S4* wasn't going to make it to the top of my head that day, nor would it at all for nearly two years: I wasn't strong enough and *S4* was too heavy. So I wedged it against my left hip like a baby, hanging on to the starboard rigger with my left arm (made strong, in fact, from carrying babies), and took care to make sure the oarlocks didn't hit the doors on the way out. Down the ramp we went, to the oars I'd put on the edge of the dock a few minutes earlier. I rigged just as I had been taught, held the tips of the oar handles together, blades flat against dock and water, put my foot on the appointed spot, and settled into a racing single for the first time.

It was like sitting on an oversized pickup stick. My legs were crammed into a narrow cockpit, feet strapped onto *S4*'s footpads (rather than the lightweight track shoes bolted by the toes on more competitive singles). My hips were wider than the beam of the boat by a substantial margin, my bottom resting on the tiny seat with dimples in which the "sitbones" nest. The only stability was that provided by the weight of the oar shafts, like a tightrope walker's balance bar, and the blades themselves which, when flat on the water nine feet on either side, offered a solid platform. Of course, once a sculler has passed the novice stage, he or she uses carbon shafts so light they would send a tightrope walker into the safety net, and the blades themselves must skim a few inches above the water before they are squared and dropped in for the next stroke. At that stage the only source of stability is the momentum of the boat itself, and the subtle, catlike adjustments of the body to maintain stasis.

I pushed off. This was a greyhound compared to broad, docile *Chelsea*. I took a few strokes. Though *S4* was still far heavier than a true racing shell, it had some of its inherent animation—sensitive and quick; designed for speed, not stability. I rowed up the harbor, turned, rowed back down. Rowed back, flipped once at the turn, rowed back down. I pulled into the dock after an hour with soaking socks and sopping T-shirt, heart pounding with excitement.

I had met other scullers those first evenings I came to row. They were quiet and watchful, like hawks on the roadside wires of midwestern back roads. There was a certain amount of banter but little bravado. Some quiet talk about rigging heights, some ribbing about how so-and-so's boat sat a little lower in the water and had he gained a little weight? I listened as they stood around in their uniforms of tired black Lycra shorts and white T-shirts commemorating various regattas. Watched them watch other scullers out on the water. When their eyes narrowed and they hummed and clucked their tongues with approval, I too watched the boat whose progress they followed. What made this sculler worthy of their attention? What could I learn from this bladework? I wanted to burn into my memory the shape of a good stroke—the roll up of the blades, the catch, the drive.

The dock "culture" at Sagamore was different from that of Huntington, where the eights and fours came in every evening. This was a collection of people united by the fact that they liked to be alone. They were all men ranging from their thirties to their sixties, and the one woman who wore the black racing suit. She was in her early twenties, had raced in college in various East Coast regattas, and like the rest of the experienced scullers, looked right through me, ignoring me until the third evening when I inadvertently got in her way as she approached the dock and she flashed me a look of irritation. She was sleek and accomplished—could walk a walk and talk a talk, eye the shells in the boathouse with the same appraising glint as the men who ran their palms appreciatively over flanks of the fastest carbon hulls. Oh, how I wanted to look casual, competent, and strong. How I wanted to row with her grace and walk my boat down the dock with her assurance.

As a newcomer, a novice, and a middle-aged woman, I was an outsider on three counts, hardly worth the most cursory greeting. While younger aspirants might have taken this pecking order in stride, sometimes I found myself feeling stung and intimidated. Sometimes I wondered what I was doing here. I had a life in which I felt important—was on boards, ran committees, hosted Garden Club seminars. Why wasn't I home typing up the agenda for tomorrow's meeting of the summer camp's volunteer mothers, or organizing the food for the Museum benefit? And I already had a perfectly good uniform. Why did I yearn for my own regatta T-shirt when I already had a lovely cream-colored linen jacket and a pair of black Joan and David shoes with clinky gold chains over the toes?

I watched the Sagamore girl lift her boat off the rack and balance it on her head to walk with a gentle sway out the boathouse doors and down to the dock, where she lifted it effortlessly off her head and set it in the water without a splash, her muscles long and taut in her racing suit. How I wanted to carry a boat with that ease. Wanted to push off from the dock with lazy confidence and hold the oar handles between my chest and knees while I tightened my shoes and set my electronic Stroke Coach whose display would give me a constant stream of data tracking my performance. How would I get there from here?

Rich was very kind to have given me an hour, but within a day or two it was clear the rest was up to me. On Friday, the fourth night I rowed *S4*, Rich determined that I had fulfilled basic requirements in the single and could be set free to sink or swim. This was the last evening I would spend on the dock for over a year, and I lingered there a few more moments before going home. I had seen the coach of the local high school crew, Al Borghardt, and heard of his skill in the single. This night Al had just sent his high school crew home after a week of afternoon practice and was getting ready to go out by himself in the last rays of the early evening. I had introduced myself to him a few days before. Though he was pleasant, it was clear he wasn't interested in standing around the dock engaging in tiresome chatter. So I watched him.

He had a lovely wooden racing single, which though it had been repaired again and again glowed with old varnish, smooth and sweet, worn and burnished. Six inches of the bow were of a different color wood, replaced after a collision. He put his beat-up oars on the dock and picked up his boat without a flourish, balancing it on his grizzled head and walking down the ramp. I watched him secure his oars, giving the oarlock nuts a practiced spin, and settle into his seat. He pushed off the dock, a tired warrior, heading up the harbor toward the osprey nests and the causeway on which the last commuters made their way to dinner. Everything about his stroke was smooth as a bird in flight, powerful and integrated, balanced and exquisitely measured.

In Al Borghardt's journey up the darkening harbor, I had my first glimpse of masterful sculling. Suddenly all my feelings of wanting a slick black suit and making a show of balancing a boat on my head, of being able to compare rigging heights with the guys and being hurt that no one would talk to me, were tossed onto the squirming heap where all the dangerous temptations of vanity, envy, and self-aggrandizement seethe; they had nothing to do with my true mission. In Al Borghardt's strokes, I saw pure beauty. In his journey down the harbor, God's hand. This, and only this, was the work of my heart. Everything else was just noise.

I longed to ask him if he would coach me, if he would be my Merlin and share with me the secrets, unlock the mystery. But I was too intimidated; his face was too worn and too tired, and who was I, after all, to ask the Master for lessons after he had dealt with legions of teenagers day after day? I watched him until he disappeared at the end of the harbor, watched his wake subside to a shimmer. Then I turned and headed home to relieve Alicja and get the kids to bed.

In a way it was a blessing that my husband put his foot down. If I had had the liberty to stay on that dock with the evening scullers, I might have been swept away by a need to belong, need to look the part, need to be recognized. Might have ultimately given up in discouragement. As it was, I got my orders—No more evening rowing.

My husband had been sarcastic about the cost of the baby-sitter and the fact that I wasn't there to greet him and hear about his day when he arrived. He told me he didn't like the frequency of macaroni and cheese. He also indicated he didn't like that I was meeting people he didn't know, was pretty sure he didn't want me to know, and was doing something that didn't involve him or our friends. And there was the matter of my not being where I belonged, doing my job as I always had.

In fact, I knew I couldn't continue rowing in the evening anyway. My children needed me at the time of day most intensely demanding—dinner hour and bedtime. They were unsettled when I wasn't there, and the novelty of Alicja had begun to wear off. So I sought another time to get to the harbor. That's when the surface of our marriage began to stir, a surface that had been so dead flat that both of us mistook it for rocklike solidity—him with a settled satisfaction, me with an occasional shiver that rattled the chains on my little black suede shoes. When I was little and was taught to sail, I came to anticipate an approaching gust, "see" the invisible wind in the swiftly approaching corrugation and darkening of the water. So I recognized a disturbance in the apparent smoothness of our marriage in my husband's cutting remarks about my new interest.

Although many of my friends spent their summer mornings engaged in tennis clinics or Garden Club activities, my husband greeted my proposal that I take to the harbor for an hour after I got the children into camp with the observation that such activity was akin to "getting manicures and wax jobs," in other words, self-indulgent, vain, wasteful. That my last manicure had been at my grandmother's hairdresser when I was nine and that I had never had a wax job was immaterial. Also immaterial was the fact that my friends were engaged in morning activities equally hardy and cardiovascular. The difference was that their cardiovascular activities were punctuated by useful conversation involving the Lantern Dinner Dance menu and the cost of Vienna Fingers versus Oreos for the annual Family Night CookOut. That, and a fact of which my husband, I suspect, was aware—that while the warp of the North Shore social hierarchy was strung in the canyons of Wall Street, the weft was woven taut as a new Prince racquet in the women's tennis clinics of North Shore clubs. So, while he may have considered a couple of hours of daily patter in Reeboks and tennis skirts on teal-colored courts a healthy and suitable recreation, an hour of solitary stroking up the long lonely harbor in a tiny boat under the watchful eye of an osprey was not. He indicated to me that the other Beach Club moms were wholesome, appropriate wives. I, on the other hand, had begun to display behavior not at all suitable to my station.

With a sense of trepidation, of the necessity to close the hatch cover and ease the main sheet, I began seeking a time I had started thinking of as "my own." The next week I started rowing at six in the morning, arriving home just before seven-fifteen, a few minutes after the children had started stirring and twenty minutes before my husband departed to catch the train to New York. I had the coffee ready and the cereal on the counter so no one would die of starvation while I was gone, and the children didn't have to pile into the car with bag lunches and life jackets for camp until nearly eight-thirty. I rowed at six for three days before my husband laid down the law. Six-thirty was "family time," and he made it clear to me that I was to be where I belonged and ready to participate.

I knew what "family time" was. For years I had played my role in it, a command performance. I had long ago discovered that failure to participate was cause for the cool and cutting sarcasm and criticism that made life hell. In my mute acquiescence to it and unwillingness to stand up for myself and face the consequences, I was a coward. My tacit complicity ultimately did him and our marriage grave ill when my resistance might, mercifully, have ended it early on. Year after year, my silent submission allowed him to maintain what I always sensed to be a rooted belief in the inalienable right of a husband to control his wife's movements, claim the use of her body.

What, then, was "my time"? What could I call mine? Not the early evening—that was time for the children. Not during the day— that was community involvement, home management, and errand time. Not at six-thirty in the morning—that was "family time." The only time I might call mine was the dark hours before six-thirty, before anyone arose, while my husband and children were still dream- ing, the fluorescent lights were still aglow in the police booth down the street, and the local baker was just rolling out the croissants on a floured slab for the first flood of commuters.

That was when I rowed. I dressed in the dark, drove in the dark, rowed in the first gray of dawn, and arrived home at six-twenty, ten minutes before the alarm sounded. I stripped off my T-shirt and leg- gings, slipped over my head a nightgown abandoned an hour and a half before, and eased myself quietly into bed once again, arm under pillow, calming my breath, closing my eyes, pretending I had never left. When my husband awoke to the alarm ten minutes later, he would wordlessly lay a hand on my hip for a few moments, then say with a chilling tone that my nightgown didn't fool him; he could tell I had been on the water because I was quivering with excitement, and it wasn't for him. For once, he recognized the truth.

Chapter Six

HEARING

THE VOICES

Janie is now of an age when she looks at me
blankly when I tell her what to do. She
wants me to care about what she feels and
thinks, but won't tolerate my attempt to shape
her vision of the world or how she acts on it. I
figure my job as mother is to let her know
that I love her, fasten my seatbelt, and
trust that the voice of reason,
common sense, caution, proportion, self-
preservation—in short, my voice—has become
so much a part of her that it speaks from within,
not beseechingly from outside her closed bedroom door, from which drift the smell of
incense and the throb of a Sarah
McLachlan song. Except as supplier
of cash and transportation to the mall, I understand that I'm pretty inconvenient. I can only hope

my voice rings out clear and convincing in her head, has become part of her own and helps her steer her path through the world.

We find our way guided by a host of external and internal voices. The trick is to figure out which ones to trust, to make part of a daily chorus, and which to tune out as tiresome, or whose message is insidiously destructive. Somewhere along the way we make our selection, as Janie did when I got a new car recently. She jumped in, smelled the new car smell for a few moments, then went right to work on the radio, choosing her favorite stations and working the buttons so she could permanently skip all but a few frequencies.

Sometimes we make bad choices, tuning out stations with important traffic or weather updates or vital civil defense instructions. Sometimes we end up accidentally listening to those malignant commuter-hour talk shows that fill the car with a chatter of leering vulgarity, poisoning our morning drive to school. Once the choices are made, sometimes long ago when lives and "issues," as Janie says, were different, it takes an act bordering on insurrection to change them, as if the act of choosing, itself, had some kind of authority.

My first year on the water, I became aware that some of the station selections I had programmed into memory were reporting news and making editorial commentary that no longer served me. I was aware, too, that there were stations I had heard once upon a time, but which had been drummed out by the numbing monotony of one powerful station—"The Voice of Acquiescence 24/7." In some ways I felt I had for nearly thirty years been driving behind an endless hill that blocked reception to the frequency with "my song." If I were to hear the voices again, find the rhythms to guide me on the harbor and at home, I'd have to have the courage to dump the station that obscured the others, and retune my heart and head to listen for the clear, resonant voices singing my truth, speaking my heart.

On a practical level, I needed to find the voice that could teach me how to row. Day after day I churned up and down the harbor, thrashing and flipping, and no Merlin miraculously appeared to take me in hand. I found it ironic that as a child of relative affluence growing up in a university town, I had had access to any lesson I could possibly want. Classical guitar, medieval calligraphy, country dancing? All were available, and my mother, wanting her children to experience a diversity of the arts, dropped us at our lessons with a check for the teacher in our pockets and a promise to pick us up in an hour. As an adult of relative affluence I had a host of diversions to choose from—faux finishing workshops, tennis clinics, English garden design classes, and stress management seminars to help my friends and me deal with it all. But now that I had found the discipline I most ardently wished to pursue, I was bereft of teacher, seminar, and workshop. In Boston or Philadelphia it would have been a different story, but in Huntington, New York, there was no one who could, or would, impart the arcane knowledge of single shell sculling. There were no classes, and as far as I knew no coach willing to give private instruction (and, of course, no one but me seeking it). So I turned to the ultimate authority. I went where every mother finally goes when she needs answers to life's questions. I went to my reference librarian.

I walked into the Cold Spring Harbor Library late one afternoon in June, past the children's section, my usual destination, and on to the desk across the hall. Nancy Savas had helped me before and I knew her skills verged on the oracular—to no question would she respond, "Gosh, I don't know if I can find the answer to *that* one." She was always behind her desk tapping on her computer or flipping purposefully through an enormous tissue-leafed volume in search of an arcane fact.

Nancy glowed with purpose—her eyes bright and alert, body barely settled in her seat, always on the verge of jumping up to slash through the thicket of trivia and ferret out an elusive morsel of information. Her domain was orderly, tools lined up ready to spring to her service: microfiche, *Reader's Guide to Periodicals*, computer, *OED*, card file. I presented my case. "No problem," she said with the gleeful anticipation of the hunter who hears his dogs baying just over the rise. Within a week I had all the books on rowing in the state of New York interlibrary loan system, a copy of every article that had appeared on rowing in the last five years, and the information number for the U.S. Rowing Association from which I could order a thick sheaf of free instructional pamphlets.

First thing in the morning after breakfast and before setting off in the station wagon, I pored over my books and pamphlets for a few minutes. I toted them in my car to read at the gas station, stacked them next to the toilet, and piled them on the corner of the kitchen table to dip into while the eggs fried. As I rowed at dawn every morning, I thought about the components of the stroke, tried to imitate what I had read. I checked in regularly with Nancy, who promised to leave no stone unturned.

We made a great team. I heeded her voice, but she heeded mine as well. As that summer passed, then the next, I reported my progress to her nearly weekly (the local library being the apex of a triangular circuit including the grocery store and nursery school). As time went by, we both had the pleasure of knowing that her participation in my quest had started to reap tangible rewards. In early August 1996, fourteen months after we had started working together, I walked into the Cold Spring Harbor Library one morning and laid my first medal on her desk. Wordlessly she stood and clasped my hand, raising it overhead in a victory gesture.

Two weeks later, she stopped me as I checked out a stack of children's books and handed me a gift-wrapped parcel. "It's taken me nine months to have this autographed, but I was determined that you should have it." I opened the wrapping. It was a copy of *Assault on Lake Cassitas* by Brad Lewis, the story of a great iconoclast rower who defied a rigid establishment and seemingly insurmountable odds to win the Olympics. I opened the cover. Inside, written in black felt tip, were the words: "To Sara, Best of luck with your rowing. Brad."

Less than a year later, Nancy sold her house and moved with her young daughter to Sioux City to join the reference department for the library system there. We went out for tea, the first time we'd met outside the library, just before she left. "You know, you had a lot to do with my decision," she said. "I was in a rut here, and I don't think I would have had the courage to take charge of my life, to try for the new position, if you hadn't shown me that it could be done. You're my shining example." Two weeks later, Nancy and her daughter went west to start their new life. I'll always remember her, and I'll always treasure the book she gave me for its message of defiance and triumph, and for its source—my local reference librarian, the fairy godmother in the middle of every town, who plied her skill in service of my dream.

One of the books Nancy got for me was *The Sculler at Ease*, by Frank Cunningham, a devotee of the stroke and a longtime coach. Though his book was published only seven years earlier, it pointedly eschews up-to-date lore on training techniques and lactic acid tests. In his first chapter he gives the best advice I could have heard that first summer. He told me to put down for a moment all the magazines and how-to books (of which his was one) and attend carefully to the example of nature. Find an aquarium and watch the fish, he tells us, then move your own hand through water like a fishy fin, feeling the drive and the feather. Note that nothing in a fish's movement seems forced or awkward, jerky or extraneous. In the rhythm of the gills, the seemingly effortless propulsion of the stroke are the fundamentals of fine sculling where nothing can be "muscled," the movement of the vessel never dominated by brute force. I imagined a stroke liquid and powerful at once, calm as a trout feathering its lateral fins in the current, biding its time under a rock.

So I watched the fish in my son's ten-gallon aquarium as they lazily moved in and out of the submerged castle with its crenellated turrets, around the green plastic palm trees. I lay in the bathtub at night after the kids were in bed, stroking and feathering the water with my palms, feeling the resistance, moving my palms and fingers like a dancer. Then I practiced on the water, hour after hour, day after day.

In summer, bluefish ran just off the shores of Long Island. Bluefish are voracious feeders and drive legions of smaller fish—bunker—to the surface, where they leap and boil as if they're already in the soup pot. Bunker sometimes hit my blades and banged against my boat; one actually jumped over my stern one morning, to my delight. Sometimes in the dawn when the bunker surged and their white bellies flashed around me as they twisted, I felt as if they were minions sent to me on a mission from another realm, like Cinderella's singing mice, making a blue and pink ball gown to clothe her for a new and better life.

Ultimately, though, it was as much the birds as the fish that taught me what I needed to learn of grace. Every morning I watched the osprey leave its nest in the salt marshes at the end of the harbor and skim the water in search of breakfast. I listened to its whistling cry and the whisper of wings as it stroked past me, hunting in the first light of the morning. Its creamy underside glowed in the dawn, modeled and voluptuously smooth. The tapered, balanced bulk of its fuselage was held aloft by the liquid grace of its wings carrying their cargo of blood and bone, hooded eyes, honed senses.

The stroke of its wing was a miracle of nuance. Good sculling, even at race speeds, looks like this from shore—effortless, instinctual, relaxed. To describe the exquisitely complex system of wingbeat or sculling stroke with words is nearly impossible. How can you delineate the flex of each joint, flare of each feather, profile the application of energy on each axis through the course of each beat?

At some point after studying all my books and rowing thousands of strokes, I realized that ultimately I would have to strip away all the mechanics—the intellectualizing and theory that confounded me—and simply trust that God wouldn't have sent me on this mission if He hadn't granted me the measure of grace to move as a mermaid, a bird, a fish. If the osprey seemed to proclaim, "I am bird. I fly, I fish, I rule these waters," it was time for me to say, "I am sculler. I stroke,

I drive, I balance like an angel dancing on the head of a pin." A hunting bird doesn't wake up every morning asking itself, "What is my purpose? Are these wings really going to work?" It arises and flies efficiently and instinctually, with the least amount of effort, fewest calories to catch the most fish. Period. The ability to fly comes from being a bird, not from acting like a bird.

I practiced a few more thousand strokes until the trees turned russet and the frigid water felt thick as maple syrup, the cold wind blew down the harbor and the osprey went south. From June until the end of October 1995, I rowed over a hundred hours and five hundred miles with no other instruction than books and fish and birds.

Turns out I was pretty terrible.

While my instinct was sound—the elements of grace, rhythm, and a sense of line are something you either have or you don't—sculling, like playing Bach or dancing *Swan Lake*, calls not only for talent but also for the technique to make it manifest. I still slapped my blades at every release, lunged for every catch, and rushed every slide; in short, I woefully lacked the technical skills acquired only by working with a coach whose experience and analytical eye hones the stroke to a fine point. In November, then, when I saw an old *U.S. Rowing* magazine in the boathouse and found an advertisement for a sculling school in Florida, I thought if I could somehow convince my husband to let me go for just three days this winter, I might actually get lessons.

I longed to go alone. I longed to take an airplane by myself and row from dawn to dusk, get a deli sandwich for dinner, collapse in bed, and row from dawn to dusk again the next day, and the next, like an initiate undergoing a solo rite of passage in the Outback. I quailed at the prospect of asking my husband. Discussion, if it had anything to do with an autonomous act, was exhausting and anxiety-ridden for me. Generally I didn't even try, and when I did, I caved in to his point of view soon after my first carefully crafted overture.

I couched my proposal in what I thought were appealing terms— if I fill the fridge with food? Find a time you're traveling anyway? Only three days? No, it made no sense at all, he told me. Sure I could go—he wanted me to be happy—but not alone. He would come with me; we would have a lovely vacation. He would learn to row, too, and from now on we would have a wholesome time on the water together, the two of us, a recreational couples activity. I wouldn't ever row by myself again, because he would always be there by my side. Besides, it wasn't natural or right that I was alone out there every morning. I think even then he was afraid I would row away.

We flew to Florida together in January 1996. He arranged the tickets, getting the best seats because he knew from years of experience the best first-class seats on every type of aircraft; he knew the gate agent, and thus didn't have to flash his mileage card. He handled the rental car, getting us something large and safe, checked into the hotel, tested the bed. In the morning he greeted the coaches, two men and one woman, with a comradely quip and guffaw, a hearty handshake, as if this were another exclusive club and they were a team of tennis pros whom you address casually as Rick or Marty and who cheerfully and deferentially address you as Mr. or Mrs. So-and-So. They thought he was a swell guy and wasn't it nice that he wanted to learn this difficult sport just to be near his wife. While I still feel angry that he couldn't leave me alone for even a moment, now years later I can also imagine he was trying to convince himself that it was safe there and was just like the Beach Club or the Skating Club or the Yacht Club. Convince himself that by rowing I wasn't really escaping the life we had known. (And later that year when we took the children to a rowing camp in Vermont for a few days, I could sense his desire to take in hand the boundless energy of my passionate quest and put it into a tightly lidded box labeled "Fun Family Activity," like the fishing trips or family drives we sometimes took on weekend mornings.)

At the time, though, all I wanted was to cut through the club banter and work with the coaches for those three days until I dropped with exhaustion and they beached their launches drained. This was my one big opportunity and I intended to take it. The coaches quickly picked up on the fact that my husband was relaxed and convivial, happy to knock off a few minutes early; I was inconveniently demanding and intense. Of course I was demanding and intense—I'd rowed five hundred miles to get here and had only three days to learn everything they could teach me.

On Day One, the voices of the three coaches yelled over the sound of the launch, "No, your elbows are still too low. Didn't you hear what I said? Up, up!" "You have to hang on the oars, hang!" "Keep your head up and your back straight!" "Don't let your midsection collapse at the finish like a broken beer can. Stay strong!" "Don't yank with your arms; drive with your legs!" On and on. I listened, worked, wrote down everything I'd learned in a red spiral-bound notebook, making notes after each practice, summarizing after drying the boat and placing it on the rack. At the end of the first day, my muscles ached, my hands were a welter of blisters, my knuckles nicked and scabbed.

That day, it was hard to hear the magnitude of my stroke's inadequacy. I'd worked with such ardor all those days on the harbor, tried to do what the books and the birds had taught me, tune myself to the sweetness of the rhythm. Now I found myself rowing to the strident complaints of my bruised ego, an exhausting riff of righteousness and indignation at high volume inside my head as each coach tore my stroke apart. Turns out my capacity for self-delusion was substantially more developed than my rowing technique. Silently I protested, "But I've done what you told me, you can't be seeing my elbows drop." "What do you mean, my finish is a mess? Can't you see how hard I'm trying?" "Why are you telling me I'm missing water at the catch when I'm doing everything you're telling me?"

Hour after hour I rowed what I thought were lovely strokes; hour after hour that first day one of the coaches would ride alongside, squinting at my efforts in the bright Florida sun, trying to decide which of my many defects to address first. About five o'clock, I started to feel my throat tighten and the corners of my mouth quiver, and tried to get a grip before exposing myself as not only vain and inept but pathetically weepy and thin-skinned. I was thin-skinned, though. (And I do cry often, and messily, for which I do not apologize.) It had been years since I'd experienced biting criticism outside my domestic existence.

Luckily, there was another station on the airwaves. This was the fundamentalist South, after all, so it's no surprise another, vastly nobler voice began to drown out the oppressive discord and self-pitying strains of my indignation. The voice that rang out posed all the predictable evangelical rhetoric that, on another day, in another place, might prompt my hand to flick the radio dial quick as a slap to a mosquito. *Why are you here? What is your mission?* But I listened, realizing that all the obstinate whininess in my head was nothing but the normal freight of human vanity, which unless it were pitched overboard now, this afternoon, would slow my boat as surely as if I were dragging a sea anchor of snake grass and old fishing line on my skeg. *Why are you here? What is your mission?* By Day Three, I noticed the boat was beginning to feel lighter, quicker.

By the time I peeled off my wet Lycra and said my last goodbyes two days later, I began to hear a new message, one unexpected and unnerving. Driving to the airport, flying home, lying in bed in the dark late that night, and the next, and the next, I heard from some long-forgotten place a chorus that became increasingly clear and free of static, as if I were emerging from behind that interminable hill and were once again within radio range. Night after night I heard the murmur of voices, low and melodious, sweet and urgent. It was as if pale faces hovered near my bed—a thirteen-year-old, thin-cheeked and dizzy with sorrow; a Little Mermaid, tongueless and yearning: a forty-three-year-old mother, pinioned by the hand of a man who seemed forever angry. *Speak for us*, they seemed to say. *Race for us.*

Win for us.

Chapter Seven

HEEDING

THE CALL

Race? Win? What happened to a
life in which finishing all the shopping
for the camp's crafts classes was basis for personal satisfaction? Wasn't caring for children,
home maintenance, and community service
enough? For heaven's sake, I wasn't Joan
of Arc getting her marching orders
from God to take up a sword and
head out into the fields to rally an
army against an oppressor. It wasn't as if
I were saving a nation, was it? And yet there
they were—the voices. There the mission, clear
as cold water. There the yearning, hot as a
flame. Although the call of the voices
was, at the time, neither convenient
nor particularly welcome, it wasn't really
such a surprise. In the summer of 1995, my

first summer on the water, I picked up David Halberstam's *The Amateurs*, an account of rival athletes striving to make the Olympic Rowing Team. I began it one afternoon at the playground, the other straw-hatted moms and me all reading our paperbacks and glancing fondly at our toddlers. However, unlike the other moms (as far as I know), I soon began silently to seethe, like some heroine in a French movie who rides a bus home from work with an impassive face and a head boiling with rich and lurid fantasies. The story of rowers expressing their own fierce competitive desire on the race course was hugely, startlingly stimulating to me. While we waited on the bench, placid as robins, listening for the distant jingle of the ice cream truck, I began to burn with a lust to put my own bow on the line and unchain the killer within. So aroused with competitive desire was I that I closed the book and shoved it deep in the bottom of my canvas tote, like tattered erotica.

Then one day at the end of October, three months before going to Florida, I found on the log stand in the boathouse a magazine article on the Masters National Championship in Minneapolis that year. I sat on the damp boathouse bench in the early morning cold, poring over photographs of adults like me wearing wraparound sunglasses and flexing their shoulder muscles in the heat of the race, sweat and spray flying. Once again I found myself filled with a longing both visceral and embarrassing. A surge of desire to be in the world, in the race, and on the line issued from what I had thought to be an emotional life securely and rigidly contained by daily ritual and responsibility.

At first I tried to turn away from urges quickly becoming overwhelming. "I'm not good enough," I told myself. "I don't have enough experience; don't have a coach, don't have a boat . . . maybe in a few years when I feel more ready, when the kids are in college." "No, I'm not the least bit competitive—a nurturer, not a killer." And finally, vainly, "I only row to feel the water and watch the birds. A gentle meditative thing. No, no. I can't possibly race."

I didn't mention all this to my husband. I felt sure that for my husband, I, with my new desire to race, would bear an alarming sim-

ilarity to the kind of woman I sometimes heard him ridicule at cocktail parties to a chorus of laughter and spray of crumbs, the pleasant,
obedient wife who suddenly cuts off her long hair or joins a women's
discussion group. Either seemed a sure sign that she has spun out of
control and teeters on the brink of deserting her family to join the
circus or become a militant homosexual—funny when it comes to
another man's wife, frightening when it comes to your own.

But the strength of my desire felt frightening to me too, not least
because I had no idea what racing a single shell entailed, and I was,
apparently, to do it. Soon. More frightening, though, were the personal implications of heeding the call. If my intuition told me that
racing would wreak havoc on the status quo, it was recognition that
told me my husband's power to keep me nicely at heel depended on
my willingness to remain as I had been.

I found myself facedown on the sofa in the family room one
afternoon about a week after coming back from Florida, sobbing as
if I were turning inside out. One part of me demanded that I let the
woman hiding inside show at last all the passion, worship, and rage
that would become, for me, the essence of racing. The other was sor-
rowful and wheedling, telling me I lacked the strength and courage to
go the course. After all the years of convincing myself that the con-
strictions of the life I had built, and the man with whom I had built
it, were just fine, in my desire to race I faced a new dimension of
engagement and expression that felt both utterly enlivening and terminally dangerous—a beginning and an end. The risks and rewards
of putting myself on the line, on the water and off, could overturn
life as I knew it.

On an April morning three months after the Florida trip, I
rinsed and dried *S4*, went home to get everyone on the school bus,
made the beds, and dialed the phone number I'd gotten from U.S.
Rowing in Indianapolis the day before. Bill McGowan, the competi-

tion coordinator for the Northeast sector, answered. I said, "I want to race. How do I start?"

After recovering from the astonishment of discovering that not only was I a housewife with minimal experience but I intended to race a single, he responded. "Nice and easy," he said. "Low key. Enter a small race, no pressure. Something local, with familiar faces . . . " He suggested the novice race of the Derby Sculls and Sweeps in Connecticut at the end of June. Very laid back. Perfect for a first race. "Here's the phone number." That evening I called the regatta chairman and signed up for the Sculls and Sweeps, eight weeks away.

The only time I'd experienced as much urge to throw up as I did in the following weeks was when I was pregnant for the first time and lay on the sofa every morning groaning and wishing for quick death. Every evening I barely resisted calling the regatta secretary to withdraw. Luckily, the first week in June I ran into a sculler named Jeff Schaeffer on the dock one morning as I was heading home. I'd met Jeff once before, at an evening meeting of the Sagamore Rowing Association. At thirty-five, he was the only masters competitor I knew of at Sagamore, had a lot of national and international racing experience, and seemed to be a knowledgeable person to whom I could relate my fears. In a friendship that has lasted some years now, I've found Jeff to be easygoing and friendly, and not nearly as burdened with a need for agonizing introspection as I. That morning on the dock, I told him I wasn't sure I could survive another three weeks of sickening anticipation; the race itself could hardly be worse than the agony of waiting. We talked about nerves for a few minutes, then he paused for less than a second before saying, "You don't have to wait three weeks. Come to the Empire State in Albany this weekend with my girlfriend and me. You can race Masters and Novice." He gave me the name and number of the regatta chairman, told me to say, "Jeff sent me," and assured me I would get in despite the fact that it was well past the entry deadline. He was right. They did let me in, much to my surprise and horror. I was going to race this weekend. Five days away.

The Empire State. This was insanity. I'd read the magazine; I knew the Empire State was a major East Coast regatta. "But, Jeff," I had said that morning, "I don't have any experience, don't even know how to do a racing start. I can't go in a straight line yet." I protested with all my season of 1996 objections; he replied with what became his season of 1996 responses. "Sure you can. I've seen you out there. You're good enough—you'll be fine." This was the sum of Jeff's pep talk. I heard it over and over that summer as we became training partners and started to row together more and more. Over and over I decided to believe him against all the evidence of my inexperience. It was the right decision.

Diamond State Championships? "Sure you can!" Maine State Championships? "Sure you can!" The Royal Canadian Henley, one of the largest regattas in the world? "Sure you can!" U.S. Masters Nationals? "Sure you can!" Finally, Head of the Charles, the most terrifying, technically challenging, mettle-testing single scull race on earth? "Sure you can!" I don't know that Jeff gave more than the most cursory of thoughts to his assurances, but I persistently took them as gospel, in spite of the fact that he soon emerged as a character so perennially optimistic that I suspected he would have delivered the same encouragement to anyone who could put three strokes together. In 1996, I raced regattas I wouldn't have dared enter for another three years if it hadn't been for Jeff's casual "Sure you can!"

There are men out there, some women too—mostly young ones who have had the benefit of the enormous boon Title Nine has been to women's sports over the last twenty years—who hear me talk about crying on the sofa, or trying not to throw up, or wrestling with angst, and say, "What's the big deal? Stop sniveling and row your race."

But it was a big deal in a lot of ways. I hadn't ever had the courage to test myself in my marriage, or in the larger world. That was a big deal. The extraordinary mental and technical demands of the single shell were far different from those of the eight-man sweep boats to which most women my age were drawn. That was a big deal. But finally, if the idea of racing was a big deal to me, it was also a big deal to many women my age, for whom competitive athletics was unfamiliar and frightening territory.

Competitive sports had no place in their lives after childhood swim teams and maybe a season or two of field hockey in high school. In the days before the Title Nine legislation required universities to spend an equal amount on men's and women's athletics, very few women played college sports. It is the rare woman who has competed enough on a regular enough basis to make the testing and confrontation of competitive sports as much a part of her daily life as it is to a man. As a result of Title Nine, which was passed in the early seventies but not really enforced until ten years later, there is a large population of seasoned women athletes currently in their twenties and thirties, but few in their forties or older.

One reason most of my competitors in the single shell have been Olympic athletes and professional women is that in the mid-seventies when I was in college there was very little collegiate women's rowing. The few programs available produced a small pool of women who, if they were good, went on to the then-new U.S. Women's National Team. The first Olympics to include U.S. women rowers was 1976, and a number of those women would become my competitors twenty years later. The balance of my competitors were almost exclusively single, childless female professionals, who display the kind of drive and competitiveness in their careers that suggest a lifelong relish of confrontation and aggressive engagement.

So, while the age categories below mine were full of women who had competed throughout their lives, my own category of women in their forties was both far smaller and populated by a Darwinian selection process that produced, in the competitive sense, killer personalities. No wonder Bill was taken aback when he learned what I was and what I intended to do. No wonder he cautioned me to start "low key." And now, in the spring of 1996, I was about to start nowhere near low key, about to race the best masters women scullers in the Northeast without even knowing how to row a straight line.

Suddenly it was real. Suddenly I was making reservations at a motel in Albany and calling Triple A for a map, checking the tire pressure, clearing the use of *S4* with the club secretary. My husband offered little resistance. I would be gone for less than twenty-four hours and was taking only Janie, having gotten a sitter for the boys. But mostly I think he hoped my likely humiliation on the race course could cure me of my temporary madness.

I went to a Sagamore Rowing Club monthly meeting two nights before the race. The club president, Andy Krause, came over and sat next to me for a few moments before the meeting began. His face was serious, almost stern. "I hear you're headed to Albany this weekend," he said with a hint of *There, there, little lady* in his voice. "Not really a race for beginners, you know. The Hudson can kick up a lot of chop; loads of trash and logs on the course, too. You'll be up against tough, experienced competition. You sure you really want to do this? Think you're ready?" I watched his lips move, listened attentively. I paused a moment, then replied in as steady and casual a voice as I could, "I'm going to give it a try. Don't think I'll actually drown, and I'll do my best not to run *S4* into the bridge. I'll be okay."

Andy shook his head sorrowfully, as if I were bent on a suicide mission, and abandoned me for the podium, where he called the meeting to order. His empty seat was filled a moment later by one of the high school coaches, Peter Bisik, whom I had met once before on the dock and who, I was sure, didn't know or care to know the middle-aged woman fumbling with her oars. He leaned over and beckoned with a finger. He sounded excited, almost conspiratorial. "When I heard you were going to the Empire State, I couldn't believe it. I've gone ahead and rigged *S4* high so you won't have to worry about your blades clearing the waves," he said in a whisper. "You're going to be fine if you stay loose and keep a steady head. Knock 'em dead, kid. I want a full report when you get back." He clasped my hand for a moment, then slipped away.

The next morning when I tried to eat breakfast, I was lightheaded and my hands were shaking. I felt dizzy with vertigo. By the end of the day I would be on the Long Island Expressway heading north to Albany with my little girl beside me and a tiny gray boat overhead.

I did the morning dishes, got in the car, and drove to the water. There is a rock on the quiet, wild side of the harbor, the south side, a rock I had rowed past four times a day for much of a year—the "loaf of bread" rock, I liked to call it. I sat on the loaf of bread rock that morning, closed my eyes, and asked for help.

Where will I find the strength to endure this ordeal? How will I keep my heart steady enough to mark my stroke for eight minutes? How will I find the balance of my little boat when I'm trembling with fear, be brave when all these years I've been a coward? I looked up the harbor, still and dark green, the shadows of trees just shading the southern perimeter.

I remembered a morning five years before—my cheerful, bossy, maternal sister Annie as serious and troubled as I've ever seen her, sitting in my warm kitchen with me. I was five months pregnant with William, my youngest son. She had taken my shoulders in her hands and looked into my eyes with pleading and anger. "Sara, you have to wake up. You can't let him treat you like this. You have to make him stop, or you have to get out. What he does to you—there is a word for it. Can you hear me? Listen to me!" Then she said the word. But I was numb and sleepy and pregnant. Where would I go? How could I ever get free? She let go of my shoulders and went back to Colorado two days later. Every few months she called after my older two had been tucked in bed and the baby nursed, flushed and sleeping on his yellow flannel crib sheet. Was I okay? Had I thought about what she said?

And now, almost half a decade later, the time had come to give birth to yet another new life. My new life. How many women feel the first pang of labor and are overcome with fear they can't withstand the pain, that they won't survive (and before my grandmother's time, how many didn't)? How many women clutch the corner of an apron, grip the edge of a kitchen table, gasp at the knowledge of what might befall them?

I sat on the rock, my arms clasped around my knees, eyes pressed tightly shut, and asked for the words to take me through. Within a breath of wind, a whisper of wings, a musical ripple of water on the sand near my feet, I heard a voice clear and sweet as the peal of a tuned bell. This is what I heard, this and only this. *Do your best. Love your competitors. Feel the rhythm.* That was all. That was enough.

Chapter Eight

THE SHINING

ARROW

On my desk at home is a framed, matted
photograph of a single shell floating absolutely
still and ready at the dock, port oar resting on the
wooden boards, blade turned up to the sky, starboard oar secured in the oarlocks, suspended
just over the water. The harbor is a dark
mirror with streaks of pink and silver
from the dawning sky, the far shoreline a
black margin, neatly and finally defining the
parameters of the world it contains. The boat,
Sagamore 4, is in reality a dull gray; but in the
photograph it has a luminous silver quality
and appears slender and clean as an
arrow, waiting to leap with the touch of blade
to water. The dock leading to the shell descends
from the boathouse and narrows, funneling from
the shelter of the warm boat bays, fragrant with the
smell of wood, varnish, mildewed towels.

The photograph has both a mythic quality—a serenity associated with destiny already charted by the gods—and the immediacy of impending day, of energy to be joyfully expended. *Sagamore 4* waits for my hand to bring it to life. Waits for us to incise the silvery meniscus of the water's surface, the exquisite band where every human story takes place, pressed, in our course down the dark harbor, into the tiny zone of human survivability between endless sky and drowning deep. The image of *Sagamore 4* reminds me of those photographs of the Earth from the Moon, so precious and fragile in a vast black universe, glowing from the surface of the page with the beauty and possibility of life.

I took the photograph at five o'clock one morning in late May 1996, shortly before the race in Albany. I had learned a few weeks before that I was to be driven from (all of us were to be driven from) our treasured decrepit home on the harbor. The boathouse, nearby defunct buildings, and all the land on which they stood had been sold to a real estate developer who planned to dock his motorboats and entertain his guests there if the structure were sound enough, or tear it down and build something far nicer if the dry rot, drafts, and bird droppings were insurmountable. We had learned of the transaction five weeks before the eviction date and were told we would have to vacate the structure by mid-June—boats, oars, gas cans, rotten shoes, and all—and start over in Huntington Harbor, three miles away across open water tossed by the swells and weather rolling in from Long Island Sound.

There is a fifteenth-century fresco by Masaccio, *The Expulsion from Paradise*, in which a sobbing Adam and Eve stumble unhappily from the Garden. All I can think of when I see this utterly crestfallen pair is that their sorrow is so real—not abstract, heroic anguish, eyes cast heavenward, titanic limbs raised in graceful supplication. The faces on these two are the faces of children from whom the candy has been yanked, whose favorite toy has been torn apart by the dog, whose mother has kissed them, given instructions to the new, unknown baby-sitter and walked cheerfully out the door.

These are the faces of visceral sadness, faces clotted with tears and runny noses.

This was the face I wore when I contemplated my own impending expulsion from paradise. I sat in the doorway of the boathouse one afternoon as the rain pounded on the roof and fat drops rolled from the eaves, striking a steady cadence on the wooden planks of the dock, and cried a harbor of tears. Fast approaching was the moment when I would have to row to the end of the harbor, thread my way through the narrow opening clogged with boats and mooring cables, the spiky remains of an old pier at low tide, and head into the deep, open water on the other side, never to return to my beloved new home.

In the early eighties, I lived in San Francisco and had been married about three years. For two years I had tried to conceive and suffered all the tests—the dye and the swabs. Finally my breasts swelled and the plus sign appeared in the little plastic window of the pregnancy kit, and for a few months I thought of nothing but booties and knitted caps. Then I started to bleed, a drop here and there at first, then a slow flow. In the fourth month, I dreamed one night that I was swimming in San Francisco Bay with a tiny black baby whale and that the little whale turned from me and swam with a flip of its tail through the narrow channel under the bridge, and off into the open ocean, out of sight forever. "Too soon, too soon," I cried in my dream. That morning I awoke to a rush of dark blood.

But for me in 1996 it wasn't too soon; I'd had my full term in Lloyd Harbor. The time had come to get out and get tough. I took a baby step one morning about a week before the exodus. After the children were in school, I drove down to the boathouse and rowed *S4* to the end of the harbor. Then I took a deep breath and rowed to the other side, into the vast openness of the bay. I was scared shitless. When you fly on an airliner or travel by ship, you maintain the illusion on some level that you are traveling on a little piece of solid earth that happens to be surrounded by air or water. To realize you are nothing but a tiny speck hurtling through a medium in which mankind was not designed to survive causes considerable anxiety and prompts you to devote scrupulous attention to the in-flight movie or gossip magazine. Likewise, my terror of the open harbor had little to do with a realistic fear of hostile storm or death by hypothermia (though both were possibilities). It had much more to do with the image of my fluttering human heart and soft freckled skin perched on a ridiculously inadequate sliver of carbon, alone far from shore and without any illusion of comfy protection. Below me were leagues of dark, cold water and a host of slippery, unsentimental creatures that would never bear names like Bambi or Thumper. Above, a vast uninterested sky. I made myself row a quarter mile straight out into the open, turned and scurried back through a rising chop to the safety of the harbor.

Then, a week after the race in Albany, it was time to go for good. The day before the locks were to be changed and the boat-house doors rolled shut for the last time, the members of Sagamore gathered a motley collection of trailers and station wagons outside the boathouse and spread a lifetime's accumulation of equipment and assorted junk on the green lawn. Some was to be transported to the boathouse in Huntington, some to the Dumpster. All the gas cans and life vests, the milk crates filled with pads and old seats were loaded into the backs of cars. The high school's eights and fours were loaded onto trailers, marked with red stern flags, and hauled away, bouncing over the rutted dirt road in a plume of dust, out of sight up the hill. By the end of the day everything was gone, even the eight-track stereo and rusted folding chair from the balcony. Only a lone coaching launch and the single shells remained. It was easier to row the shells to the new boathouse than to de-rig and load them on a trailer. They would be rowed to the new boathouse by their owners and the volunteers who had been called to help with the mournful exodus.

The next morning at six we met on the dock. We stood fidgeting, longing for and dreading the moment when someone would say,
"It's time, now. Let's go." We were very quiet. Unaccountably, I found
myself thinking about the time I waded through a snowstorm to use
the rowing machines upstairs, remembered how cold and silent the
unheated boathouse was in late December, how I had to wear mittens
and my breath hung in the air, but the eight-track player still worked,
blasting someone's abandoned Barry Manilow tape. Mine were the
only tracks to the boathouse for a week or more.

I knew the other scullers had to be thinking about sitting on the
red bench outside the big doors and watching the water of the harbor turn color, remembering the first time they flipped at this dock
and the first time they smelled the drooping white spirea on a June
afternoon as they headed over the shorn meadow to the boathouse
and water's edge. We all signed the log for the last time, entering our
names, the names of our shells, the time. Then one by one we lowered ourselves into our boats, stowing our shoes in the tiny cockpits
because we were never coming back. Someone rolled the big doors
shut and clasped the new padlock. One by one we pushed off and
hovered offshore, waiting for all to be waterborne.

At some signal I could never discern, we began stroking at once,
like migrating birds beating their way to the mouth of the harbor.
The coaching launch, with its life jackets and megaphone, chugged
along behind to protect us. Then we plunged through, bursting in a
wave of frantic exhilaration to the other side, into the wide, cold,
choppy expanse. Wind whipped at our blades, a hat blew off. We
headed east, toward the new sun, the spray stinging our cheeks.
We clung together in a flock, blades flashing in the open water as we
crossed. At the lighthouse we turned as if in formation, wheeling
south toward the channel buoys. We were swept now by a tidal current into the boat basin, where we scattered to find paths through the
powerboats and fishing boats, and a half-sunken dry dock, all of us
seeking a glimpse of a stout, graceless, cement boathouse that was our
new home.

If Lloyd Harbor had a dreamy, protected, isolated quality—the watery version of an enchanted forest—Huntington Harbor teemed with all the human vigor of an airport or a shopping mall. The new boathouse from which we rowed was on public land located next to the town gas dock and thus witness to a constant stream of thirsty pleasure craft and fishing boats of all sizes. The parking lot serving both docks was gargantuan and provided some of the local residents rich opportunity for languorous afternoons of beer drinking, lazy hours of smoking dope, frenetic evenings of sweaty necking. The boathouse dock did double duty as prime fishing venue for the town and was host to a population of mostly Spanish-speaking men meticulously baiting hooks, casting into the tidal waters, and settling down on aluminum lawn chairs with a bag of chips and a can of Bud for a pleasant afternoon of quiet talk and infrequent reward. Sometimes whole families would make a day of it on the dock, with a litter of children and toys and a collection of Styrofoam coolers. In all there was a sense for me of beginning to ply my craft in a larger, more public arena. I really had "come into the world."

At first I simply rowed to the end of "Puppy Cove," a protected thumb of water off the main thoroughfare, and back. With a length of only fifty strokes, this was like trying to jog in a basement playroom. Then I rowed down the harbor toward CoCo's and the repair marinas. Soon I discovered that to operate successfully, or at least safely, in a larger, more populated world, I had to pay a lot more attention to where I was going than in Lloyd Harbor, where the worst that could happen was to run the boat up on a sandbank if I forgot to check my course. How many times those first days in Huntington was I concentrating on some technical aspect of the stroke and felt a prickling on the back of my neck, a tiny alarm in my head shrilling with the sense of a kind of magnetic field of mass fast approaching. Instinctively I would brace with my blades, slamming to a stop inches from plowing *S4*'s tiny, tender bow broadside into a forty-foot steel fishing boat. Rule One: Survival in the big world requires staying alert.

Within a week I outgrew Huntington Harbor and longed to escape out the channel and head like a homing pigeon for Lloyd Harbor, nearly three miles away. The club frowned on this. It was one thing if a rower were experienced and had his own boat, like Jeff Schaeffer—free to endanger both boat and life at his own risk—or was traveling with a group under the protection of a launch, as we had in our transit to the new boathouse. Even then, a solo trip to Lloyd Harbor across the great gulf of the bay was thought to be as foolhardy as cliff diving, or climbing a sheer granite face without ropes. It was quite another for a novice—admittedly, since Albany, a modestly accomplished novice—to head out alone into the open ocean in a narrow racing single. But there was no rule on the books, probably because at that point no one but me wanted to do it. So, while the club scrambled to come up with a policy, I made a run for it. That's when I discovered Rule Two: Make adversity your friend.

There are single shells designated "recreational," or "open water," like my first boat, the *Chelsea*, designed for rowing through the swells and choppy water of exposed bays and ocean. Wider and more stable than racing singles, they also have "self-bailers," little ports that dump the water waves have poured over the gunwales. I didn't have an open water single, but I figured *S4*'s cockpit was so minimal it could only hold about four gallons tops. Anyone could row with four gallons in the boat, right? And I wouldn't be foolish, I would only go out in fair weather and make a beeline for Lloyd Harbor, taking care not to impale myself on the sharp rocks of the harbor entrance just beneath the water's surface at midtide, scuttling for cover if a storm threatened. The dark of predawn seemed, on reflection, an ill-advised hour for such an undertaking, so I parked in the giant lot next to some amiable dope smokers at nine-thirty one morning after the children were safely secured in day camp.

One of the reasons I ended up doing well in competition later that summer was that I not only knew my way around adverse conditions, I assumed adversity to be the norm; it didn't really occur to me that most people row on flat water contained by narrow banks because I had never experienced flat water and narrow banks. It was only a year later, when I began rowing on the Charles in Boston, that I discovered the felicity that is a nicely controlled river punctuated with friendly boat clubs and decorated with a nice mirror surface. My trip across the open water to Lloyd Harbor that morning in June bore no resemblance to river rowing and turned out to be chockfull of the character-building challenges to which I was beginning to find myself strongly attracted and which I soon accepted as a matter of course. First was the powerful tide.

Huntington Harbor opened into the larger bay through a channel grievously undersized, given both the quantity of boat traffic passing through it and the vast amount of water flowing one way or the other during a run of the substantial tide. So narrow was the channel that, when the tide ripped through, flooding into the harbor, rowing to the other side was like fighting your way upriver in a kayak. Unlike a kayak, however, a racing shell is designed to cope with neither the channel's current nor its standing waves, and responds to both with bad behavior. Many a sculler has swum there. So the experience of fighting my way out of the harbor was, as my mother says, "excessively exciting."

Once on the other side, I followed the channel markers to the dark stone lighthouse, an incongruous Gothic affair ringed by sharp, slimy rocks on which stood black cormorants with outstretched wings. The whole thing had the look of an outpost of some Evil Empire. I rowed around the lighthouse twice to ratchet up my courage, buy some time, and show the birds who's boss. Then I sighted the entrance to Lloyd Harbor in the distance, took a bearing on the Eaton's Neck power stacks off my stern to guide me, and struck off through a light chop, taking care to avoid the rocks I knew lay just under the surface to my port. About halfway across where the water was deepest I began to hear steel halyard shackles striking the sailboat masts, *clang, clang, clang,* at the distant entrance to the harbor. Steady now, I told myself, keep an eye on the power stacks. Then I caught my port blade on a soggy half-submerged kapok life jacket someone had made into a buoy.

Singles flip easily, but not quickly. Usually they go over with a slow, inexorable fatality. When my blade entangled with the life vest, I knew the damned owl was calling my name. But the stupidity of a soggy life vest moored out in the middle of a harbor was so irritating that I angrily threw my weight to starboard, bracing and yanking, and out popped my blade. After a moment of trembling and teetering on the edge of disaster, I realized my gunwales were still dry. I let my heart steady, and moved on.

The clanging became louder. Suddenly I was sliding past a big white cruiser on one side, a little ratty mustard-colored launch on the other. I picked my way through the clutter at the entrance to the harbor, careful not to become entangled in mooring cables, noting that the flooding tide had hidden the sharp pilings on port. Then I was home.

Oh, the joy of rowing to the end of my harbor, all the way to the osprey nests. I felt like a freshman who has come home for Christmas after the first semester of college, full of a new worldliness and confidence, smug with the experience of recent adult, high-risk behaviors. I rowed right up to the base of the nests that perched, ruffed by grasses, on their tall platforms. One of the osprey peered over the edge at me, whistling angrily; the other wheeled overhead, impatient for me to be gone.

I turned and stroked slowly back down the harbor, past the fallen tree, past the boathouse, shuttered and empty, dock covered now with Canada geese. Back through the sailboats, back across the open water, not quite as scary as before, round the lighthouse, triumphantly back down the channel markers toward the narrow harbor entrance. Then I noticed a large, very large, fishing boat. It was closing steadily at two o'clock on port.

When you have steam heat radiators, and you have babies, you know the two will get together sooner or later and there will be tears.

So it was with me and the fishing boat. The allure of rowing near its stern and showing off a little to the laconic fishermen standing at the railings was irresistible. Look at me, I wanted to shout, I'm almost as fast as you. I had no experience of boat wake, Lloyd Harbor being off-limits to motor traffic, and thus no healthy respect for its ability to throw off a wave that can swamp a shell and dowse a rower. I was busily impressing the fishermen with my best strokes when I noticed, too late, the tsunami quartering toward me. I'm sure the fishermen barely raised an eyebrow, watching it all unfold not with admiration but amused speculation.

The wave quickly caught up to me and washed over my decks, rolling up my stern, filling my cockpit to the brim, soaking me to the skin, and tossing *S4* to the side like an empty Coke can. In an instant we were transformed from fighting machine to flotsam. The fishermen were kind enough not to laugh; they turned away lazily to tend their gear and prepare to land at the dock. Thus I learned Rule Three: Best to move faster than other boats. This one I took to heart.

With the passage of weeks I came to use the fishing boats as a training tool. Sometimes I purposely sought them out, pulling alongside, then rowing like hell to stay ahead. It became a game, and I started to feel a wild, ferocious joy in my chest, a new surge of power in my body when I could hold off a fully loaded trawler bearing down on my stern. The fishing boats, the ripping tide, and the high chop challenged me to punch through the waves aggressively. They made me strong. The fog daring me to cross the bay guided only by the sound of seabirds, clanging shackles, recognition of distinctive buoys, made me canny. Each day, I got tougher. Each day, faster. Each day, more aware that the fragile seed of strength and sureness growing inside me was developing roots, bark, leaves. Looking back on that summer, I can see that leaving my ramshackle Eden in Lloyd Harbor was the best thing that could have happened to me because, though I didn't know it yet, I was getting ready to take on the world.

I never saw anyone else out there, except the oystermen with their long rakes, portable radios, and yellow dogs perched on their bows like figureheads. They came to know me and greeted me every morning, chiding me on windy mornings with a warning, "Take that greyhound of yours back to shore before it breaks in half and you drown!" One morning in late June about three weeks after Albany, I was crossing the bay and nearly collided with Jeff Schaeffer, wearing a perky formerly white tennis hat and rowing equally obliviously in the opposite direction. Neither of us expected to encounter another rower. We stopped, a half mile offshore, both sitting calmly in our inadequate and unseaworthy crafts, rising and falling on the big swells rolling off the Sound. We traded the news, talking awhile about the inhospitable conditions in Huntington, the byzantine nature of club politics, the next big race on the calendar—the Diamond State, in Delaware at the end of July. Then he suggested we train together. Just like that.

Train together. Why would Jeff want to train with me? He had a pile of gold medals from all over the world and I didn't know the first thing about training—I was busy staying upright and alive. But yes, he really did want to train with me; there was no one else in Sagamore who both rowed a single and was infected with a desire to race. Jeff needed a sparring partner because training with a partner, even as inadequate a partner as I, was better than going it alone.

Since that summer I've drawn some conclusions on the effectiveness of different training styles. Most serious scullers with the good fortune to row on a river with a sculling community train in wolf packs under the watchful eye of a coach prowling alongside in a motorized launch. They meet on the dock, chatting and laughing as they get ready for a morning of drills and mock races. There is a quality of interaction in the roving pack best characterized as both purposeful and jolly, involving a lot of banter, but also a good deal of anxious, covert comparison. Thoughts like "She has more body angle at the finish than I do, maybe I should try that," or "He barely bends his elbows before he's out of the water—that must be the key to his speed," constantly bedevil the wolf pack sculler. For most of my rowing career I have gone down to the boathouse alone, launched alone, rowed alone for an hour or two, wiped down my boat and put my oars in the rack alone, and headed off to greet my day, alone. I prefer to train by myself, or, as I was about to find in the summer of 1996, with one other sculler with whom I can experience the intimacy and challenge of sparring but maintain the inner intensity that can be lost in the conviviality of a group.

I know a young, immensely talented sculler who tried out for the National Team sculling program in Atlanta a few years ago and was rejected. The sculler didn't hang up his blades and resign himself to becoming a CPA; he moved to Boston, where his friend Jamie Koven, then reigning World Champion, trained on the Charles every day alone. The two men started training together, rowing intense "pieces"—timed periods of hard rowing—day after day, staging mock sprints, rowing the three-mile Head of the Charles course. When the sculler went back to Atlanta for the yearly National Team selection trials the next season, he was "off-the-charts" fast, simply blew everyone away. A few months later he won Henley, a spectacular achievement. Training with one partner, particularly an exceptionally skilled partner, works.

This was to be our daily drill. Jeff would send me out ten seconds ahead of his start, then chase me down with the determination of a hungry bobcat closing on a stringy jackrabbit. My job as prey was to row like the wind to avoid becoming part of the food chain before crossing the finish line. I soon learned that we would enact this nature drama up to ten times a day, day after day, week after week. Jeff's mission was to turn a housewife into as fast a rabbit as possible, as quickly as possible, so that he could gain maximum training benefit. What kind of magic turns a mother into a jackrabbit? Hour after hour of grueling work and sickeningly high heart rates, buckets of sweat, bleeding blisters, and muscles screaming day after day from lactic acid overload. Presto.

Jeff told me on our first day together that we would follow the Junior National Team workout, designed for eighteen-year-old pre-elite men in top condition. The workout varied every day but consisted of an hour of "pieces" alternating hard and easy work, plus warm-ups and cool-downs. At ages thirty-five and forty-three respectively, Jeff said, we should have no problem.

I thought I was going to die. We rowed every weekday morning after I got the kids in camp (Jeff wasn't as fond of dawn as I, and the heat I was getting at home from my predawn routine was reaching boiling point). By six every evening, I felt an overpowering urge to lie very still just when it was time to boil up another pot of pasta, nuke the frozen peas, and pour the milk in "tippy cups." But I didn't succumb to the siren song of the sofa. I did the dishes, read the stories, lanced my blisters and soaked in Epsom salts, and finally, slept like a rock. Jeff was a serious athlete and competitor, and if the program worked for him, I would make it work for me. It never occurred to me to moderate or modify the regime which, after all, had come by mail from U.S. Rowing.

My husband said little about my new regime, and the children seemed hardly aware of it. I rarely cut into their time, almost exclusively rowing on weekday mornings when the children were in camp and my husband was at work. He grumbled occasionally about my body, which was losing some of the softness and bulk left over from the years when I was pregnant or nursing; but mostly if he mentioned my rowing, it was as my "little recreational diversion."

It seems bizarre to me now that I didn't even consider trying to claim an hour from my family to get on the water Saturday or Sunday morning, as another woman might jog or take an exercise class. To ask my husband to baby-sit, what other mothers might have called "shared parenting," was to invite his criticism that I was selfish and negligent in my duties. He had made his position abundantly clear on this years before, and I hadn't the courage to challenge him. The idea of approaching him in his study some evening and attempting to negotiate an attitude adjustment, gave me a lump in my stomach like a stone.

Three weeks after Albany, he had come to the Derby Sculls and Sweeps where I raced the Novice Women. It was one of the few of my races he witnessed, and when I pulled into the dock, I was very excited—I had come in second. I asked him breathlessly how he liked the race. He said only, "It should have been me out there, not you," and turned away. I felt stung and confused, not sure what he meant. But one thing was certain: by no interpretation did his comment suggest support. I asked if we could stay so I could race the Masters Women, a race I would win a year later, but he had things to do and said he couldn't hang around all day.

By this time I had already begun to be, if not exactly secretive about my rowing, at least acutely aware of the necessity of keeping my head down. I never lied about what I was doing, but I certainly never waxed on at the dinner table about the thrill of sweat and speed, or the gratification of working with a partner who supported my dream and wished me success.

One morning after the Derby Sculls and Sweeps, Jeff suggested we try a double scull (a two-man shell) to work on timing and balance. In the double we were both rabbits, chased by the clock, which in this case was a cheap digital watch the plastic band of which was lashed to Jeff's shoelaces. Jeff rowed stroke—rowed from the stern seat and set the cadence—and I rowed bow. In theory, I was to steer, but my steering skills were so dismal that Jeff steered from the stern (my collision rate in the single would have been even worse that summer if I hadn't had Jeff nearby yelling "Boat!" just in time again and again). Suddenly in the double I could *feel* good sculling for the first time.

In the double, I could learn Jeff's timing both by watching him and by feeling the movement of the sensitive boat. I could time my blade's entry, or catch, and release to match his, adjust my slide, the rate at which I rolled toward the stern on my little wheeled seat, exactly as Jeff did. For the first time I was in a boat with enough balance to get my blades off the water and feel what a real stroke can be— perfectly timed, blades perfectly rolled up and squared, dropped in at just the right depth and just the right time. It was poetry.

We didn't engage in much talk on the water, just executed the plan of the day on water flat or choppy, bay calm or windy, sky rainy or sunny. Jeff called the workout. "Three and ten in two at thirty-two" (two more easy strokes, then five strokes to build power and raise cadence, then ten powerful strokes at a rate of thirty-two strokes a minute). "Two on, one off, times three, paddle six, times three" (two minutes of intense work with one minute of light work repeated three times, then row easy for six minutes, repeat entire cycle three times). "Sixty steady state" (sixty minutes steady rowing, no stopping). Experienced rowers time themselves and tune their performance with the help of a Stroke Coach, an electronic device mounted just above the feet which gives a constant readout of performance data: elapsed time, number of strokes per minute, current "splits" (the time it would take to row five hundred meters at the current speed). I used a plastic digital watch from Wal-Mart fastened to my foot straps with a pink barrette from Janie's dresser drawer to clock the pieces and help me calculate the stroke rate in my head.

We rowed the double for three weeks before returning to singles. When I got back into S4, I was an entirely different sculler. I could feel S4's center of balance, could sense S4's need to "run" (the ability of a racing shell to take the power of the stroke at the point of the blade's release, and glide while the blades are swung clear of the water for reentry). I was significantly better, significantly stronger. Most of all, I felt a new connection to the boat and to the water.

There is a point in learning any discipline when the equipment, which feels so alien and awkward at first, starts to feel like part of your body. A beginning pianist one day feels a surprising tactile quality to the keyboard, a new sensual connection to the keys. A woodworker begins to feel as much as see the pleasing texture and irregularity in the grain of a fine piece of oak. A skier finds she no longer feels lashed to slippery, unpredictable boards and experiences her skis as a pleasing extension of her body that allows her to flex, carve, fly. At that point the body's own instinct and intelligence begin to take precedence over the intellect. Henceforth, the analytical mind no longer attempts to strictly control the body but merely gives suggestions, tweaks some subtle aspect of technique, yet never attempting to quash or constrict the creative source itself.

My body had begun to experience the timing and balance of the stroke and the blade's connection to the water in a whole new way. I have a friend in her early fifties who has won numerous championships in the single shell. Often we go for breakfast after an early morning on the river. One day she looked at me and said, "I was embarrassed to tell anyone about this, but I get such a feeling of connection to my boat by the end of every season that when I row long pieces, I actually start to fantasize that my boat and body are a fish. I *am* a fish in those moments." I, too, found myself becoming a fish once again in the summer of 1996.

I began to experience the myriad personalities of water. No longer was it just wet stuff against my blade; it seemed to change character and consistency from day to day. It felt thin as rubbing alcohol on some days, difficult to grab and lever against. It was thick and satisfying as maple syrup on others, with a viscosity I could bite into and lean on. Sometimes it seemed oily and smooth as butter, sometimes sticky, sometimes elusive as dots of mercury escaped from a broken thermometer. Sometimes my wake closed and smoothed so fast it seemed to forget in an instant my passage, so insignificant in the total scheme of things. Sometimes it remained rent and roiled, retaining the ruthless cut of my boat and plunge of my blades as I tore down the harbor, slowly sewing itself back together in long stitches after I had moved on.

Some of what I experienced had as much to do with how I passed through the water as the nature of water itself, but one thing was clear: no longer a creature of dry land riding the water's surface, I began to feel the boat, the water, my body as linked in a rapturous system. Every day was a bliss of sweat and sensual reward. Every day replete with a gratification quite different from the slaking of thirst or purchasing of a longed-for treat, a gratification that came from doing, not having. And every day, too, I was becoming a jackrabbit more likely to live to see another sunset (until Jeff shaved down my ten-second head start and the death struggle commenced anew).

Then one day in mid-July Jeff said, "Word's going around the club that we're getting pretty fast. Delaware is only two weeks away; I think we ought to send our entries in the next few days." In my mind, the universe of two in which we sweated and sparred day after day immediately expanded, widened once again. From the narrow, private world of Lloyd Harbor to the larger public orbit of the bay, now to the widest world yet—the regatta that drew the best masters competitors from New York to South Carolina, the most seasoned and formidable scullers from Philadelphia, Washington, and Virginia.

The narrow focus of our weeks of training suddenly led somewhere: a point on the map, a moment in time when I would sit on the start line once more and take the sum of all my mornings threading my way through the fog, all my crossings tossed on the chop, all the jackrabbit chases with Jeff hot on my heels, all the breathless wonder of balancing *S4* for the first time, and put it to the test. Time to pack up the boat and head out into the world once more, to the largest masters regatta on the East Coast. The Diamond State.

Chapter Nine

STRIKING

GOLD

Three days before the Diamond State, Jeff
taught me what he called "the Thirty-five-Year-
Old-Guy Start." "Time you got professional," he
said. "Pull out this one and watch 'em sweat."
Right, I thought. From dead last to
watching 'em sweat in six weeks, like the
Miracle Diet. The Thirty-five-Year-Old-Guy Start
involved four short, quick strokes. From the "ready"
position at the start line—blades buried, seat rolled
three-quarters up the track, back straight and
braced to take the strain, head upright—the start was
an explosion of strokes powerful
enough to "lift" the boat and get it off the line and
moving, but not so violent as to make the blades "rip"
the water (like cavitation on a propeller, the air
bubbles created by ripping reduce the
efficiency of blade through water).

The key was lightness, quickness, and an exquisite ability to control power—measured in part by the force exerted by the body on the oars, but secondly by the degree to which the legs are compressed. Like a spring, the greater the coil is pressed down (the legs drawn tight to the body but not so close as to overcompress the knees), the greater the force when it is released (legs extending explosively to drive the boat). The first stroke was to be light and at three-quarters compression—to take the first stroke from a dead standstill at full compression would center the entire weight of boat, sculler, and water resistance on the sculler's lower back, possibly herniating disks or tearing muscles. The second stroke was a more powerful stroke, at half compression to bring the boat to speed. Then another half. Then one more stroke at three-quarters before launching into ten full-power, full-compression strokes, a power ten, designed to put the sculler out front where she can dominate the race. From that point she drops the *rating*, the number of strokes per minute, while maintaining maximum power on the blades, called *full pressure*. The rest of the race is rowed at that pace, except at approximately five hundred meters when the sculler might throw in another power ten to break the spirit of an advancing opponent. The last thirty seconds of the race are a sprint to acquire or assure the lead, depending on position at that point, and "empty the tank," expend the last ounce of energy. That's the theory.

Jeff watched me practice. "No, you're ripping the water! Easy, easy with the first stroke." "Quick, quick, quick, bring up the rating, we want these fast and light." "Again." "Again." "One more time." I flailed and ripped, sometimes digging in with one blade and nearly flipping, sometimes the other. The key was to make sure both blades were perfectly square to the water and fully buried at the moment I applied pressure. If one were anything other than square, the power of the first stroke would drive the blade diagonally toward the bottom of the harbor. The only way to be sure was to actually look at them, but the simple act of turning my head often upset the balance of the boat. More practice. Any error, any slight angle in the blade's attack, and I remained askew at the start line, wasting precious milliseconds finding my balance once again.

The first time I executed the start correctly was like the first time I did a good spin on figure skates—a whole new game. Both are a maneuver you either nail or you don't; there's nothing between failure and success. My first successful racing start was like flooring a hot rod—I felt I should be wearing a seatbelt. By four-thirty in the morning on race day, when I lashed *S4* to the roof rack of the station wagon and loaded the kids and a cooler of juice boxes inside, I knew I could do the start successfully about one try in three. I hoped my start in Delaware would be one of the ones.

After two hours on the New Jersey Turnpike, the children wanted breakfast. We stopped at a fast food plaza with an ocean of cars, three of them with boats and "U.S. Rowing" stickers destined for Delaware, one of them Jeff's. I had asked Jeff once about his scientific pre-race dietary policy. "I eat anything I can get my hands on and lots of it." I found him inside wolfing down cinnamon rolls witnessed by his less ravenous girlfriend, Kristen. While I've never been known to turn down a cinnamon roll, this morning was an exception. As we rejoined the line of traffic, my eight-year-old son John offered me part of his breakfast. No thanks, I told him, I'm too nervous about the race to eat. John, who was an experienced soccer player, replied helpfully, "Mom, butterflies kick butt." So I choked down a banana while the children tore apart their sticky buns and we pushed on through an increasingly hot, humid morning toward the Delaware Bridge and the long road to Noxontown Pond.

As we turned from the eight lanes of the New Jersey Turnpike to the four lanes of the long straight highway heading south from the Delaware Bridge, then to the two lanes of the country road leading through the woods and toward the end of Noxontown Pond, we saw trailer after trailer filled with fours and eights stacked one atop the other, tail flags flying, and car after car with singles and doubles riding high, cutting through the thick summer air. There were license plates from Virginia, Philadelphia, New Jersey, New York, Washington, D.C. These cars were filled with grown-ups, not college kids with baseball caps and beer hangovers. These were men and women old enough to have careers, families, mortgages, leaking roofs, bills, insurance—all the rewards and baggage of adult life. But here they were, many with their children, headed through the humidity and haze to the Diamond State Regatta, the largest masters event on the East Coast.

Masters racers are just like young elite athletes in some ways, not at all like them in others. Masters rowers—men and women from twenty-seven to whenever they decide to hang up their blades for good (I know of one competitor over ninety)—are passionately dedicated to their sport, but have to carve the time to train and race from real life. Sometimes I think about the incredible privilege of college athletes who have a nice thick wedge of their afternoons designated to row or run or swim. Masters athletes have to find the time in the hours no one else wants—when the world is sleeping, or during the early evening and Saturday morning if they're lucky enough to have a mate who understands that getting an hour on the water, or on the road, or on a bike will make them happier, and therefore a better partner.

The people who flocked to Noxontown Pond this hot morning in Delaware reflected, for the most part, the demographics of the masters rowing community. The majority rowed sweep boats. Many of the men had rowed in college and never stopped, or took up an oar again after a hiatus; many of the women under forty had done the same.

There was a large contingent of women sweep rowers over forty who, like me, began rowing eights in community and club programs and stayed, drawn by the camaraderie of team boats and the relative accessibility of sweep technique (out of any ten masters women competitors in their forties, probably nine are sweep rowers). Unlike the

My uncle Tucker,
Robert T. Hall, circa
1990.

Below: My parents,
Patricia and Richard
Hall, circa 1987.

Being a fish, age ten.

At the ranch, age eleven.

Going into eighth
grade, the year
"everything changed."

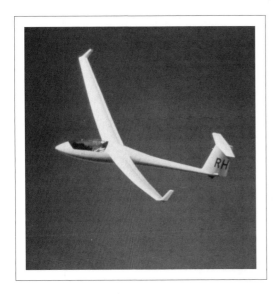

My brother,
Richard, circling
to land after a finish
at the 15-meter
Soaring Nationals,
Hobbes, New
Mexico.
(Credit: Steve Hines)

With six-week-old Janie,
March 1985.

With my siblings, Colorado, 1988.

With my sisters in
1999 at our parents'
fiftieth wedding
anniversary party, which
was held in an airplane
hangar (Mother chose
the music, Dad the
location). From left:
Caroline Otis,
Annie Hudnut, and
the author.

The Reginald Minor Boathouse,
Lloyd Harbor, New York, my dearest
home on earth in 1995–96.

The photograph I took a few weeks before the loss of the Lloyd Harbor boathouse. The Shining Arrow of chapter 8.

Packing up the Lloyd Harbor boathouse for good, 1996.

Moments after receiving the bronze medal for the Womens Lightweight B Single, 1996 Masters Nationals, Lake Onandaga, Syracuse, New York.

Below: The world's first "coxed" single shell, 1998 Maine State Championships. Son William insisted his Beanie Baby, Dobie, would help me win. He was right.

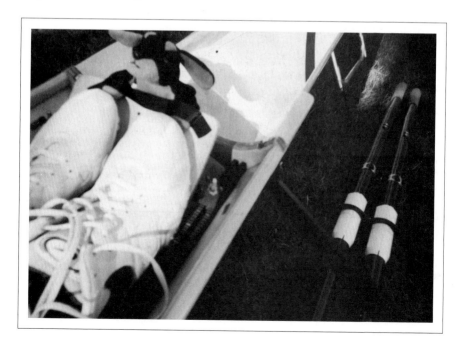

With the Sharrow after racing
the 1998 Green Mountain
Head, Putney, Vermont.

Below: Maiden voyage of the prototype Resolute lightweight single,
1998 Head of the Charles, Boston.
Though we met the production
deadline, the hull paint is barely dry.
(Credit: John Thompson, Jet Photographic)

Above: Gold Medal Quad, 1998 World Masters Games, Portland, Oregon. From left: Chris Ives, the author, Judy Davis, and Henry Hamilton.

Below: Congratulating our competitors at the medal ceremony for the Quad, 1998 World Masters Games.

Above: With Carie Graves after winning the double at 1998 World Masters Games.

Below: With Carie Graves, carrying our Cambridge Boat Club double, *Cabot,* after our win, 1998 World Masters Games.

Readying the Staempfli quad, *Mary Oliver,* 1998 World Masters Games.

Checking the race line-ups,
1998 World Masters Games.

Race Day: four minutes of excitement, eight hours
of hanging around.

Moments after winning the single,
1998 World Masters Games.

After my big race. The oar-bearer is my father.

Medal ceremony for Women's C Single, 1998 World Masters Games. From left: silver medalist Elena Morozova of Russia, the author, bronze medalist Paula Loane of Australia.

Above: Our mighty Cambridge Boat Club Quad winning the 1999 Head of the Schuylkill. From left: Henry Hamilton, Judy Davis, the author, and Al Flanders. *(Credit: Sports Graphics)*

Below: Dawn in the double with Al Flanders, upstream of Cambridge Boat Club, 1999. *(Credit: Joel W. Rogers)*

Winning the 2000 U.S. Masters Nationals in the double. From left: Linda Kennett, bow; author, stroke. *(Credit: Joel W. Rogers)*

Heading downstream for a morning workout,
5:30 A.M., Charles River.

stringent technical demands and relentless solitude of the single, a sweep boat provides the comfort of companions and the not inconsiderable relief of a coxswain who makes all the decisions and steers the boat. It also offers the forgiveness of a technique that, though it is as physically demanding as sculling, is initially much easier to learn. I risk alienation from every quarter of the sweep rowing world when I suggest that in terms of a mental game—and rowing is at least as much a mental game as it is a physical one—sweep rowing is to single sculling as a vigorous hike with friends is to a solo ascent of Annapurna. I have even found that racing the double scull, while nearly as technically demanding as the single, is vastly easier psychologically than the terrifying isolation and pressure of racing alone.

Masters racing itself is organized around the inescapable fact that physical performance declines with age—not necessarily much, but enough to make a difference. The handicapping system, applied mostly at small regattas where there aren't enough participants to divide the age groups into categories, is based on this principle, and makes for some juicy competitive politics. The standard handicapping system provides an incremental time advantage for each year of age—a fraction of a second per year in the thirties and forties, around a second per year after fifty. I've been told by those who have watched the scene over decades, and seen the aging of athletes whose skill and strength is well established, that the system is a surprisingly even-handed leveler.

Where it gets interesting is in a race in which there is a wide range of ages. Many times I've sat on a start line and heard, "I'm thirty. And you're . . . ?" Once I heard all five other competitors query each other. "I'm twenty-eight," one said. "Well, I'm thirty-one," said another. This went on through the lanes, the oldest crowing about her advanced age of thirty-six. Then it got to me. "I'm forty-five." A groan went up all round. Not only did they have to beat me, but they had to beat me by enough to keep me from winning with my handicap. Thus, there is a whole science to rowing a handicapped race. The first year or two when no one knew me, I looked young enough that my handicap was a secret weapon. Another woman may have crossed the line a fraction ahead of me, but I was the one on the medal stand. By my third year, I knew the players and they knew me.

The Diamond State, however, was large enough to break us down into the standard letter-denominated age categories: competitors in the A category were between twenty-seven and thirty-five, B between thirty-six and forty-two, C forty-three to forty-nine, D fifty to fifty-four, and so on. There is no handicapping within these narrow categories, so again, there's a science to working the system. Many competitors plan their lives to be able to train and race in the years when they enter a new category and are thus the most competitive in terms of physiology: an "old" A might take a year off to have a baby and reemerge as a "young" B. An old C might decide to throw herself into her career for a year until she becomes a young D. A competitor is allowed to "race down," or enter a race in a category younger than her own, and I have done this many times just to get more practice. This year, 1996, I would race only the C Single in Delaware. In 1998, I would race the A, B, and C Single, and in other regattas I even raced Open Class against the best twenty-three-year-olds, who always beat me but gave me great racing experience.

Races are occasionally run in a "finals only" format, either because there are only six or fewer participants (the standard course has six lanes), or because the schedule doesn't allow time for heats and a final—the standard elimination system used in most large regional, national, and international events. The exception is the International Rowing Federation masters competition, an annual event in which gold medals are awarded to the winner of each heat, a practice that produces as many as three or four "World Champions" in any given age category. The apex of the masters racing world is the World Masters Games, which occur every four years and attract over ten thousand of the best masters athletes on earth, much like the Olympics. Using a true elimination system, the World Masters Games produce one, and only one, "World Champion" in a category.

If masters competitors play an age game, it is one entirely peripheral to the stringent requirement for a high level of technical skill, an
extraordinary level of physical fitness, and the intensely competitive
outlook demanded by competitive rowing at any stage of life (though
in top masters competition, unlike elite competition, the depth of the
field at any given event is always affected by the demands of careers
and families). Our ranks are studded with men and women in the
backs of whose closets there are still old National Team T-shirts commemorating various Olympic and World Cup events. I have always
found the opportunity to compete against athletes of this caliber to
be a privilege, but it is one available to anyone willing to get up before
dawn, work hard, and lay it on the line.

We had rounded the end of Noxontown Pond and drawn up
to the gates next to the shore. Uniformed officials directed traffic and
we threaded our way through a sea of trailers to the parking lot. Jeff
hadn't arrived yet, so I found a shady spot on the grass beside the
pond and set up *S4*. The children helped me move the oars and the
toolbox. John took a rag and a gallon of water to wash the road dust
off *S4* and the other kids ran off to the pond to cool down.

An hour later, I was on the water. John carried my oars to the
dock and I pushed off only to find that, once again, I had put my
oars in the oarlocks backward. I backed down to the launch dock and
reversed them in full view of the sea of spectators. Once again I wore
my step-class shorts and the Sagamore jersey sized for a Sumo
wrestler, my hair in a sensible-mommy cut held out of my eyes with
a hairband. The day was like a steambath, breathless and sweltering. I
picked my way through the children, some of them mine, swimming
and splashing in the shallows to keep cool. "See you, Mom," they
called cheerfully as I waited for the signal from a race official to cross
the course for the half-mile trip to the start.

S4 was looking as spruce as an old club boat could. John had spent an hour on it, carefully polishing its hull and making sure my seat tracks were free of grease. I rowed down the lake, past the start, and warmed up in the swarm of singles and fours in the shallows beyond. Then my race was called, my competition materialized out of the crowd of milling scullers, and we backed to the line and the waiting hands of the stake boat attendants. All was quiet.

I looked to starboard. Two women tightened their laces and took a last gulp before emptying water bottles. I looked to port and realized with a shock that the woman to my immediate right was Sara Sargent, whose photograph I had seen a few months before in *U.S. Rowing* magazine. A fiercely competitive sculler from the vaunted ranks of Boathouse Row in Philadelphia, she was known for her indomitable racing spirit and dazzling muscle definition. She had a hank of white hair in a ponytail and cheekbones that would have looked great on the cover of *Vogue*. Her one-piece outfit coordinated with her boat and her eyes were impenetrable behind gray wraparound sunglasses. I looked past her to the far lane. There, calm and inscrutable in a sleek black unisuit, white cap, and mirror sunglasses, was Vicki Reynolds, reigning National Champion.

When I was little, one of my favorite books was *The Three Little Animals*. The three little animals lived in a forest quite happily until they discovered the existence of the Big City, to which they became irresistibly drawn. Problem was, they had no clothes, just furry paws and fuzzy ears and soft furry bellies. So they fashioned shoes from bark and hats from leaves to cover their animal ears, skirts and pants from more leaves. Off they went to the Big City, where their leaves and bark fooled no one, but no one had any interest anyway, and the three tossed off all their silly pretend human clothes and ran back to the forest to live happily ever after.

I felt very much like one of the three little animals as I sat at the start of the Diamond State in my bark shoes and leaf hat next to Sara and Vicki looking drop-dead cool. I was totally out of my league, in the wrong glasses, wrong haircut, wrong clothes, wrong everything. Even loyal *S4* with its silly footpads seemed chunky and crude next to their beautiful, bright boats.

The race official started calling the role: "Ready Pamlico? Ready Fairmount? Ready Sagamore?" I checked my blades. Then I looked across at my hopelessly squared-away competitors and said, "You girls look lethal." The flag raised. The starter called, "*Attention.*" Pause. "GO!"

When the flag dropped, I started the sequence Jeff had taught me. My fingers more than anything else sensed the lock of my blades on the murky water of Noxontown Pond, and the first four strokes were right on the money. I'd nailed it. What happened next so confused me I nearly stopped. Five strokes into the race there were two women, the ones to my left, who apparently hadn't known that the race had begun because they were back at the line just starting their first strokes. In my peripheral vision I could sense that to my right I was neck and neck with the two juggernauts. What was going on? Was there a false start? Should we stop? Then it dawned on me—Jeff's Thirty-five-Year-Old-Guy Start worked. I launched into a power ten.

Five strokes later, Sara Sargent yelled that I was about to hit her, "Number three to starboard! Number three, you're in my lane!" I was really sorry to be in her lane, truly I was, but my steering skills were not nearly as developed as my new starting skills. I pulled to starboard and tried to sight on a landmark to stern. Soon I was veering into Lane 4 again. "Number three, watch your course!" Again I veered away, ultimately zigging and zagging all one thousand meters.

Think how fast I might have been if I'd rowed a straight line. At about eight hundred meters, Sargent yelled that I was going to hit her. I wrenched *S4*'s bow to starboard once again, and realized suddenly that if I were about to hit her, my bow must overlap her stern. If I were that close, then I hadn't been left in the dust and, to my astonishment, was *in the running*. We crossed the line. I was third.

Later, Sara Sargent apologized for yelling at me, though she had every right to do so, and I apologized for careening into her lane. Jeff reported to me a few days after the race that Sara had told him, "She's going to be good—she's got the head for it." I was flattered that she noticed me (though given the circumstances how could she not), but I wondered, what did my head have to do with it? The answer became clear over the next year.

In Albany, I had won all I ever needed to win. The fact that I crossed the finish line nearly a minute later than all the other competitors was beside the point; I had conquered a lifetime's accumulation of self-doubt and a mountainous belief that I could never, and would never "lay it on the line." I had raced my own race, against my own fear. In Delaware, though, I began to experience a new strength and skill that placed me in a larger arena—geographically, and in relation to my competitors. Instead of the long solitary slog of dead last, my experience of the race in Delaware had sparked a competitive spirit that excited and inspired me not just to survive and stay upright over a thousand meters but to excel.

Someone asked me recently what I love about racing. It is this: there is no greater terror and joy than to take the whole sum of who you are and express it in four minutes. As I told my friend, if orgasm has been called a *petite morte*, racing is a *grande morte*. In racing, your fuel must be all the courage, skill, and strength in your tank, including your spare tank, and you must plan to run dry just as you cross the line. When you do finally cross the line, the expenditure leaves you writhing in pain and gasping great tearing sobs for oxygen. This may not sound like fun. It isn't fun. It is totally fulfilling.

By the time I packed the cooler and the children in the car, lashed the boat and oars to the roof, and started back up the New Jersey Turnpike that July day, I had tasted, if not triumph, at least a sense that the greater my willingness to reach beyond my limits, the greater the reward. A week later, when Jeff suggested I go to the Canadian Henley, my heart pounded, my stomach turned, and I said, *Yes.*

"It's a great international event on a famous course. *And* it's got divided lanes so it'll be great for you—for once you can go straight, as long as you don't get your blade caught in the lane buoys and flip." Jeff's voice didn't have a hint of sarcasm and clearly he felt he was doing a fine job selling me on the trip to Ontario. "Look at the brochure, 'Biggest Regatta in the Northern Hemisphere.' " From Lloyd Harbor to Huntington Harbor to the East Coast to the Northern Hemisphere in nine weeks. When were we going to take on the galaxy? "This is a regatta you really want to win," Jeff said enthusiastically. "They don't give silvers or bronzes but the gold medals are the best, better than Masters Nationals, real whoppers." I loved the way Jeff seemed convinced this was in the realm of possibility.

I sent my application by express mail to beat the deadline, then spent the next two weeks drilling two hours every morning and grilling Jeff on how to row the course. "Don't bother where you're going," he said, "just sight down the buoy lines behind you to stay on course. Stay off the buoys—they'll mess you up. At the seven-fifty mark you'll see a banner over the course. When you see that, put your head down and give it everything you've got."

I called the baby-sitter who had taken care of the children a few times when I had accompanied my husband on a business trip. She was available. Then I asked my husband if I could go, leaving on a Saturday, returning Sunday night. No. Later he changed his mind after talking to a young associate in his office who was a former Ivy League oarsman. Apparently he learned that the Canadian Henley was a top-drawer event in the rowing world (and thus a useful tidbit to mention at parties and business functions), but that it was also a "meat market." Therefore, he said he would go with me to protect me from the hordes of "randy rowers." He didn't seem to realize that most of the randy rowers were under twenty-five and that, as a woman of forty-three, I not only didn't register with them as a woman, I hardly existed as a person.

Then I called our club secretary. From Saturday morning to Sunday night, crossing international borders? He made unhappy sounds. "We don't generally encourage this kind of thing. More than twenty-four hours and that kind of mileage puts the boat at risk and takes it away from the other scullers for the weekend." (What other scullers? I wanted to ask.) "Well, okay. Just this once as long as you get *S4* back on time in good shape." That's when I realized I would soon need a boat of my own if I were serious about racing.

On Saturday afternoon, August 10, 1996, we pulled into a dusty parking lot the size of a football field in St. Catharines, Ontario. It was filled with hundreds of shells, a thousand or more rowers, license plates from across the United States and Canada. Guards and traffic volunteers yelled instructions and waved flags. I panicked. How would I find Jeff and Kristen? Where was I supposed to go? Would I have a chance to try the course before I had to race the next morning? My bark shoes chafed.

We parked in a far corner of the lot and unloaded *S4* onto an empty rack, then looked for the registration building where, sure enough, they had a yellow manila envelope with my name on it. Inside was my bow number, Lane 3, and instructions for my Masters Women C race at 9:55 the next morning. I asked about practice on the course and the registration official told me I could go out after racing was over for the day, about 5:00 p.m. Until then we could watch the last elite-class races of the day.

The shoreline next to the course was dotted with the banners and booths of vendors who sold everything from rowing clothes, bumper stickers, commemorative pins to racing shells from around the world—Staempflis from Switzerland, Kaschpers and Hudsons from Canada, Empachers from Germany, and Vespolis from the United States. Competitors gathered around the boats and ran their hands longingly over the glossy red and blue finishes, spun the oarlocks idly, asked the price. My husband and I looked over the merchandise in the booths. He seemed to be getting into the spirit of the event, so when I asked if we could talk to some manufacturers about their singles, "maybe for someday," he didn't object. We walked into the Vespoli tent, emptying now in the late afternoon.

The Vespoli representative, a big, athletic, dark-haired fellow who seemed to be on a first-name basis with everybody, was lounging on a high director's chair with snappy "Vespoli USA" graphics. He talked and laughed with the few final customers of the day. He looked like he was about ready to hang it up and go out for some beer. "Excuse me," I said, when the tent had cleared and he was starting to put away his promotional material. "I'd like to know a little about your singles." He yawned, asked, "What do you row now?" I told him. "How long have you rowed?" I told him. He looked me up and down, taking in my ill-fitting jersey and my age, sizing me up and coming to a quick conclusion. Then he tipped back his head, narrowed his eyes, sniffed once, and said with unmistakable sarcasm, "So, you think maybe you might go fast someday?"

I may have been inexperienced in the world but I knew a snub when I heard one. My face flushed and I wanted to disappear into the hard-packed dirt of the booth. I could sense my husband's satisfaction—maybe Sara would see now that she was way out of her league. I thanked him and walked out, cut to the quick. What was I doing here? How could I come to Canada with my clunky boat and my water-stained notes from sculling school and think I was a real competitor?

Did the Vespoli rep crush me? For a good twenty minutes or so, yes. Then I had to turn my attention to the task ahead. Certainly, I never forgot Vespoli USA's treatment of this masters woman. Turns out the next day, though, the Vespoli rep became very nice; indeed, downright solicitous. He was amazingly eager to be helpful and provide all the information I needed—not, I would guess, because he regretted his rudeness, but because the next day I won the Canadian Henley.

Sunday morning at 9:55 I sat on the start line in Lane 3 and, as usual, felt like throwing up. I dunked my oars in and out of the water and noticed that I had forgotten to replace the pink plastic ducky barrette holding my watch to the velcro straps of my footpads.

I remembered how it had looked pinning back Janie's blond bangs as she got on the school bus last spring.

The day before, after my encounter with the Vespoli rep, I had almost been barred from launching for practice because my boat "failed to satisfy international safety requirements." I had the required bow ball, a rubber bumper like a clown nose affixed to the sharp bow of every boat to prevent one sculler from accidentally impaling another. But the required heel tie-downs, that was another story. I had stood at the head of a long line of boats whose owners waited impatiently to launch while the race officials decided what to do with me. Heel tie-downs are strings that link the heel of the sculling shoes (which are bolted to the footboards by the toes) to the boat. If the sculler overturns, the tie-downs pull the sculler's heels from the shoes and she slips free, avoiding unpleasant death from hanging upside down underwater. The problem was that *S4* had no shoes, and therefore no heels. In reality, I had the safest system of all—no shoes, no need to release—just slip out. But they went by the rule book at the Canadian Henley and it took them about five minutes to conclude their summit and give me the authority to launch. To his credit, my husband, who has a quick and litigious mind, went to bat for me, arguing with the officials and wearing them down with his logic and the force of his personality. I stood in the late afternoon sun, aware of the press of scullers behind me huffing and fidgeting. They all had boats with the requisite shoes; I had a velcro strap with a pink barrette. I sighed. Then they gave me the go-ahead.

When the roll was called at the start line of the Canadian Henley, I remembered the rule from the book I had read on racing protocol, and acted accordingly. "Lane 1, Alexandria; Lane 2, Ridley Grad; Lane 3, Windsor; Lane 4, Sagamore . . . " Wait, I wasn't in Lane 4, I was in Lane 3. The book said any mistakes in the announced lineup should be brought to the official's attention with a raised hand before the start. The starter kept going. I raised my hand, confident that he would stop and rectify the situation before the flag dropped. He finished the roll. I was still waving my hand like the goody-goody everyone hates in the front row of English class, ready to give the right answer. "*Attention*" (the flag rose). "GO!"

Oh my God, he's started the race. I grabbed my oar handles and tried a start. It was sloppy and crooked. Oh my God, I'm late. I'm so stupid. Such an idiot! Ten strokes into the race I realized that it wasn't the mistake that was slowing me down, it was the panic and self-recrimination. Let it go, I thought. Just leave it behind and race this race. So I picked up the rhythm to some inhumanly high stroke rate of which I was blissfully unaware because I had no Stroke Coach and, in the heat of the race, couldn't do the math quickly enough to calculate my stroke rate. I looked neither to the left nor right—there was no sense in knowing where the other competitors were, and watching them at this point wouldn't make me any faster. I must have gone five hundred meters, about two minutes, without the slightest glance at anything but the two lines of buoys behind me, converging in the distance evenly. I was tracking down the lane in a trance of rhythm, my blades biting and stroking. The buoys passed to stern like the beat of a metronome, *tick, tick, tick*, and S4 and I were cutting a straight course for the very first time. This is *my* race, I thought. All out. Every stroke. That's the strategy.

At six hundred meters, I couldn't help but see the others. They were right beside me, right there—I'd caught up with them. Ten strokes later, I did another check. There was a Canadian behind me, another. Then I counted. One, two, three, four . . . they were all there, behind me. All behind me. . . . Suddenly something inside me felt very, very different, as if the main switch on an electrical panel had been thrown and every light in the house blazed to life. Suddenly I wasn't a nice mom trying really hard. Suddenly I was a force.

Twenty more strokes and I was passing under the banner at seven-fifty. I remembered Jeff's instructions: "When you see the banner, give it all you've got." Of course I'd already been giving it all I had for seven hundred and fifty meters. Somewhere I got more. It was torture. It was ecstasy. I didn't know how we kept going but old S4, so reviled by the Vespoli rep and the race officials, got faster and faster. I increased my lead from a half length to a length, finally to two lengths. When we crossed the line at a thousand meters, I was so far in the lead I could have paddled for the last twenty meters and still won.

Oh my God the pain! My legs and chest were on fire and I couldn't hold still in my boat, twisting and retching with lactic acid overload and oxygen deprivation. An experienced racer never goes all out from start to finish as I had. She uses strategy, marshals her energy, spending it wisely and where it counts. I had simply thrown myself at the course, reckless and passionate. I was embarrassed at how noisy I was, gulping and rasping for air. It took me three minutes just to be able to sit quietly again, three minutes during which the race official in the chase boat had hovered off my stern asking anxiously if I was all right, if I needed medical attention. All I could do was shake my head and hold up my hand. By the time I composed myself, all the other competitors had already turned and started back down the course to the landing dock. I looked at the official, sheepish that I'd worried him, and asked, "What do I do now?" His face relaxed. "Follow me, ma'am."

He led me across the finish area to a dock decorated with bunting and pots of flowers. A dock attendant held the bow of *S4* as I got out and was escorted to the medal block. I climbed onto the block, facing the grandstands. I'd like to say the stands were filled with cheering crowds, but this was Sunday morning and many of the spectators had gone home after the elite races of the days before. Nevertheless, there was a smattering of spectators.

I stood on the block while a man in a straw boater approached, bearing a velvet tray on which lay a gold medal that was everything Jeff described. He stood in front of me, holding the medal. Instinctively, I reached out to put the ribbon over my head—a mother knows that if you want to get anything done, you better do it yourself. He laughed. "We like to do this for you." He asked me to bow my head, and placed the medal with its red, white, and blue ribbon on my neck. I looked at him, at the people in the stands, at the sky, then held out my arms and laughed with happiness. Laughed and laughed. The spectators began laughing with me.

In my life I had known a Sara who was a good mother and a dutiful wife; had found on the harbor a Sara with strength and courage. But I never expected this, not after all the years of submission to the forces that bound me, all the years of turning my cheek, all the years of opening wide to take my medicine. No, there was no denying it any longer. For once, this Sara was on top. For once, this Sara was the winner.

T H E

E D G E

After I returned from the medal dock
and rinsed *S4*, wiping it down, cleaning the
seat tracks, and rubbing off a scuff mark
from the medal dock, I leaned over and
kissed its scratched gray hull. Then
I walked through the vendor tents,
a victor this time, and bought a plain black
racing suit for forty dollars—no stripes, no lightning bolts, no splashy logos. I wore it, much faded
and considerably less stretchy, two years later
at the Masters World Games.
    Packing up for the long trip home,
I stopped for a moment to take the pink barrette
from my foot straps. I went to the shore of the course,
pressed it to my cheek, then threw it across the water.
I was taking something important home with me
from Canada; I also wanted to leave something
dear, but now outgrown, behind.

After we had threaded our way out of the maze of trailers and started on the long trip back to Long Island from St. Catharines, my husband and I drove through Customs. The agent hardly looked as we pulled up to the window of the booth. "Did you acquire anything on your trip in Canada?" He was bored and wrote something on a form. "I didn't, but my wife did," said my husband. Silently, I held up the gold medal. The agent glanced up, then he looked harder—at me, at the medal, then at *S4*, riding on top of the station wagon. A moment's silence. "I don't guess you bought that, did you, ma'am?" I shook my head. "Congratulations. Pass through." Looking back, I realize this was the only time I can remember when my husband showed any sign that he was proud of my rowing. It is painful now to remember how intense was my gratitude.

It was time to start accepting myself as a serious competitor. The issue didn't really have anything to do with the world taking me seriously, it had to do with *me* taking me seriously, and my willingness to admit to myself, I'm a contender. To present myself as an ill-equipped raw novice was fast becoming a denial of hard-won truth. If I were to have the courage to pursue mastery, I needed the courage to leave behind the persona of the hapless, inexperienced underdog. Of course, I *had* been an inexperienced underdog, but as of this morning, no longer. To linger in the fantasy that, as an "old mommy," any success was a miracle was to malign both my own efforts and all the "old mommys" of the world who are making substantial contributions. I am a woman in midlife; I am a mother; I am a competitor. These were the words I repeated in the days after the Canadian Henley—partly as a statement of truth, partly in an effort to convince myself that it really was acceptable to be all three in my culture, and in my life.

Two weeks after the Canadian Henley, I went to the U.S. Masters Nationals on Lake Onondaga in Syracuse. I raced the Open Weight Cs and the Lightweight Bs—women one hundred thirty pounds or less, ages thirty-six to forty-two. I won bronze in the Lightweight Bs, rowing against women younger and theoretically faster than in my own category, and placed fourth in the Open Weight Cs against women my age some of whom outweighed me by thirty pounds or more (in rowing, weight is less an indicator of fat than of muscle mass). In just over ten weeks I had gone from finishing dead last in my first race to placing third at the national level. How could this happen?

It happened because I worked hard, because I loved rowing with all my heart, and because at the seven-hundred-meter mark of the Canadian Henley I had found the Edge.

It has been reported of the extraordinarily successful, famously competitive, longtime Harvard crew coach Harry Parker that as a young man he felt he should never be allowed to play any sport in which he was permitted to carry a stick. His observation recognizes the fact that an essential ingredient of the competitive spirit is sheer, naked aggression—the undisguised expression of a joyous, uncontrollable, and often rage-filled impulse I call "the Edge." The impulse Parker alludes to is, I believe, man's—maybe I should say "men's"— impulse to "beat the shit" out of an opponent, cheerfully and legally in athletics, murderously when it comes to possession of women or property. They slug it out in a frenzy of blood and territoriality on the battlefield and the playing field. I've heard my son talk about his opponents ("We're going to kill 'em, Mom!") and noted his lust to wear full armor and bash another kid with a lacrosse stick. Men slash and grunt, relishing the joy of rooting around in their own dark instincts, reveling in aggression the way a dog rolls ecstatically in the rotting carcass of a dead seagull while you vainly call, "Come, Sparky, come now!"

I think it fair to say that most men don't share my zeal to make competitive sports an opportunity for spiritual catharsis and personal growth. And yet, while I can sound smug and female about men's lack of evolution, I'm one to talk. I've rowed the Charles River three years now and have found that I, too, am guilty of the impromptu aggression that appears as regularly as the big, dark fish that suddenly throw themselves out of the water right behind my stern, a reminder that there's more to the river than the morning lyricism of reflected leaf and light. I've felt the moment when my killer instinct rises from a mucky deep of old boots, abandoned shopping carts, and lost keys, and flings itself in the middle of my peaceful meditation—say on a Wednesday morning at dawn when I'm rowing a long, steady piece, minding my own business, losing my cares in the calm of the river and meditation of the stroke. Suddenly I can't help but notice a sculler in the distance. Who is that? I keep rowing, admiring the grace of the waterbirds, the shimmering of sunlight under a bridge. The speck gets larger. From deep in my hypothalamus, a wolf starts to howl. Who *is* that? Is he gaining? I pick up my pace. I really wanted to go a little faster anyway. A half mile later I notice he's raised his stroke rate. I raise my rate. Now my heart is going *bang bang bang*, sweat is stinging my eyes, and my lungs are starting to burn. No way is this guy going to get past me. *No way.* And my nice meditation has become a duel to the death.

In my Lightweight B race at the Masters Nationals, for instance, I remember the instant my Edge leapt to hand. *S4* and I were laboring in fourth place as we approached the seven-fifty mark. I was feeling outclassed and very sorry for myself. With my peripheral vision, I could see the yellow stern of the woman in third holding steady off my port bow. She'd been parked there for two hundred meters and looked like she intended to stay parked there forever. In an instant I felt a welling of anger as elemental as the unexpected gust of wind that sends dust flying and signs tumbling. Son of a bitch, I thought. I didn't sweat all these weeks to come in fourth! It wasn't that I was angry with the woman in the yellow boat, or even that I was particularly angry with myself, but suddenly the overwhelming urge to slash myself free of my sorry laboring self and to *dominate* my opponent was potent as jet fuel. Five strokes later and I'd overlapped her stern. Seven more and we were bow to bow. Another seven and she was left flailing in my wake. A half hour later, after I had left the medal stand and was walking through the crowd with my children in tow, the woman in the yellow boat approached me. "Boy, when you drove through me like that at seven-fifty you just plain broke my spirit," she said with cheerful equanimity, her spirit obviously restored. We laughed, introduced ourselves, shook hands, and have been friendly at regattas ever since.

The Edge is visceral. The Edge is empowering. The Edge is overpowering. I'm convinced it springs from the same deep well of instinct and desire as sex. Wielding the Edge on the race course, I am not a pleasant, moderately cultured college graduate with a mortgage and a library card who happens to be racing. I am an organism operating on pure instinct, like a cheetah chasing down a gazelle—unstoppable, wholly focused. The Edge is a moment-by-moment, *I give it all here and now* feeling, not an *if I try really hard maybe I'll win* feeling. It is empowering in that I suddenly gain access to another, hitherto unsuspected dimension of strength; overpowering in that the civilized persona on which my everyday life is based becomes, for a brief time, pure directed impulse. As one friend puts it, we "go animal."

For many athletes, including me, the Edge is a mixture of wild, ecstatic fervor, rage, and a determination rooted and reflexive as a pit bull locked onto the neighbor's shin. From an alloy of the three was born the sword I pulled from the stone in the summer of 1996 as a woman of forty-three, ready, finally, to start fighting for my kingdom. It was a new and powerful weapon in a hand more accustomed to scrubbing crayon marks off the woodwork.

My Edge was a lethal weapon on the water. Ironically, though, the impetus behind it had nothing to do with my competitors or the race at hand. My rage on the course was directed at two opponents:

one usually a hundred or more miles away; the other a constant companion, in my boat, my car, my kitchen, my bed. During most of my races, the first was making business deals on the telephone in a sunny living room with the nice flowered curtains I got on sale. The second weighed down my racing single like a grotesquely oversized coxswain. She was the confused, defeated part of me, who was afraid to stand up for herself. This was the real foe, the one to vanquish once and for all. There was no room for her in my narrow vessel, and at the seven-hundred-fifty-meter mark in Canada I left her, for the first time, in my wake. Later, much later, I recognized there was not only no room for her in my little boat, there was no room for her anywhere in my life. One of us was going to have to go.

So my zeal on the race course had nothing to do with the chauvinism of team rivalries or some grown-up version of school spirit. And my determination had nothing to do with some arbitrary invisible line across a river. None of it had to do with beating the other women in my race; but the result was that I beat many. Sure, I wanted to win. Recognition felt wonderful after having no value other than that of good mommy and agreeable wife. But the fury and desire in my heart was not to decimate the woman next to me. For her I felt gratitude that she'd had the courage to come out on the course to do battle, for without her there is no race, and without the race there is no opportunity to confront, to surmount, to be fully alive—the true substance of victory. To turn the base metal of my rage into gold—the Alchemist's trick.

What *is* the fury that powers the Edge? I'm not suggesting that all athletes operate from a deep reservoir of anger, but I have spoken to a number of highly competitive women, and men, who tell a tale not just of the normal ups and downs of existence but of real emotional hardship somewhere in their lives. One man told me that when he and his seven crewmates sat talking quietly in the warm-up area before they were to compete in a national-level regatta, they discovered that seven of the eight highly successful athletes in the boat were sons of alcoholics. I know of other women competitors who suffered sorrows similar to mine. This is not to say that competitive athletics is the province of the physically strong and the emotionally crippled. I suggest that we are not only physically strong (and perhaps unusually pain-tolerant), but we are able to use the adversity in our lives—and specifically the inevitable anger that springs from it—to surmount what are, in some cases, devastating emotional wounds. We are able, through competition, to convert the very thing that would defeat us into a potent resource, powering us to achieve extraordinary competitive goals.

Even though by the time I found rowing in 1995 I had allowed my awareness of my anger to be submerged by the demands of raising three children, four years earlier, just after my youngest son was born, I had specific reasons for the anger swaddled tightly under my damp nursing pads—an anger sharp, hot, and thirsty for blood.

It wasn't just that I'd lain in bed at home on enforced bed rest for five months, like my first two pregnancies, then in a hospital bed for another two before the baby's birth, and thus had a fair amount of pent-up physical energy. More volatile was the outrage that had been building quietly for years and that reached a boiling point during what turned out to be a very frightening pregnancy. Because of the position of the placenta, my doctor had explained, the possibility of bleeding to death was very real, particularly given the distance of our house from the hospital. By the end of the fourth month of pregnancy, he had urged me to interview the local ambulance services to determine which could get me to the emergency room the fastest. Yet during all the weeks of waiting and fearing that each night would be the one when I'd wake in a pool of bright blood, my husband vented his own apparent anxiety not just in the clever verbal feints and jabs I knew so well but in a daily barrage of criticism. As my sister, having witnessed only one of many evenings, had said to me in the kitchen, "What he does to you—there is a word for it. . . . Listen to me!" The word was "abuse." And that was an evening when my husband had been on "company behavior."

Home was a war zone. Every night I could hardly keep myself from taking a blanket and hiding in the dark woods behind the house when I heard the slam of my husband's car door and the click of his heels on the front walk. I wanted to burrow in the deep leaves and vanish like a mouse in winter. But of course I couldn't leave the children. Every night in our pretty, civilized rooms, my husband attacked me with brilliant, cutting derision—he was angry at his new job, he told me, a job that was not going well, angry at me for being in a nightgown when he left in the morning, a nightgown when he came home at eight, angry at the baby whose conception had been a miracle but an unexpected miracle. Of course it must have been scary as well as frustrating for him—his wife bedridden, his job tenuous, his burden as breadwinner about to grow heavier; but his stream of sarcasm, belittling me and accusing me that I cared more for the baby than for him, forced me nightly into a frantic dance to appease him.

Many nights, the palpable tension and hostility of the situation actually sent me into early contractions as soon as I heard his tires on the gravel of the driveway, faintly at first, then stronger and more regular. One night when I was just over five months pregnant, the contractions had been strong enough and regular enough that my obstetrician feared I had gone into premature labor. As I neared six months, I was frantic. If the baby were born now it might survive, but with a high probability of lung or brain damage. I begged my husband to act friendly even if he couldn't feel it. "Pretend you like me. Please. Pretend for the sake of the baby." Once I tried the only argument that I thought might move him: "Think of your life if the baby were born now." I hoped that the idea of appearing at the Yacht Club Fourth of July supper with an obviously impaired child in a blue blazer or a smocked dress would move my husband to do whatever it took to help keep the contractions at bay. But it didn't.

"Don't point that thing at me," he said more than once of my swollen belly as I lumbered naked from the shower, as if the baby were a mortar. The more I scrambled every evening to appease him with the right combination of flattery and commiseration, the more stimulated and angry he seemed to grow as the night wore on. Nothing I said appeared to make any difference, nothing. Almost nothing. There was, he suggested to me one day, something I could do for him that would "help us get along better," and he described it. I needed peace for the sake of the baby, and for my sake—I was going into contractions nightly now. So I gave him what he asked for.

He called it our "little date"; I thought of it as prostitution. Even if it had been possible to raise my voice in outrage, I hadn't the will to do it. That was, for me, the deal. That had always been the deal.

Finally I began to bleed and was taken to the emergency room one gray March dawn. I thanked God to be out of that house, and thanked God, too, for my mother, who had come from Boulder to care for the children during my absence from home. I was in the hospital for almost two months. I remember drawing pictures of birds for the kids, watching old reruns of *Magnum, P.I.*, and feeling very grateful to be in a place where, even in the ceaseless noise and bustle of the high-risk maternity unit, my baby was safe and I could be calm.

William was born in late May in an emergency operation that fulfilled all but the worst of my doctor's predictions: the bleeding was so catastrophic that my total blood supply was transfused twice over; there was no time to separate placenta and uterus so they took it all.

When I went home at last on a green spring afternoon, the baby left behind in neonatal intensive care, I was angry. Oh yes. I was very, very angry.

I went to a therapist to help me find a way to stay in my marriage and somehow live with the rage. The psychologist counseled me to "be nicer to yourself and never have sex unless you want to," useless advice but not atypical of many therapists' inability to recognize and address situations such as ours (though I've heard of worse—women who are told by their therapists that it is *their anger* at a controlling husband that is dysfunctional). A few weeks later, a friend gave me the phone number of a divorce lawyer. I kept it on a tiny piece of paper in the back of my calendar, nervous as if I had hidden a bomb in the basement. When I finally worked up the courage to dial, though, I looked at my newborn in his little plastic tippy seat and realized it was too soon.

Sometimes I had dreams about getting free; but with two small children, a premature baby, and the debilitation of seven months of bed rest and major surgery, where would I find the energy to fight a man who, over our years together, I'd seen respond to the possibility of litigation with an alert and watchful relish, like a cat seeing the flick of a mouse tail under the refrigerator? I'd watched him take on a former employer and the local government, use his mind to dominate an opponent not just at home but everywhere in his life. He seemed to feed on it, growing larger and stronger with every skirmish. Divorce papers could stimulate *his* Edge. My worst fantasy was that the affront of my defiance would empower him to "morph" from mortal man to superhuman monster, like a character in my kids' afternoon TV show. I wasn't prepared for Armageddon. Yet.

So I learned how to hit tennis balls.

In the backboard I found the perfect partner. It slammed as hard as I, accommodated my schedule with the children, and didn't require chicken salad and pleasant chatter afterward. That summer, I developed a stroke that made its resonant plywood ring like the rhythmic report of a well-used rifle range. The moment of connection with the ball—the ringing of the strings, invincibility of the stroke, snap of my head with the impact—satisfied something famished inside.

The few times I did play with other women, they always beat me—I was a raw beginner and didn't have any sense of timing or strategy—but I could slam the ball low and fast over the net right at their feet. While their yelps and hops were gratifying, my gratification in their reaction made me nervous; they weren't, after all, the target of my missiles. Thus, I met at last a killer instinct—sprung from my nursing bosom like newborn Athena, tall and dangerous in her shiny breastplate, idly thumbing the sharpness of her blade, testing her Edge. But was she really quite the thing to unleash in combat with nice ladies on suburban tennis courts?

So I made her wait. She retreated into the shadows, quiet and watchful, while I devoted myself to raising my kids and doing community volunteer work. Waited, sword in hand, for the right place, the right time. She waited five years.

Then I found rowing, and at last my waiting warrior found her place, an arena in which competitors vie alongside one another, not face to face. In rowing, competitors engage in fierce struggle, but also maintain a deep feeling of common endeavor as they stroke in the same direction. Unlike tennis, where one hits a missile *at* a competitor, in rowing each of us strives as an individual among individuals, parallel rather than in opposition. In other words, no hitting with sticks. Sometimes I tell my children, probably to their irritation, "It is important not to deny your feelings, but to express them appropriately." In competitive rowing, I finally found "appropriate expression" for the bloodthirsty goddess within ("Xena," as my husband laughingly referred to me), and discovered in the last two hundred and fifty meters of the Canadian Henley that the bright blade of my competitive instinct was very sharp.

At first I thought my competitiveness might be the sign of some lurking deviancy. The contrast between nurturing mother and armor-plated Athena was hard for me to reconcile. Now that I've known many hugely competitive woman athletes—some of them mothers, all apparently productive members of society—I know that both instincts can coexist. But back then I was afraid that my competitiveness had been so long imprisoned it might, like a convict set free after serving his term, do something stupid and unacceptable. I would make the monumental fool of myself and be sent right back to serve the rest of my days in confinement.

Someone asked me once if I have a strategy for my races. "None," I replied, "except to row as fast as I can." But this is not exactly true. Although I didn't have a conscious game plan, a pattern emerged of which I became more and more aware. Racing in my first two seasons, I never looked to right or left in the first half of the race—rowed like a slave, lashed and laboring, keeping my eyes to myself, not interacting with the other competitors. But then something happened after five hundred meters. Suddenly, like a scene from *The Three Musketeers*, the Edge leaped to my hand as if a comrade had tossed me a sword from the sidelines and it landed square in my palm with a pleasing slap. No more the diligent downtrodden slave, trying so very hard; in an instant's metamorphosis I became Master—of my boat, of the race—armed with a weapon of lust and aggression honed to a fine point, which I wielded to sever the momentum of my competitors and drive to the finish. The third season I raced, 1998, my Edge sprang to hand earlier and earlier as I learned to use the pressure of my competitors to make me faster, smarter, more lethal. Finally, by the end of that summer, I left the slave on shore altogether.

The Edge is irrational, irrepressible, elemental. Expressed in the service of religion or nationalism, it wreaks havoc in the world. At its best, though, it offers us opportunity to experience a self stronger, more vibrantly alive, more intensely focused than that of our everyday lives, a self armed to take on the darkest forces in our own, inner territory. Not only did it give me the opportunity to express my most volatile, potentially destructive impulses in an appropriate context; using it again and again on the race course gave me much-needed training in honing the power of those impulses, readying myself for the time when I would reclaim and reshape my life.

Chapter Eleven

LETTING

GO

About three years ago, I was being
coached on the Charles River just upstream
of the North Beacon Street Bridge. My coach was
Ted Benford, a measured, serious man, unflappable
and kind. I was concentrating so hard my jaw
ached as I tried to assemble all the myriad
elements of the ideal stroke for at least a
few seconds. Ted was driving his battered green
aluminum Community Rowing launch, one hand on
the throttle, one on his megaphone, a simple cone,
spray-painted "CRI." He lifted the cone to his
mouth. No, not another thing to remember, I
thought. "Lose the grip," Ted said calmly.
"You're killing 'em."

Ted was referring to an image many
coaches use to convey the need to keep a loose grip
on the oar handles in order to feel water pressing on

blade. The image is of the rower holding a sparrow in each hand. Too firm a grip and the little bird is dispatched to sparrow heaven; too loose a grip and it flies away. A just right grip allows the sculler to maintain control, yet avoid throttling her own tiny author of instinct, energy, rhythm, connection to wildness. If she can keep the sparrows alive, she gains a formidable competitive weapon—finesse. When Ted said I was "killing 'em," he was saying my hands were clenching the oar handles so tightly that I hadn't a hope of feeling the water through my oar blades. In addition, when hands and jaw are tight, so is the rest of the body, making it impossible to find a natural rhythm or sense the subtle movement of the boat. In other words, I was trying so hard I had squeezed the life out of my stroke and might as well have been on a machine in a gym. Time to let go.

There is a saying in rowing circles, "Life is rowing in miniature," and rowing is nothing if not metaphorical. It is a process in which one is traveling swiftly forward through time and space while facing backward—chockablock with hindsight, but blissfully unaware of the bridge abutment dead ahead. It is, of course, the ideal image of life itself. The principle of letting go is another of those rowing metaphors exquisitely reflective of human experience.

The necessity for letting go, on the water and off, is hard to grasp and harder to execute because we humans, so gloriously smart, are so afraid to trust our own instincts. We have to control everything—our bodies, our lives, our relationships, our physical environment—and we often try to do this by force, by exercising the strength of our muscles and ego to bend the world to our command. We think if we get a grip on whatever challenges us—a good, hard, take-no-prisoners grip—we're golden. But we're not. Sometimes, in fact, the best solution is, as my mother says, to "turn it over to God." Let go. I have a friend, a coach, who says that often the strongest rowers are the hardest to coach because they think that strength is the key to going fast. They end up like eggbeaters, all splash and thrash, no forward drive.

A fine sculler knows how to play the delicate line between control and obeisance to the water's subtle demands. He has developed an exquisite feel for the delicate interplay of muscle, boat, and water—drawing his blades with all the power and confidence of his body, yet always remaining keenly sensitive to the well-being of the "sparrows." He is willing to relinquish some of his human need to control in order to become attuned and responsive to the elemental world he inhabits. If the expression of the Edge is all about the assertion of my muscle, my will, my passion, the impetus behind the just right grip is the abandonment of self to a greater imperative. The combination of the two makes for a hell of a fast boat.

Sometimes I swim laps at the local YMCA. It always amazes me that one strong man can finish a lap in half the time it takes another, apparently equally strong man. The difference is that one strokes at a frantic pace, stiff and awkward, floundering his way down the pool looking as if he simply can't get a grip on the water, and the other courses down his lane with a natural, loose, rhythmic stroke, locking on and twisting past his steady hand, and flipping with a splash at the wall. It looks almost as if one swims in thin water, the other thick. Both swimmers are strong. Only one will win a race.

There are a number of extremely fast scullers, many of them lightweight, whose source of speed is a mystery. Ironically, the answer lies in their lack of bulk. Their size forces them to row smart, not just hard. They will sometimes challenge a heavyweight and emerge the victor as if by magic. Where does it come from, this ability to slip through water with the natural ease of a fish? The finesse sculler, like a trout, is beautifully adapted, senses perfectly attuned to the language of the water. The "eggbeater" may be highly trained and working hard, but he is still a human at odds with an alien medium. That's not to say the finesse sculler isn't expending a great deal of energy, but he has become *of* the water, not on it or against it. Of course, the fastest sculler of all is the heavyweight who also rows smart. He is unbeatable.

My sister Caroline, the darling and glamorous one (as opposed to Annie, the sunny, well-adjusted one), told me recently she couldn't figure out how our parents produced out of four such apparently unambitious siblings my brother Richard, a National Champion in the fifteen-meter glider, and me, a World Masters Games Champion in the single shell. I think it has to do with our mother's having read *Mary Poppins* to us as children. Mysterious, instinctual, intimately connected to nature, Mary's enormous power had nothing to do with muscle tone.

It's been forty years since I lay in my parents' bed under the blanket with my brother and sisters while my mother read *Mary Poppins* to us. The chapter is absolutely clear to me. Mother read about the newborn Banks twins, Mary's charges, chatting with the sunlight and the wind, and with the starlings that landed on the windowsill next to their crib to wheedle a crumb of cookie. The starlings tell John and Barbara that the time will come, on their first birthday, when they won't be able to talk to the birds, the wind, the sunlight any longer. The twins don't believe it, of course. "Do you really mean we won't be able to hear *that* when we're older?" they say of the wind whispering in the trees of Cherry Lane. And both burst into tears. A few months later, the starlings arrive one day to find the babies babbling and kicking, oblivious to their questions. The secret language and instinct of the natural world is lost to them forever, lost as surely as the tadpole loses his tail. They will grow up, acquire book learning and furniture, dress in suits and silk dresses. Most horrifying, or maybe most comforting, is that they have forgotten they ever had the power to understand the language of, as Mary says, "the sunlight and the stars." My mother closed the book, hugged and kissed us. Time for bed. It made a big impression.

The magic and power of Mary was that she never forgot how to talk to the starlings. Somehow, Richard and I have been able to hear them in distant whispers, sometimes farther and farther away (and for nearly thirty years, almost obliterated for me), sometimes closer and stronger, there in the sky for him, the river for me. Like Mary and her umbrella, when we can hear the language of the birds, we fly.

My brother and I are different versions of each other. We feel each other's failures and triumphs, mourn each other's sadnesses. Richard and I joke that we have carbon fiber bones, for both of us are enraptured by long white wings, narrow white boats. Recently he told me about the day when he was thirteen and saw a glider for the first time. "It was simply the coolest thing I had ever seen," he said, the guy-talk version of my falling in love with a boat.

Both of us had spent long periods of our lives hobbled by what we experienced as terminal limitations—mine the darkness of adolescence and constriction of my marriage, his the impaired vision in one eye that left him without enough depth perception to play ball with the other kids on the block. He fumbled and flailed when they caught and jumped. After years of painful and ultimately unsuccessful treatments to restore use of the eye, he approached the age when all real boys joined the football team. In a stroke of luck, he was taken by our parents to the Boulder Municipal Airport one day where our father flew a biplane on weekends, and found the love of his life on a dusty dirt runway.

Within a few days of his first lesson it was clear he was designed for wings, not shoulder pads. In the air, he had the instincts and grace of a hawk, even as a gawky teenager. From that day he happily left the ball field ten thousand feet beneath his fragile fuselage, his narrow young face intently focused on his variometer and altimeter, his boy's palm on the stick lightly, keeping the wingtips level, his "good" eye scanning the horizon for thermals. At eighteen, he became one of the youngest competitive soaring pilots ever.

In 1992, when Richard was thirty-six, he took his lovely white sailplane with the call letters RH (international call sign "Romeo Hotel") to the National Soaring Championships for the thirteenth time. Year after year he'd earned first or second place for the first five days of the event, then clutched on the sixth, the last day, "killing the sparrows," pulled to earth by his overwhelming need to win, to "show them." Year after year he'd landed out on the last decisive day and placed a dismal fortieth or fiftieth for that day, though in the top five or ten overall. His crew, of which I was sometimes one, would drive the long straight prairie roads in the lengthening afternoon and find him in a stubbled wheat field a hundred miles from home, his beautiful long white wings covered with silt, his face stricken and stoic.

But in 1992 there was a different sixth day. I was in Lloyd Harbor, three thousand miles from his competition in Nevada. Late in the morning when the kids were in camp, I walked to a high ridge and sat overlooking the water. I said a prayer for him: *May he feel the glory of those wings, and know the grace of moving through the heavens. May the sorrows and yearnings that pull him to earth drop away. Please, God, let him simply rejoice in the beauty of Your gift.* If he could experience what I hoped for him, his flight would be complete, and whatever place he earned quite beside the point. Later, my father told me what happened that afternoon in Nevada.

Richard went into the sixth day in the lead. He took off and waited for the perfect moment to fly the start gate, then went through on course and at speed. He flew the three-hundred-mile task over high desert in record time. By late afternoon, he was thirty miles out over the sage, over the mountains, hurtling down the last leg to the finish. Then the sky grew dark.

My father saw the storm bear down, heard the thunder roll across the mountains. His son was airborne and alone, his fragile carbon plane a straw in the wind. The radios started crackling. Pilots reported rain, lightning, high winds. Crews hovered for news in the growing chill of the storm.

My brother radioed that he was just on the other side of the range, holding firm in strong gusts, waiting for a break in the curtain of rain and lightning to slip over the mountains and land. All that kept him aloft was his experience and his hand on the controls—firm enough to pilot the plane, sensitive enough to respond to the will of the wind. Here was the moment. Here was when he could have clutched, when he could have said, "I can't wait, I'm just going to muscle this thing through the rain. I'm so close to winning . . ." But he didn't. He let go. He waited patiently, feeling the wind on his fingers, riding the current like a salmon in a river, nosing into the rapids, waiting for the moment to make a dash. One pilot could stand the suspense no longer. He plunged into the wall of rain, desperate to land, and got lost. My father said everyone could hear his transmission, "Heavy rain . . . zero visibility . . . out of altitude . . ." Minutes passed.

"Romeo Hotel to Ground. I see a break and I'm coming through. Five minutes, Dad." Oh man. My brother has this perfect pilot voice. So cool he could have been ordering toast, buttered. Nothing can make him sound panicked. My father, who is himself a cool customer, could hardly tell me this story for the tightness in his throat. Then there was my brother skimming the last ridge, lightning flashing behind his tail. He tore through the rain, letting the wind hold him in its embrace and carry him safely home. "He came in fast and low, and I could hear his wings whistle when he dove for the finish," my father said. "He was just as easy and smooth as a hawk. Smooth as a hawk." When he touched down, my father ran with the ground crews to get him off the field and out of lightning's reach. He became National Champion that day.

"What was different?" I asked him the evening after his victory. This is what he said: "It was the first time I allowed myself to let go of the need to beat everybody. I made up my mind I would fly just for the joy of it. That's all, the joy."

When we let go of our ego's need to bend the world to our will, we can, at last, worship the beauty of this glorious water, this embracing air: God's miraculous world. At last we can hear the language of "the sunlight and the stars." Like Mary Poppins, all of us can tap a source of power vastly greater than that of our mortal bodies, our petty desires. When I won the World Masters Games, three years after the first day I put hand to oar, I was a lightweight in a heavyweight event. That morning, my friends, gathered around our club banner, asked me why I wore an old, faded black racing suit for the biggest race of my life. Why not wear my new club suit with the graphics and the logos, show the team colors? This is what I told them before I had a chance to be embarrassed: "The single I race for God."

Chapter Twelve

THE

SINGLE

For two years I rowed *Sagamore 4*, my
companion from my first time in a racing single
in June 1995 to my races in Albany, Connecticut,
Delaware, Canada, Syracuse, and finally the Head of
the Schuylkill, the famous Philadelphia distance
race, in late October 1996. Nearly ten pounds
heavier than a competitive racing single,
which, at approximately thirty pounds, is so
unsubstantial it is virtually a figment of a boat, *S4*
placed me at a real disadvantage. I liked to think of
it as a noble, earnest Labrador retriever finding itself in the lineup with greyhounds; loved
the idea that, like me with my ill-fitting
racing outfit, it was going to strive valiantly
against seasoned competitors and superior equipment. But in the autumn of 1996, the time had
come to leave *Sagamore 4* to be loyal Labrador

to other new scullers and aspire to a true racing shell. To pretend that sculling was just a pleasant hobby, for which I needed and deserved only the most rudimentary of equipment, was to ignore what I had done and who I was becoming.

Then, in early October, Sagamore Rowing Association decided for me. After the Head of the Schuylkill, the board said, *S4* would be confined to the boathouse permanently. My homely little gray companion was to return to the quiet life. If *S4* could dream, slumbering in its wooden rack in the cold cement boathouse on Huntington Harbor, surely it is dreaming now of afternoons in 1996 when it nosed through the hot winds of the New Jersey Turnpike at seventy miles an hour from its perch atop my old station wagon with the blare of rock music and piping of children's voices. Would dream of starts so quick and ragged that both of us hung on for dear life. Dream of pulling into the lead. Of crossing the line.

Late in October 1996, we drove past the refineries of Newark for the last time. When we got to the boathouse, I wiped *S4* down and put it on the rack, gave it a kiss on its old gray bow, and locked the boathouse. Now the need for a boat of my own, my very own, became acute.

I feared in my bones that my husband would not allow me to have something of my own, particularly something that gave me as much pleasure as a single shell, sensed there was too much at stake for him. Though I knew he would have gladly bought me the nice watch or pair of diamond stud earrings in a brown velvet case that were standard issue for North Shore wives, he knew I wanted neither, and I suspected that my lack of longing for them infuriated him. I wanted a boat in the boathouse, not diamonds in a jewel box. This was to be more evidence of what, I understand, he eventually began to call "Sara's sick obsession."

No, it wasn't a watch I coveted. I wanted a featherweight carbon racing shell, with a wooden deck and seat and a white cathedral hull with blue stripes—purchased for my solitary pleasure and expression. In the prickling of my scalp and pounding of my heart I could feel the danger of my longing. The question was not, Could we afford to buy a good racing single? The question was, *Could I afford to want one?* Because to allow myself to want a boat meant recognizing that I had the right to pursue fulfillment as an individual, and to assert such a right struck at the heart of my marriage.

Now, as nothing had in the past, not even William's birth, my desire for a single forced into the open what I had sensed to be the central truth of our relationship, a truth that suddenly appeared in my path as from a darkened doorway, as if I'd heard its footsteps behind me on a night street a hundred times. The issue of the single made real the obduracy at the heart of my marriage, an obduracy I had felt, but could never see, always hovering in the shadows, kept at bay with acquiescence, flattery, and "little dates."

What were the chances I could save our marriage with persuasion? About the same, I thought, as the chance that a woman confronted in the dark alley can talk her way into a warm, mutual relationship.

One evening after my husband got home and settled in his library with a glass in hand, I came in and shut the door. I needed to talk to him about something important, I said. Then I explained carefully and calmly how vital it was for me to have his support. I made myself talk as if I had some reasonable expectation of it, as if expectation of it *were* reasonable. He would be with me every time I rowed, I said, if only he could find it in his heart to let go of me just a little, to give me the right to be my own person just a little. If he would freely give me wings to fly, he could trust me to fly back. We had been married for sixteen years—our anniversary was in a few weeks. Would he consider giving me a boat as a token of his willingness to recognize and honor my needs? Might we go into the next sixteen years with a new feeling of partnership? "Could you give me a boat because you love *who I am*? That's all I ask." He looked at me as if I were a snake coiled and rattling on the bright chintz slipcover of the sofa. Then he said one word. "No."

Pinned above my desk in my little house on Elm Street is a clipping from the *Boston Globe*. Last year, on a warm morning almost three years after the conversation in the library in late 1996 and many months after I told my husband I was leaving forever, I ate breakfast and read the *Globe* at my kitchen table after getting the kids to day camp. When I turned to the "Sports/Women" section, I found on the front page a large photograph of a beaming woman sprawled on a backyard rope hammock, surrounded by her four young children, also beaming. The headline read: "Marshfield Mom hoping to reach finish line in Vermont endurance race." Mary Kate Shea, mother of four small children, Sunday School teacher and ultra-marathoner, was quoted in italics. *"You can be happy with your life, have your children, and still want to set goals that challenge you physically and mentally."* Her husband, Richard, who, it emerged, steps in on weekends to make sure she gets training time, said, "We try to give [her running] the priority it deserves. She'll always be trying to put the children first, but she has to be sure to cover her own needs as well." I lay my head in my arms on the kitchen table and wept—for all I had lost in those long years, for my little children and all they had lost never bearing witness to parents who loved and supported each other.

For sixteen years I had gotten into bed every night with a man who showed me in a hundred subtle ways his antipathy for who I was and what I prized in myself. I experienced him as the man who would rather incapacitate the woman he claimed to love than see her know a pleasure he himself hadn't granted.

On most days, newspaper stories are very different from that of

Mary Kate Shea. Most days there are stories with headlines like "Prominent Physician Beats Wife to Death," or "Woman Shot by Husband on Courthouse Steps," announcing the final chapter in a long, harrowing tale of battering, sometimes physical, always emotional, always devastating. We usually don't hear a woman's story of suffering until her husband succeeds at last in extinguishing her body as well as her spirit, and it makes the front page. In my story, the final chapter has yet to be written.

I'd like to say we were unique, that no couple had ever been locked in just the same dance of domination as we were—a dance in its own way as rigidly patterned and ritualized as a waltz on a wedding day. But there was nothing unique about us, nothing except that he was smarter and more subtle than most (and if the pen is mightier than the sword, in our case the tongue was much mightier than a fist that might have driven home what was happening to me). I believe I was like any of thousands of women in thousands of marriages in which a man's apparent need to control and subjugate is expressed the same way, using the same time-honored methods. It's all there in black and white at every women's shelter, though I got my fistful of fliers from my Episcopal minister, a woman, with the warning, "These are dangerous. Hide them where you're sure he can't find them."

The result is the unraveling of both the woman's sense of self-worth and her trust in her perceptions and values; the loss of her reality. In many marriages in which the damage is emotional, not physical, she becomes so confused and diminished that she blames *herself*, again and again rationalizing her husband's behavior as a reasonable response to the myriad shortcomings from which, he has convinced her, she suffers. She even comes to lean on her tormentor, grateful that he sticks with her. In many of these relationships, the batterer doesn't have to murder his wife; she does it for him. Surely I might have died—in spirit, possibly in body—if I hadn't fallen in love with a white boat

on a windy harbor one spring afternoon. Even then, it took four years
to find the strength and clarity to row my way to freedom. I was a
lucky one.

How do women get into such relationships? And *why do they stay?*
I'll tell you how. I'll tell you why.

W e married with the best of intentions, on a cold day in mid-
November 1980, just a few months after meeting. It had been a blind
date. I carried ivy as my bouquet—resilient, graceful and evergreen, I
thought, as I wanted to be in my marriage. I made my dress on my
grandmother's sewing machine. My sisters and brother made the
cake; my mother played Bach on the harpsichord. Few of our friends
were there, so we faced the minister on November 15 witnessed only
by our families and one or two family friends.

A work acquaintance had introduced us six months before, and
the man who became my husband called to ask me out on Good
Friday, an omen excellent from one perspective, chilling from another. The first thing I noticed was his lovely voice, melodious and beautifully modulated. He could say anything, read a menu, and it would
sound delightful. On our initial date, I was dazzled. He was wonderfully articulate and discussed issues from art to finance with a quick
and fluid intelligence that knocked me off my feet. He knew his classical music, his botanical prints, his French sauces. He could say
something bitingly clever about local politics, then play a breathless
riff on his banjo—a Renaissance man.

He was funny, he was brilliant; he was hurt, he was vulnerable. His
first wife had deserted him for another man, he said, and he hoped
someday to find the one good woman in the world, "not a bitch" like
the others. I heard in his anger the sorrow of a man rejected.

As the weeks passed, it emerged that I was to be the one good
woman. I listened patiently all the times he explained the depth of
female deceit, "except for you"—described a woman's faithless

nature, so different from that of a man, which, he said, was based on logic, honor, and the value of commitment. "Except for you, most women are terrorists," and he explained how they held a man hostage with their tears and emotional blackmail, as immune to his suffering as a hijacker or a letter bomber. Oh yes, women were terrorists. And "cunts" (a word whose hard consonants he always carefully enunciated over the years). As despicable, he told me, was that they're constantly on the lookout for "a better offer," ready to abandon one man in favor of another with bigger or better hardware. "Except for you," he said. I was different—I had "integrity." I listened, confused and repelled by his condemnation of women, which was delivered in a conversational tone as if his opinion were unassailably reasonable. I wasn't sure whether to be pleased at his praise, or outraged at his criticism; it didn't seem possible to be both. But I was sure his first wife's infidelity had made him bitter; and I could sense the sadness and loss at the heart of his bitterness. Of course, he felt women were untrustworthy—he had been terribly hurt. I would show him a different side of femininity. I would be the one.

Within a few weeks we were saying the three words and making meaningful allusions to long-term plans. He told me he was delighted that I didn't seem to be a woman whose hormonal cycle caused me to suffer the violent mood swings that sent most women "out of control." I got the impression that the poor man thought a woman's periods, in fact a woman's very femininity, rendered her somehow physically and emotionally pathological. But of course he had been a warrior, not a lover. His world was of men—of the all-male military academy, of all-male clubs, and the mostly male oil company for which he worked. How could he possibly know anything of women?

This was my fatal mistake. I was so bewitched by his intellect, and my nurturing instincts so aroused by his sorrow, that I discounted the hostility that seemed to radiate from him. Surely this was a temporary symptom of the breakup of his marriage and would pass with the experience of our love. If I had paid more attention to the message behind his words and less to the perception of his sadness that played on my empathy (and my own woundedness), I would have walked away and never turned back. Instead, I dreamed my dreams of the edifice we would build: marriage, children, home.

Oh yes, I planned to heal him with my tenderness and truthfulness, and I would heal too, for I had my own lingering pain about my female self—sorrow about the fact that my father might have liked me better if I'd been a boy; grief over my terrible stillborn love for the rancher; and fear that I might never be able to bear a child. So I looked to a life with him to give me opportunity to demonstrate to myself my ability to conceive and deliver love. To become a whole woman.

It was a bargain. I would cure both of us of our sorrow, and banish once and for all our deepest fears—his with my demonstration of loyalty and reliability year after year, mine with the experience of marriage and motherhood. I would be the woman he dreamed of—honest, forthright, faithful—and he would be the man who needed and loved me, treasured me for offering him succor and safe harbor in my body and heart. I hardly reflected a moment when he said to someone, "The only thing that keeps Sara from being the perfect companion is that she's not a man." He would come around. I knew it.

Sometimes we would wake in the morning to the classical music station and he would identify, out of a deep sleep, the work of some obscure eighteenth-century Italian composer. I would laugh with delight and we would kiss. We loved to play in bed. My mind might be almost as good as a man's, but he relished the part of me that was a woman with an urgency that left me sometimes feeling that, in his embrace, I was playing in ocean waves just a little too big to be fun.

He couldn't seem to get enough of me, even when I was sleepy or tired. The insatiability of his apparent need to fill me and, even more, somehow to be filled by me was both thrilling and disquieting. Sometimes I felt he invaded me as if I were a vast continent with rich loam and sunny skies—setting his stamp on every inch of me and growing full on my richness. But every once in awhile he was like a child nestled safe inside, famished for my warmth and love. So, in the early days, I felt both the shiver of lust any woman feels in the heat of the sexual game—the delicious moment of yielding to the invader—and a protective tenderness for the needy little boy. Both conqueror and boy seemed to yearn insatiably for my womanly body, my loving heart. We made love night after night, then told each other our scariest secrets.

We'd been in love three months when my sister Annie and her new husband stopped by one day to visit us in California on their honeymoon trip. That afternoon, Annie and I danced a little maiden "I'm in love" dance, arm-in-arm, in the sunny driveway as her husband watched, smiling. My soon-to-be husband came out of the house and found us. "What are you two elephants pretending to be, a couple of Vestal Virgins?" His tone was difficult to decipher—friendly enough that we were clearly meant to take his comment as a joke, but with a hard, sarcastic edge. I felt as if a bee had stung me, a bee I hadn't seen. Later, Annie took me aside. "You *can't* marry a man who talks to you like that. You *can't!*" That night I told him his comment felt hurtful to both Annie and me and I didn't want him to do it again. "Can't you take a joke?" he said fondly, as if I were a silly, oversensitive little thing. "Don't you know I love your goofy-sister act?" I guessed I was oversensitive because—though his explanation, which hadn't an echo of an apology, seemed reasonable, sort of, and his tone affectionate, sort of—I felt stung again, by a bee I hadn't seen.

A few weeks later, we, or rather he, addressed the issue of friends. It had become clear to both of us that he didn't like my friends and my friends too were dismayed with my choice of him. While he had tennis and sailing acquaintances, he didn't seem to have the kind of "bosom buddies" I did. Over a candlelit dinner he told me I had a choice: I could have my friends or I could have him, not both. He gave me an explanation that played on my particular vulnerabilities. He told me gently that a healthy adult woman should want no other confidant than her mate. The "best friends" I sometimes talked about with affection? For me to continue to want such an intimate connection outside our own trusting intimacy was symptomatic of a lack of emotional development (a defect on which he was willing to "work with me"). Most women grew out of "best friends" after adolescence, he explained. Emotionally undeveloped? I already suffered from what the gynecologist had called an "infantile uterus." Was my emotional development stunted as well? Maybe he was right, maybe there *was* something wrong with me.

So I gave them up. Just like that. After all, it was with him that I would live my life, he who might give me the chance to bear a child. It was to our love I would turn for sustenance. How often does a woman have a chance to build a family with a good man?

In losing contact with the people who knew and loved me, I eliminated one of my only sources of "reality check," people who might have said, "There's nothing wrong with you; he's playing mind games." Much as I wanted to reestablish a connection with them over the years, to meet my old friends outside my marriage would both confirm his diagnosis and invite his accusation that I was covert and disloyal, just like every other woman.

He made it clear he didn't like my family, either. Oh, the men were fine, my father and my brother; but my mother, he told me, was the kind of eccentric, New Age character he hated. "She's self-obsessed," he told me regretfully, like a doctor informing me that my mother had breast cancer or a brain tumor, then went on to point out how she pursued her music at the expense of my father. Surely I knew that a normal wife would want nothing more than to share her husband's interests so they can spend more time together. (Did he think she should give up Bach and learn to fly a stunt plane? I wondered.) And not only was my mother dysfunctional, my lovely sister Caroline he considered superficial and vain. So, like my separation from my friends, I soon learned to keep my family at arm's length. My friends and family tell me now it was as if I went into a tunnel and didn't come out for nearly two decades.

A few weeks before we were married, we visited my husband's parents. His father, who died just after our daughter was born, was always cordial and pleasant to me and I liked him. His mother, who had the lovely, modulated voice my husband inherited, was welcoming and inclusive. We hit it off. But the first evening in the middle of dinner, something happened that chilled me to the bone. His father started needling his mother, just a funny little poke at first, then more and more angry, less and less funny. His voice took on a new tone—louder, deeper than before. She responded with her own new tone, a little shrill, a little desperate, talking faster and faster in an effort to give any answer to satisfy him. They wound toward a crescendo as if in a well-rehearsed duet of his criticism and her cringing appeasement. He chided her about misplacing his fishing vest in loud, demanding tones as if she were a simpleton hard of hearing, or a hotel maid who speaks no English and can't tell you where to get your fax sent.

Yet my husband, his father, and his mother, for that matter, seemed to think that this was a reasonable dinner table exchange. I guessed it was one in which they had engaged countless times over the years. I certainly witnessed it every time we visited them, heard disquieting shadows of it in my husband's voice when he talked to his mother on the phone as if she were a wayward child or an errant puppy needing correction. I was shocked that she took it. It was as if she had gotten so accustomed to this brand of humiliation over the years that she didn't see it for the grotesquely degrading ritual it was—like those people who come to tolerate lethal doses of poison by increasing in tiny increments the amount they ingest daily. I was appalled. Oh my God, I thought on that first visit, don't let me ever end up like this.

If I'd allowed myself to pay attention to the distant alarms in my head, I would have begun to see the trap I was about to step into. If only I had read even one of the pamphlets handed out at women's shelters—*The Characteristics of a Batterer*—I would have checked down the list with a pencil, tick, tick, tick. If only I had had the conversation back then that I had on a research trip this spring to Sanctuary for Families, an organization in Manhattan that offers victims of domestic abuse shelter, counseling, even job training for a new life. In my interview with Beth Silverman-Yam, the clinical director, I had talked about what happened to me in some detail when, in a pause, she lifted her hand. "If you're in any doubt that what you're describing is domestic violence," she said, "it is." She explained that it didn't matter if the attack is as obvious as hitting a woman with a tire iron or as subtle as disparaging her with a cutting remark disguised as a joke, or even as praise, the agenda is the same: Power and control. She went on to describe a pattern of behavior that resembled what I had experienced in my marriage in uncanny detail—jealousy, isolation from family and friends, "mind games," sexual coercion, rigid gender roles. "Psychological battering is real. Like physical abuse, its purpose is to gain control, not by attacking a woman's body, but by destroying her sense of self." If I had known even the most basic warning signs, she said, I would have run the first time I heard him call a woman, any woman a "cunt."

Three weeks after the scene at the dinner table with my husband's parents, I married him.

On our honeymoon it became clear to me that, though I was the one good woman, he was still afraid I would stray from his side like a poorly disciplined dog to a stranger bearing a bone. We went skiing in Switzerland. One afternoon when we walked into the mountain lodge for lunch, two men who had skied nearby raised their steins to us in greeting. I smiled and nodded. My husband turned to me in a cold fury and accused me of flirting. I was baffled. I remembered how he had talked bitterly about "the better offer," but surely *this* didn't count as betrayal. When we got home, though, I realized that he needed the security of knowing I was safe from contact with other men—at least for our first year or two of marriage until he could learn to trust me. I took a job and enrolled in a master's program at a nearby women's college, "so he won't have to worry," I told myself. Thus I entered our first year of marriage without friends and family, stripped of the routines and interests that had supported me in my single life, and in the equivalent of a nunnery, all of my own free will. Why didn't it feel like free will?

After we settled down, things started to change, or maybe they didn't change. Maybe his little jokes just started to get to me. If in our first year I felt hurt by his comments, it was the predictable nervous strain of being a new bride, he said. My new husband rarely raised his beautiful voice and most of his little quips were said in the guise of affectionate banter.

"I love your enthusiasm," he said to me one afternoon. "When you get excited, you're just like a cocker spaniel running around in little circles and piddling on the floor." If this was supposed to be some kind of compliment, I experienced it as painfully derogatory. Yet when I defended myself, he said I was overreacting. "I love spaniels," he said. Then he told me I should be happy he was comparing me to one, that it was endearing the way they "quiver and lose control." Was I, perhaps, getting my period?

At his response, I felt a spinning sensation almost like vertigo. His comment about the spaniel was humiliating, yet he told me in an exasperated voice that not only should it *not* hurt but that I should be sensitive enough to feel gratitude at his "compliment." So I was doubly in the wrong. (Triply if you accept his suggestion that my female hormones had somehow impaired my ability to perceive his "compliment.") I felt hurt and confused. It was as if my own experience of the situation, my reality, was suddenly slippery and elusive. Which way was up?

This was one of thousands of similar moments over the course of sixteen years, each one whittling down my trust in my own perceptions. With each little remark I felt smaller and less solid, and he seemed to get bigger—somehow harder and immovable.

There were other remarks, always delivered in a low, chiding voice with a twist of sarcasm, remarks about "wagging your tail" and "scarfing up dinner," as if I were his favorite pet. I didn't feel flattered, I felt degraded, but he made it clear that my hurt was the result of my feminine tendency to "take it personally." He told me he knew I would do my best to overcome my defensiveness and honor his loving remarks in the spirit he intended. "After all," he told me then, and dozens of times over the years, "no one could love you as much as I do." "No one," he told me with an affectionate grin, "would put up with you!" I guess I was a lucky woman. Again the earth shifted under my feet and my head spun.

Sometimes he told me sadly how disappointed he was that I was so selfish and immature. When I protested, he accused me of being insensitive to his feelings of disappointment, another sign of my selfishness. I felt helpless and paralyzed, wondered if I was losing my mind.

Early on, I learned to gauge his mood and wait for the moment when he might be most amenable before I made the smallest request—to take a class or go to the city for the day. I found that my life was closely confined by his stated belief that my job was to stay at home where I belonged. My few trips to visit my parents he punished with frequent evening phone calls accusing me of negligence—to him, to the children, to the house whose gutters clogged and roof leaked as soon as I got on the plane. I learned to walk on eggs, to phrase and time my comments and requests to avoid the accusations, the little stabbing blade of sarcasm; learned to avoid the requests I knew were hopeless anyway. I remember one day when I overheard two other mothers talking about going out for dinner and a movie. How did they get permission to *do* that? I thought.

After we married, the sex changed, or maybe it didn't change. His urgency during courtship became a demand that I be available to him every morning whether I was asleep or awake. Sometimes, early on, I protested. Then he punished me with a cold shoulder and sarcasm about the mess in the house ("a shithouse," he would say). For all that day and sometimes the next, he sulked, ignoring me. When I asked if he was mad, he would say, "Of course not. You always think it's about you, don't you?"

In fact, I thought it was less and less about me. In our sexual interaction, I began to have a disquieting feeling that the need I perceived in him to drive into me with the relentlessness of a machine had nothing to do with who I was or what I wanted. That I was occasionally ill or tired or busy didn't seem to affect his ardor at all. My willingness to participate seemed entirely peripheral to his experience of "making love."

The only time I refused him was just after William was born, when my level of rage made it impossible even to go through the motions. Six weeks after the baby's birth, I faced the day when I would have to, as my husband put it, "open my doors for business." When the day came and I found myself simply incapable of "opening my doors," he responded with anger for only a moment, then delivered a lesson in female pathology in cool, dispassionate tones, as if, in addition to his career as an investment banker, he had miraculously become a credible clinician and I an addled female patient. My rage, he said, was not the product of his mistreatment, which was a figment of my imagination; it was a dangerous condition known as postpartum depression, a debilitating mental disorder in which women have been known to kill their own children. He added that he had also been concerned for some time that I was suffering from both a case of classic sexual frigidity—of which my present refusal to make love was evidence—and a structurally malformed clitoris. His unwillingness even to acknowledge my position without branding me as deformed and demented left me feeling I was caught in a nightmare.

Over the years if I'd had friends close enough to ask, they might have told me that he was violating my mind as surely as I felt he had violated my body. But I had no friends close enough to talk about such things.

My husband consistently asserted in the exasperated tones of a long-suffering parent that he was doing nothing I could reasonably experience as hurtful, and that I should be more grateful for the lifestyle he provided. Yet I hurt as if an unseen assailant were stabbing me with the small, thin blade of a penknife—so quick I couldn't identify the attacker and almost couldn't see the wound. Always my hurt feelings were the fault of my flawed perception; my reasons were illogical, my pain the result of some pathological feminine weakness. By the time we had lived together a dozen years or so, I had begun to feel our "conversations" were a nightmare in which I was paralyzed and disoriented while he lopped off a finger or a toe, an earlobe or the tip of my nose—nothing major, just a carving away of my person, bit by bit. I was disappearing before my eyes.

Except for the brief period around William's birth, the overwhelming emotion I felt in my interaction with him was not anger. It was confusion. I felt his inability to understand how his words hurt had to be the result of my inability to communicate adequately what it was about them that bothered me. If only I could find the right words, I thought again and again, he would understand and surely he would stop. But I was wrong, because all those years I innocently assumed a mutuality of empathy. Ironically, it was my own assumption that both left me feeling defective and inadequate and made it impossible for me to see that he was surely operating from a very, very different agenda.

He was reasonable, he was smart, he loved me, of that I was convinced, partly because *he* was convinced. So, maybe the intensity of my pain and paralyzing confusion were symptomatic that something really was very wrong with me. I assumed at one point that my experience with the rancher had damaged my ability to love and was at the heart of my pain in my marriage. As you might imagine, my husband jumped on this bandwagon, since it exonerated him and placed the blame for my pain squarely on my shoulders. He seemed to grow plump with satisfaction in his role as concerned, nurturing spouse to an emotionally damaged wife.

But, though the impact of the rancher on my life had been substantial, and as my husband asserted later, central to our relationship, it was not for the reason he thought. No, if it hadn't been for the numbing of my ability to recognize the danger he posed, I would, in fact, never have married him. And if it hadn't been for my lack of a strong, clear voice to protest his treatment of me, I would certainly never have stayed with him as long as I did. My ability to love is just fine, as it turns out, and it took two years of therapy for me to realize that my experience with the rancher, though traumatic, was really nothing but a red herring in the context of my marriage. How do I know? From the moment I decided to leave my husband over three years ago, I have felt dramatic and immediate alleviation of the confusion, pain, paralysis. I've started to feel whole again.

No one outside my family, and certainly not the friends we had acquired as a couple or the neighbors and acquaintances where we lived, had the slightest hint of what was going on. Usually no one does, even in cases of physical abuse. The community at the clubs and schools thought he was a nice guy. They didn't see him often because of his travel schedule, but he held the kids' hands as we walked the brick sidewalk to the church door. The parishioners must have thought, What a good Dad! They didn't know that at home he called an errant child a "little shit" (not in anger, he said, but in "fun"), or that he told Janie, in front of her little brothers, that her fourth-grade teacher, who had given a difficult assignment, was "a dumb cunt." He was a wonderful conversationalist and could be very charming at cocktail parties where he often lavishly praised my handiwork as a homemaker. "What a devoted husband!"

Sometimes he seemed to want to remind me of what a caring, feeling man he was. He had a habit of tugging on my sleeve in the sentimental parts of movies to make me look at him. Once I was looking, he would turn slowly toward me in the flickering light so I could see the tears rolling down his cheeks. If I didn't turn and acknowledge his tender heart with an empathetic smile, he would tug my sleeve harder. I admit this was one of the only times I did not feel confused. I was repulsed.

I had a dream about a decade into my marriage. I dreamed that I was being executed by excruciatingly slow lethal injection, so slow that I knew what was happening but had no strength to tear out the IV and leap from the table. In my dream, I was conscious but dizzy and confused, paralyzed by the poison, and awaiting with desperate dread the moment I would slip into unconsciousness forever.

If my husband had hit me—broken my nose, split my lip—I could have seen him for the enemy he was. I experienced his form of "love" as a torture so subtle, so effective, that sometimes I just wanted an ending, any ending.

There is a terrifying old movie called *Gaslight*, with Charles Boyer and a lovely young Ingrid Bergman. Boyer is smooth and debonair, with that great accent and deep melodious voice. Bergman is all quivering innocence and alluring femininity. He marries her apparently for her freshness and beauty, in spite of the fact that she, like me, had suffered a youthful trauma that posed the possibility of a "nervous condition." Then Boyer, for material motives we slowly come to understand, proceeds to systematically drive her insane by playing on her particular vulnerability. The gaslights in her room dim and flare night after night, the result of his machinations, yet no one will believe her reports of this. He gives her a valuable brooch, steals it back, then casually asks to see it. When she searches for it, increasingly frantic, he tells her in those wonderfully solicitous tones that her mind must be going. He secretly takes a painting from the wall and, the next day, looks at her with tender and exasperated reproach when she cannot remember removing it. Throughout, he seems the ideal husband, nurturing and concerned, distraught that his young wife is disintegrating before his eyes. She is frantic and confused, acutely embarrassed every time he says, "Oh Paula, it hurts me when you're so ill and fanciful . . . "

As with my husband and me, *his* reality becomes more real to her than her own. If he says she hid a painting, she comes to believe it. If he says she lost the brooch, then she accepts that she did. If his watch is missing and he suggests she stole it, she simply bows her head in shame. These days, this subtle, devastating brand of torment is actually called "gaslighting," and is known to every domestic abuse counselor in the country. But during the years of my marriage, I had no idea what was happening. All I knew was that something was very wrong with me.

Unlike most cases in real life, the movie has a happy ending, because, unbeknownst to Boyer, handsome Joseph Cotten, suspecting foul play, has hovered on the curb outside Bergman's London house, gazing up from the dark street at her gaslit window. One night when she collapses in a state of nervous despair, Cotten manfully forces his way through the front door and up the main staircase, and rescues her from her torment at the hands of this monster—her loving husband.

Like most of the thousands of women in my situation, I didn't have a Joseph Cotten hovering nearby.

Sometimes I shook off my confusion and paralysis for a moment, like the last rising of a drowning swimmer, and knew with despair that only the most diabolical man on earth would devise a system of torture so efficient that the victim is manipulated into believing she deserves her punishment. But then I realized that, to me, he was more terrifying than the evil plotter, like Boyer, who simply sought the treasure in the attic. No, my husband seemed to be the man who has truly convinced himself of his righteousness; the man whose fear of an "Other," both threatening and alluring, he expresses in a missionary zeal to control and subjugate. God's work.

What made all the years worth it? The children. To feel my baby quicken within me, to smooth the downy hair of my newborn, to feel a little fist hold my finger tight as a limpet made it bearable. To watch them grow tall and run down the front steps to school with their Power Ranger lunchboxes, and to greet them in my bright kitchen for a snack and a report of the day when they came home, made it bearable. To rock them when they fell off their bikes and hug them when they wrote their names for the first time made it all bearable.

I got my boat. I finally had to beg for it, so I begged. But if he was counting on the paralysis that had always assured my acquiescence, he made a terrible mistake, for I had already experienced a win—on that bright morning in Canada. Mutuality, partnership? At last it was clear to me they were not to be part of our marriage.

From the moment he finally wrote the check and handed it to the boatmaker, I resolved never to associate him in any way with the vessel about to be built. I earned it—in the kitchen; on my back—and I deserved it. Because, at last, through the mastery I gained from all those dark dawns on the still harbor, from the strength and vision I built from racing my course ever more straight and true, I knew I had the right to something of my own. Me.

Chapter Thirteen

MOVING

ON

In March 1997, my single arrived in the
middle of a cold night when the old snow lay
in patches and the last vestiges of ice clung to the
bluestone in the shade of the porch. It was
delivered wrapped in yellow quilting and
nestled in a wooden shipping cradle,
as if the stork had rested for a mid-night
moment in our dark and frozen yard.

The trucker had called from the outskirts
of Baltimore late in the afternoon. "Lady, says here
I got a boat for you." He needed directions and said
he figured that, with a break for dinner and a few
stops for gas, he'd be in Lloyd Harbor around
two in the morning. "Where you want me
to leave this thing?" I thought for a moment.
Leave it under the apple tree near the kitchen door,
I told him.

At three-thirty, I woke with a start and lay in the dark with my eyes open, my heart pounding. The alarm clock glowed by my shoulder, and the only sounds in the room were the breathing of my husband and click of the steam radiator. It was here. I knew it. Slipping out of bed, stealthy and eager as a woman on her way to meet a lover, I found my slippers and robe, felt my way down the long staircase and out the front door into the freezing night. It was too early for dawn, but the sky glowed with the faint gray of city lights on low clouds, just enough to see the shape of the car and the outline of the driveway, just enough to see something very long and very, very narrow underneath the apple tree: my boat. My single. I picked my way across the icy stones to the dim shape, clutching my old bathrobe across my chest. Then I knelt in the snow, wrapped my arms around the slender bow, pressed my face against its cool nylon quilting, and christened it.

Has there ever been a boat as sweet and dear as mine was to me? I know now what I didn't know then, that the boat favored by champions is the yellow boat, the Empacher, produced by the dozens in a German factory and raced to the roar of the grandstands. But my boat, the Sharrow, is the most graceful thing I have ever known.

It was mine—built for me alone, tailored to my body. I had chosen the color of the hull, a snowy white, and the rich dark blue of the narrow racing stripes that tapered to nothing at each end of the delicately arched cathedral deck. The bow curved sheer and clean as a carving knife, and the stern was an elegant reverse transom that lent to it an illusion of quickness, of yearning forward. The seat decking and paper-thin gunwales were of pale beech, with a rippling, delicate grain suggestive of movement and water. The seat itself was beautiful. It was molded exquisite as sculpture, a ply of beech and carbon only a quarter of an inch thick. Even the width between the sitbones holes in the seat matched the width of my hips.

I had chosen the Sharrow partly on the basis of a coach's recommendation; partly on my interview with its builder, George Sharrow, who interviewed me as much as I him; and partly on the legacy of having read Shel Silverstein's *The Giving Tree* to my children probably fifty times over the course of their childhoods. George, who custom-builds performance racing hulls for women and lightweight men, is known by a small circle of scullers both for his uncompromising workmanship and for the materials he uses: carbon fiber for its stiffness, wood for its beauty and resilience. In his obsession to create the perfect boat, he insists on building each one personally, and thus only ten Sharrows a year leave the doors of his workshop.

When I talked to him on the phone for the first time, I liked what I heard—a man who felt strongly that a boat should be quiet ("that's where the wood helps, it dampens the noise of the slide"), quick ("darn it, no one else builds a performance hull for the needs of a sculler under a hundred forty"), and light as a feather. "Some production boats come from the factory with gobs of adhesive and old paint sticks left inside where you can't see them," he said. "That's sloppy workmanship, and that's *weight*!" To George, workmanship and weight were inextricably linked. "You'll never find so much as a glue drip in any of *my* boats."

But as much as I liked the technical advantages of George's boat, and as much as I liked George himself, I liked most of all the idea of a boat that incorporated the "soul" of wood. I had always loved the notion that the clapboards of my house or the planks of my kitchen table retained in their grain the aliveness of the tree from which they were made—a memory of flexing in the wind of a summer storm and bending under a load of snow on a December night. Every piece of lumber was a piece of a "Giving Tree," Silverstein's tree that self-lessly shares itself with its human companion. I wanted in my boat the same kind of ally. Wood was no longer fashionable in a racing shell, but I was going to need all the help I could get. My Sharrow and I have raced together coast to coast, in calm and storm, for four years now, and my tender vessel, and the Giving Tree of which it is made, has not let me down.

In the first days of spring 1997, then, I found myself owner of a new racing shell that had no home except the narrow space next to the bushes and under the apple tree by the back door. Rack space in a boathouse anywhere is always at a premium. Sagamore didn't have room for my Sharrow in Huntington, so it was up to me to carry the boat atop my car to Lloyd Harbor every day.

The first time I "car-topped" took all morning. Getting the boat on the padded rack and strapping it down with blue nylon webbing was easy. Getting launched at the other end was not. For one thing, there was no dock. A rowing dock is lower than a standard dock to accommodate a shell's riggers, and Lloyd Harbor's rowing dock had, by that time, been replaced with one suitable for powerboats. Sagamore's dock in Huntington was impractical for car-topping—it was at the end of a winding, thickly forested path. So it took me half an hour to find a spot on Lloyd Harbor where I could both hide the car (parking next to the harbor was illegal) and wade in safely. Then I had to find a place to set up the wooden stands for the hull—the slings—where no one would tamper with them.

After unloading the boat onto the slings and placing the oars at the water's edge, I walked into the icy March water at low tide across the mud with the boat balanced on my head (unlike S4, the Sharrow was light enough that I could finally get it atop my head) and set it in the water for the first time. Then I ran for oars before the slight breeze could blow the Sharrow into deep water where I would never get it back, because to swim in that water, on that day, would have been madness. Now, with feet and legs numb below the knee, I settled myself into the tiny seat, nesting my sitbones in the holes, and slipped lifeless feet into the lightweight track shoes bolted to the footboards. I balanced very, very carefully, wedging the oar handles between knee and chest to brace the boat so I could use both my hands to tie the shoelaces (another first—S4 had no shoes, and therefore no shoelaces to tie). All this while taking care not to drift onto submerged rocks that would put a hole in my new craft before I ever took a stroke.

At last we were ready. I was frozen. My hands were raw (I hadn't heard yet about the special mittens for scullers, called pogies, which encase both hand and oar). My breath came in clouds. I took a stroke. This was *definitely* different from *S4*. Took another. My Sharrow seemed twitchy and alive, a frisky little mare anxious to be given her head. We made our way cautiously down the harbor, hugging the shoreline. I rowed very carefully. This was my first time on the water this year and months out of the boat had made me rusty and tentative. That and the fact that I knew I would quickly perish of hypothermia if we flipped. "I'm not giving you free rein yet," I told my little mare. But clearly the Sharrow longed to be let loose. I rowed into the shallows near the sandbar midway down the harbor. "Okay, let's see what you've got." And I put on the power.

Lord Almighty, what had God and George wrought? This boat really was a thoroughbred—everything about it longed for speed. We flew up the harbor. *S4* had been a dear friend, but the Sharrow was as responsive as *S4* had been steady and plodding. Everything about it was quick and spirited. I adored it.

My hands could hardly grip the oars, they were so cold. All the way back down the harbor, I stopped every minute or so to stuff one or the other under my armpits to warm my fingers enough to go further. When we finally arrived back at the narrow launch site, the slings were gone. They had simply floated away on the rising tide. I still had a lot to learn.

As the spring passed, I developed a routine precise as a rifle drill for getting my boat from home, to water, and back home with a minimum of fuss. My neighbors noted the frequency of my boat on top of the station wagon and one of the other nursery school moms, Betsy Roche, whom I liked and who could be counted on to say her mind, looked at it one day as we stood next to the playground. "Well, Sar," she said, folding her arms across her chest, "it's a hell of an accessory!"

It *was* a hell of an accessory. It was everything a woman, or at least this woman, could want. Every morning I drove to Lloyd Harbor at five, left the shell on slings, and drove up the street to a friend's house where I could leave the car. After every row the process was reversed, with my arrival home in just enough time to wash down the boat, dry it, and put on its yellow cover before the morning wake-up ritual began. Often I looked out the kitchen window during the day just to see again the slim shape, quiet under its quilted cover.

Now I was a free spirit, at least on the water. I no longer relied on Sagamore for a boat, no longer had to ask permission to use club oars. After the Masters Nationals in Syracuse in August, I had worked briefly for a local high school as interim coach for their crew team and used the few hundred dollars I earned to buy a set of ultra-light carbon "hatchet" blades and a Stroke Coach of my own. Cartopping was arduous, but the sense I had of being truly independent, with all my own equipment, even my own launch site on the public beach in Lloyd Harbor (no more odysseys from Huntington Harbor), was heady. And there was no getting around it: though there was no one against whom to test my speed, I could feel by the way the boat moved through the water that my Sharrow and I were getting damned quick.

Our first test was in Boston in the middle of May. It was also my first introduction to racing on the Charles River.

The Charles is not designed for racing. In fact, the Charles is not designed at all. It meanders maddeningly in long loops that ensure the wind will blow from every quarter during even a short workout. In addition, it is studded with picturesque bridges supported by stout abutments guaranteed at best to scrape an oar, at worst to stop one dead. There is one section of the lower Charles, the Powerhouse Stretch, on which a thousand-meter course is laid out, a course that takes the sculler downriver through two bridges. So narrow is it that only four competitors can race at a time, necessitating an unusually stringent elimination process: the final can have only four, instead of the usual six competitors. These four competitors have to divvy up the available river width, one through the Boston Arch of each bridge, two through the larger Center Arch, and the last duking it out with upstream rowers going the opposite direction in the Cambridge Arch.

The Riverside Sprints is a yearly event about which everyone says, "It's too soon for a sprint. I'm not *ready!*" Well, I was ready. I had driven to Boston with the Sharrow the night before and the morning of the race dawned windy and bright, the water of the Charles a deep, roiling blue. I recognized a couple of competitors I'd seen in Albany the year before, and one from Derby. Otherwise, I knew no one and no one knew me.

I rowed to the start line of our heat, a start line bereft of stake boats—the Charles is so narrow a starter can stand onshore, sight the mark on the far shore, and call the scullers into alignment. When the flag dropped, the Sharrow and I jumped, as we had practiced dozens of times. In the next lane was a woman who had won the Head of the Charles in the single a few years before. We swept down the course and through the bridges, she out front, me trailing by a length. With twenty strokes to go, I felt my Edge leap to hand. The Sharrow and I found our new rhythm, catching the leader in ten strokes and inching past her just before the line. In the final that afternoon I met the winner of the other heat, a powerful woman in her early thirties. We rowed a good race, and she beat me decisively. But I was elated. I had placed second in Boston.

In late 1996, a few weeks after the discussion about the single, my husband had accepted a job offer in Boston. It appeared from the blue (and sometimes I really did wonder if God had a hand in it), and arrived with extraordinary timing. It was a very good offer, from a well-regarded investment firm that wanted my husband to select a team and lead a department, a role he had long sought. He was excited about it, and I too was cautiously optimistic about our family for the first time in a long while. He talked about less travel, shorter hours, more time for the children. I thought there was a chance, a very long chance, that in Boston we might begin to heal as a family.

I know it's hard to imagine I wasn't considering divorce after everything that had happened. I can hear women out there yelling, "Are you crazy? Leave him! Do it now!" and my own sisters and mother would lead the chorus. But the truth was, with the advent of the job offer, I started imagining that we might be able to find a peaceful accommodation—like those turn-of-the-century upper-class couples with separate bedrooms and, except for the children, separate lives. If he really meant what he said about wanting to become involved with the children, and if he could come to live and let live with me, it might be enough to carry us through. It was wishful thinking, outdated thinking, certainly foolish thinking (and the literature from the shelters is full of women who keep deluding themselves that *if only*, then he'll change, and *this time* it's going to be different). But I did wish it. And I owed our children my willingness to try.

I would be lying if I said I didn't know that Boston was the epicenter of rowing in the United States, maybe even the world, and that I wasn't wild with glee at this stroke of luck, a glee about which I kept very, very quiet. The prospect of rowing the Charles daily and becoming part of Boston's rowing community would have satisfied my dearest fantasy if I'd ever dared to dream it. My training partner, Jeff, had moved to Boston to coach at a university at the end of August 1996, the summer we trained together, and now I had no one with whom to row. Jeff and I talked on the phone occasionally, and when he told me about morning workouts in which the Charles swarmed with scullers, sparring and drilling, it sounded like the Promised Land.

So we agreed the job was the best thing for the family. In January 1997, my husband moved to a rental in the Back Bay and went to his new office for the first time. The children and I were to remain on Long Island until the end of the school year in June. Some weekends he would come home; some we went to Boston and looked for houses. We decided on an affluent suburb twenty minutes west of

Boston, where we found a house in late winter. It was a large white house, with pillars and a pond, just like the one in Lloyd Harbor, and within a few weeks of entering into a purchase contract I'd signed up the children for the summer day camp where they could make friends, and made contact with the minister of the Episcopal church across the street. The children would go to Sunday School; I would sing in the choir, as I had on Long Island.

At the end of June the children were finally out of school, the moving vans packed, the cats put in carriers, and the boat strapped atop the car. It just so happened that our route on moving day took us out the Wilber Cross Parkway and up Interstate 91 in close proximity to Derby, site of the Sculls and Sweeps that were taking place that very day and for which I was registered. My husband agreed to stop for an hour so I could race Masters Women, the race I'd had to miss the year before. We parked, leaving the windows open for the cats to get air, and I set up lawn chairs and laid the picnic. When the Masters Women were called, I promised to get the job done as quickly as I could, and I did. Before the sandwich wrappers hit the ground and the soda cans were in the garbage, I'd won my race, gotten my medal, and packed my boat back on the car.

It was ironic. Only a year before, two weeks after my race in Albany, I had seen a box of gold medals casually thrown on the registration table at Derby and wondered with a passionate and futile longing if I would ever, ever have one of my own. Now here I was again at Derby, and having won the coveted medal, found myself apologizing to my husband and children for the heat and inconvenience of attending my race. In the middle of my own family, there was no one with whom to celebrate. We got to Boston in time for me to make up the beds and cook dinner.

Less than a month later, I made the trip down the coast to Delaware and the grassy banks of Noxontown Pond and the

Diamond State. Once again the air was so hot and thick I could hardly get a breath. I raced the C Women and B Women, rowing a straight course and pulling out my Edge at the seven-fifty. I came in second in each. I was jubilant. I hadn't expected to win, but to place second in major competition, not only in my own category but a younger one, was cause for self-congratulation.

All the way back up the New Jersey Turnpike, past Newark and the tanks, I rode a wave of excitement that felt dizzying. Entering battle with my sleek Sharrow both in Derby and in Delaware I had felt like a knight riding onto the field on a brave steed, ready to leap off the line, lusting for the moment of attack. Yet as I drove home now, I began hearing an insistent and all-too familiar melody: "The Song of the Medals"—siren song of self-glory.

I was as sick of it as a shopper is of the endless chorus of "Jingle Bells" in the grocery store at Christmas time—repetitive, pervasive, impossible to expunge. The winter before, when my husband was in Boston and Lloyd Harbor was wind-whipped and frigid, I had sometimes taken my gold medal from Canada and bronze from the U.S. Masters Nationals from their bags and laid them on the bed in the afternoon while five-year-old William took a nap, the laundry tumbled in the dryer, and a fly buzzed in the corner of the window. They winked and glimmered on their bright ribbons, tailored to lie on my bosom just so. They crooned to me the story of my races and the wonder of my new biceps, sang to me of the coolness of sauntering through a crowded regatta, medal glowing from the bodice of my sweat-stained unisuit, knowing that in my world I was at last someone to reckon with. After a few weeks my addiction to this afternoon ritual grew embarrassing, even alarming, so I boxed them up and buried them outside, where they were soon locked into frozen ground until spring. I dug them up just before we moved to Boston.

Where, I wondered, did this boundless need for self-aggrandizement come from? If anyone had suspected the depth of my slavish conceit, I would have been mortified. I was mortified as it was. It was as if until I had the confidence to know that I really was the new me, and *no one* could take her away, I was still small enough and empty enough to crave constant reassurance.

A week after Delaware, I drove north to the Maine State Championships with William. The Maine State Championships is a funky, wholesome affair on the first weekend of every August, set on a beautiful lake in southern Maine and attended by a flock of Maine's best rowers—a stubborn lot used to fierce conditions and heartened by adversity. And some talent from the South: there were always a few rowers up (or rather down) for the day from Boston and Connecticut. Competitors race a nearly three-mile course marked by a buoy tower and some tiny, rocky islands—the Stake Race. Then, exhausted by the Stake Race, they are cheerfully herded to the start of a thousand-meter (or, as it said in the promotional flyer, "Kill-o-meter") sprint race, to "drain the tank"—as if the tank hadn't already run just about dry at the two-and-a-half-mile mark of the distance race. Afterward, all are treated to a picnic lunch and award ceremony.

I was warming up before the race when a woman I didn't know drew abreast and started to chat. We introduced ourselves. "Sara Hall? Oh! I've heard about *you*." I almost turned around to see if she was talking to someone behind me, realizing with a shock that in my lean black racing suit and elegant new racing shell I must look to her like one of those scary women I'd found on the start line in Delaware the year before. The talent from the South. I wanted to say, Oh no, you don't understand, I'm just me. But what, now, was *just me*? As I rowed to the start, I was reminded of the time when, pregnant with William, I had been in the hospital over a month, and my sister Caroline flew in from Minneapolis for the day to cheer me up. She had swept into my drab room like some exotic animal, flung her fur coat on a chair, and promptly painted my toenails a brilliant carmine red. Unfortunately, I was too pregnant to see past my belly, but when I did I was startled to find mine were not the feet of a sallow, frightened pregnant woman, but those of someone vivacious, well tended, and probably discreetly decked with diamonds. So *this* was me, too, I had thought.

At the races that day I crossed both finishes first, the distance race by a comfortable margin, the sprint race by a whisker. Then they posted the results. Another competitor was listed as having won the Stake Race. No, she hadn't, I thought indignantly, I'd seen her behind me all the way, everyone had seen her, and me. This wasn't a photo finish, it was a margin of seconds well in the double digits. Suddenly the exhilaration of the races was altogether lost in my anxiety and anger over a clerical mistake that would cost me my medal. My medal—mine!

I was in a state. I protested ever so politely, rage not being exactly the order of the day on a lovely lake in Maine in a friendly, low-key race. Within half an hour the confusion was cleared up and the amended results announced. But still I seethed. When I drove back to Boston with William that afternoon, my irritation was like a pack of dogs whose din was not quite enough to drown the shrill strains of the two medals singing their familiar chorus as they hung from the rearview mirror. I started to hate everything about the day. I started to hate myself. Why wasn't I taking home the memory of racing on a glorious Maine lake with strong, able competitors? Why was I driving south tyrannized by my coveted golden booty—feeling vile, inside and out?

It all came down to a critical question: Where would I locate the new goodness and strength that had emerged as a result of my rowing? In my own body and heart? Or in the success itself—the medals? After all the years of having been pared almost to the point of invisibility, I needed the medals as proof of a powerful Sara. Yet, in letting them tell me who and what I was, I was stepping into a familiar trap. In my life I had given away my authority again and again—as a teenager, as an adult, as a wife—and paid a terrible price. Would I once again allow forces outside myself define and control me? In the matter of the medals, and my life, what was it going to be, master or slave?

There was nothing to be done. I felt hopelessly and unhappily in their thrall. Then one day, about a week after the Maine State, I realized there *was* something to be done, and I knew with a chill what it was.

In mid-August, the sale of our house on Long Island was to close on a day my husband was tied up in Boston, so we decided I would go to the afternoon meeting alone and sign for both of us. The night before the closing, I drove down from Boston and stayed with my friend Terry Walton. We went out for dinner in Huntington and talked about children and change, about moving on in our lives. I remember having two glasses of wine instead of my usual one, and feeling sleepy and philosophical. Maybe I felt I needed just a drop of anesthesia. Before going to bed in her little guest room tucked under the eaves, I set my alarm for five-fifteen and laid out what was needed for the morning: shorts and T-shirt, a white silicone swim cap, and a plastic bag containing my medals. All five.

The following morning at five-thirty I stood on the shore of Lloyd Harbor next to the "loaf of bread" rock. The sky was heavy with rain, the air cool. Drizzle wetted my hair in a net of drops and darkened the rock, revealing its grain and veins like the pebbles I licked as a little girl to see the patterns inside. The plastic bag on the rock next to me was also veiled and it was hard to see the colors of the ribbons, the gleam of the gold.

At forty-four, mermaid or not, I still found swimming in a natural body of water unnerving. My summers in Boulder had been spent in cement pools filled with artificially blue water and clearly discernable black lines on the bottom showing me where to go and proving that there was nothing to be afraid of except drowning itself—no slimy, toothy critters lurking under me. Even as an adult, I sometimes have to close my eyes behind my goggles and suppress a shiver when I know that my tender human body is silhouetted on the surface for all the hungry feeders to see. On this day I was to swim in murky seawater, and do it in the rain.

The water of the harbor under the gray sky was particularly dark and impenetrable. After all my experience of Lloyd Harbor in its many states, this morning it felt most starkly elemental—not aglow with the rosy dawn I'd imagined when I'd worked out my plan a few days ago, but somehow stripped to its essence. The rain came down harder now, the water pocked and jumping with drops. No one was here; no one would wander down for a walk on a rainy morning at dawn.

I took off my shorts and shirt and folded them neatly, placing them under the corner of the rock to stay dry, then pulled the cap onto my head and tucked up my hair so it wouldn't get in my eyes as I swam. I took the contents of the plastic bag, the five medals, each on a bright ribbon, and put them round my neck. An early morning bird-watcher stumbling on my ritual would have been startled to find this rare species. But there was no birder. I was alone, was always alone on this harbor at this hour.

I could see as far west as the osprey nests in the salt marshes, as far east as the narrow opening clogged with sailboats, beyond which was the open water of the Sound. In the middle of the harbor there was a spot just opposite the old boathouse, in the very center where the water is widest and deepest—the heart of this dearest of domains. I waded up to my thighs, then struck out into the dark water with a prickle of goose bumps, looking for a rhythm, reaching out with my fingers toward the goal half a harbor away.

I had forgotten about the bluefish. Hanging like lures between my breasts were the medals, flashing and clanking. Feeling them, I remembered, suddenly, a time years ago when John was fishing, and as he worked his ten-inch striped bass up to the boat with great excitement, half of it had been bitten off by a bluefish. Fishing that day turned out to be more of a nature lesson than we'd bargained on. Though my breasts weren't exactly new—they'd nursed three babies and I didn't think my nipples still qualified for tender epithets—I was pretty attached to them and did not relish the prospect of their sudden removal by rows of sharp teeth. I turned and swam back to shore, where I twisted the medals into a ball and tucked them up under the cap. Now I really was stark naked, except for the swim cap, bulging on top Conehead-style. Janie would have said, "God, Mom, you look like a total dork!" I struck off once more through the green water. As I swam, I could feel the medals weighing down my head.

I arrived at a point exactly in the middle, and aligned myself with the boathouse on one shore and a leaning oak on the other. The osprey were at one end of the harbor, still quiet on their nests; the moored sailboats at the other rolled gently on the breast of the harbor, shackles clanging against their masts like a tolling of bells keeping time to the faint swells. I stopped, treading water, and took off the cap, putting the ribbons back around my neck. Then I took off each medal, one by one, and held it in my hand, my eyes squeezed shut.

First each of the Maine State Championship golds. I thought of the piercing blue sky of that morning—the excitement of rounding the little islands with Mary Beth Weathersby hot on my stern, the sear of pulling hard the last three hundred meters with the wind in my hair and my breath like a steam engine. Remembered the crazy joy of careening down the sprint course neck and neck with Marlene Royle, gusts snatching at our blades. Then the bronze from the Masters Nationals and my children screaming, "Go Mom!" as they ran along the shore. S4 and I had plowed through the chop and high winds on Lake Onondaga in Syracuse, so like Lloyd Harbor when a gale blew in from the west. The race officials allowed my three children on the medal dock that day to place the bronze on their mother's neck. Then the Canadian Henley gold. I remembered my incredulity at finding myself in the lead at eight hundred meters, my unmitigated joy standing on the high block of the medal platform in front of the bleachers, holding my arms out, palms up, laughing with surprise at my triumph. Then the Derby Sculls and Sweeps gold, won on the hot June day we moved and I placated my damp children and grumbling spouse with the promise that I would make it quick.

Each medal I held tightly in my hand, reliving the beauty of the day and giving thanks for the gift, the divine gift, that is the Race. Each medal I loosed, opening my hand, watching it disappear in the dark water, each red, white, and blue ribbon twisting and losing its brightness as the weight of the disk carried it out of sight to the bottom of the harbor. I made myself recognize that I might never win anything again. That after all the years of scraping Cheerios off the kitchen floor and wiping cream cheese off little faces, after all the years when I felt so very "unheard," these might be all I'd ever have to tell the world or my children of my own passionate self. The rain still fell; I cried and cried there in middle of the cold, green, empty harbor because I loved my medals, and in letting them go I risked losing forever the shining, solid proof that, after all the years, I existed at all. I opened my hand again and again; I let them go.

Then I was free. My medals were in a safe place, where they belonged, given to the place which had afforded me shelter and safety to flex my mermaid's tail, fan my hair in the current, find, at last, my way home.

A year later almost to the day I won the World Masters Games in the single shell.

Chapter Fourteen

CONTACT

A week after the swim to the middle
of Lloyd Harbor I went to Long Beach,
California, for the 1997 U.S. Masters National
Championship. The day I arrived was blister-
ingly hot and hazy with smog. By midafter-
noon I had found the regatta site, parked
my sub-subcompact rental car in a
distant lot, and located my boat
in the sea of shells and trailers. At three-
fifteen I stood alone in a crowd of a thousand
rowers as they shuffled equipment and set up tents
near the sizzling asphalt trailer enclosure. I was at a
loss. Before me was a racing shell that I couldn't
move three hundred feet down the hot tarmac
to the sandy verge where a legion of singles
waited, neatly aligned, bows to water,
ready to launch the next morning.

A fully rigged racing shell cannot be placed directly on the ground without risking damage. That is a fact of life. Yet it is impossible for one person (or at least this person) to move a single from one place to another carrying both boat and slings, then set up the slings at the destination site with a boat balanced overhead. My boat waited obstinately next to the Cambridge Boat Club trailer, on which it had hitched a long, dusty ride across the plains.

The men from the Cambridge Boat Club had arranged their battered aluminum lawn chairs in a neat circle next to the trailer and paid absolutely no attention to me. As they watched other trailers pull in and other competitors sort riggers and unload oars, I noted with a sigh their easy laughter and languid inscrutability—mark of the perennial victor. Though my family had been in Boston for just over a month, I had car-topped the Sharrow to a launch ramp upriver every day, and thus was still as fatally an outsider on the Charles as they were fabulously insider. And though I'd rented space on their trailer, to the men from the Cambridge Boat Club I was just a fluffy female stray from upriver, unlikely combination of single sculler and mommy who still wore a neat bright hairband on this wiltingly hot California afternoon, as if she were heading to a flower-arranging seminar at the Garden Club. Ask one of them to rise and help me carry my boat? I would have to be, as my daughter so succinctly puts it, on crack.

I felt weepy and tragic, like my children when they haven't gotten a nap—frantic, exhausted, fallen apart somehow. I needed arms around me and the rhythm of a creaky rocker, back and forth, back and forth, in a cadence that says the world is quiet, regular, predictable, a beat that would slow my breathing and soothe my heart. Sometimes my littlest son says, "I need a hug. Badly." I needed a friend. Badly.

Nothing about my world was then quiet or predictable. My old house was gone; my old routine was gone; the group of other mothers to share the news and the carpools was gone. The faces of friends who had peered into my children's cribs and, later, exclaimed how big they were getting when they carried their own books to the checkout desk at the library, were gone. I didn't even have a library card now. In moving to Boston we had willingly torn from its roots a life that was in many ways comfortingly regular, and we'd done it with the dream of building a better life that was, in the short time we'd been there, already beginning to fall apart.

Just before we left Long Island, I had talked to a therapist about how to use the new situation in Boston to repair our family. I had also mentioned my regattas, and the fact that the children were bored with the waiting and the heat, and they were wary—they seemed to scent in the air their father's feelings about my racing. If I get baby-sitters, I told the therapist, my husband will attack me for being selfish. "Selfish?" he said. "Wanting to do what you love isn't selfish. Besides, you would do your family the greatest service possible by leaving the children in their father's hands. Your husband might kick and scream, but you put your foot down. They need the time together to make a bond without you hovering nearby, worrying about the junk food he's giving them or the movies he's letting them watch. Go. Just go. Try it. You'll see."

Put my foot down? It had been a disaster. When, a few weeks later, I proposed to my husband that he take the kids while I went to a weekend regatta ("Take them out to breakfast, go to a movie . . . you'll all have fun!"), he responded without skipping a beat. No, he most certainly would not be my baby-sitter while I went up and down the East Coast amusing myself with my little hobby. What did I take him for? If I wanted to neglect my children, I would have to hire a baby-sitter; he certainly wasn't going to abet me.

Everyone was here with someone. Everyone had a friend, a fellow club member, or a spouse. Competitors and their supporters had arrived by the planeload, or in vans bristling with boats and bicycles. They laughed with friends in the shade of nylon club tents with team logos. They leaned against fenders, balancing water bottles and talking in tight groups, unloading coolers and toolboxes from the backs of station wagons under the watchful eyes of mates who worried that the shoulder surgery they had had this spring wouldn't hold up in the final sprint on Friday, or that their lower-back twinge may be a flare-up of last year's disk problem.

Out of over a thousand competitors, I was surely the only one here completely alone. I had no club and wore no special jacket with club colors, having resigned from Sagamore last April when it was clear we were moving to Boston. I was here in Long Beach rowing under the designation "Unaffiliated," the no-man's-land for those who rowed alone and whose boats lived on top of their cars or under tarps in their backyards. Although I recognized some names and faces, I had no friends here, and certainly no one who knew me well enough to yell, "Go, Sar, Go!" for my race. My only competitive friends were Jeff Schaeffer, and my new doubles partner, Carie Graves, and both remained in Boston. I looked over to the men from Cambridge. They were talking quietly and tinkering with riggers; a few pored over the race lineups for the next morning. From the feeling in my throat, I knew I might soon start to cry—just the thing to disgust them thoroughly and ensure my permanent exclusion from their cozy circle.

Still my little boat waited.

Two weeks earlier, in a moment of defiance, I had said no for the first time in my long marriage. My husband told me he planned to come with me to California. Then he demanded to come with me to California. I said no quickly, before I could imagine the consequences and change my mind. A minute later, when I could feel my heart pounding and my stomach in knots, when I understood exactly what this no meant, I said no again. Louder, this time. He was speechless. He looked at me as if I were suddenly possessed, suddenly speaking in tongues. But there was one thing more frightening to me than facing his anger, more frightening than flying three thousand miles by myself, renting a car by myself, signing into a motel by myself, and racing a single shell a thousand meters by myself, and it was to face those thousand meters already beaten. I couldn't allow him to shred my concentration and confidence before a race; heading to a start line in a single was difficult enough. So, after all these years, I finally summoned the courage to say out loud the word I've heard echo in my head like a muffled persistent voice shouting from under the kitchen floorboards. "Say no. For once, say no!" *This* must be what it felt like to "put my foot down." Sickeningly scary.

I'd rehearsed defiance. Since the night last March when my Sharrow arrived in the dark, I had practiced courage as I would a technical drill to address some thorny aspect of bladework or body swing. I forced myself to face what frightened me again and again, going out when the winds howled the length of the harbor and the waves rolled down the Sharrow's bow, crashing into my back and filling my tiny cockpit with icy seawater.

On Mother's Day last May, I had risen at five and faced a gale that turned the harbor inky black and angry, a wind so strong it wrestled my blades from my grasp and threw my bow to port or starboard with each gust. The oystermen called to me, hands to mouths, "Go back!" But the wind carried their words away toward the lighthouse, toward the far shore and the Eaton's Neck stacks.

What kind of woman do I want to be? I asked myself that morning as my husband and children dreamed their dreams two miles away in warm beds. *A brave one.* What kind of mother? *A strong one.* Two hundred strokes into the teeth of the wind, I told myself, my voice shouting the strokes in a frightened but defiant cry swept away by the gale. "Forty-seven! Forty-eight! Forty-nine!" When I went home and got back in my nightgown, the children awoke and brought me a fistful of dandelions and a cup of tea in bed.

Yet this no had frightened me beyond measure and I felt as if I were driving late at night in a state of dangerous fatigue. A week before Long Beach, getting ready to race the Masters Nationals in California, I'd had a coaching session with Ted Benford and rowed a thousand-meter course with such reckless intensity that my vision blurred and I began to pass out. I started feeling "empty alone," not "full alone"—the isolation of the single and the loss of my old life since the move to Boston leaving me with the feeling I'd broken loose from my moorings.

There was no mountain of laundry big enough to hide the fact that what had been the semblance of a marriage was disintegrating, even more so since the move. It was becoming clear that nothing was going to change. A few days before Long Beach, I had asked my husband to go to couples therapy with me in the fall, but he denied culpability for any part of our anguish and flatly refused (*"You're* the one to go. It's for sick people"). But still, as I stood in the parking lot in California, I was sad for us. The amount of sheer, dogged momentum in a marriage as hopeless and sordid as ours was appalling.

For the first time since Albany over a year before, I could feel in my bones the fear of rowing to the line by myself tomorrow morning. I wondered if I had what it would take here, and at home. And I wondered how I was going to move this boat and these slings three hundred feet by myself. Do something, Sara. Anything. So I walked up to someone passing by and asked for help. And that someone, life's random *someone*, smiled and said, "Sure! We're in this together." Simple. We're in this together.

By late afternoon, my boat was safely tied down near the other singles and I had just signed the forms at the registration tent and claimed my entry ID with the list of races—the C Single, B Single, and Mixed D Quad with three West Coast rowers who, on my friend Carie's recommendation, had agreed last week to let me join their boat. Competitors were allowed to register for five races. As I left the tent and turned down the long road to the parking lot, I was feeling silly to have flown all this way for only three. Silly and terminally "Unaffiliated"—embarrassed that I was on no one's list of candidates for team boats.

The road was nearly deserted. Most competitors had adjourned for motel pools and plans for dinner on the beach. I was resigned to picking up a sandwich at the grocery store and reading a book in my room. Then I noticed a lone woman trudging toward me through the heat. She was carrying an oar in each hand and talking to herself. She looked about my age and walked with a stride that suggested a lifetime of serious athletics. We were about to pass and I could hear what she was saying: "I need to find a forty-five-year-old sculler. I need to find a forty-five-year-old sculler. I need to find . . . " Now we were abreast, each locked on a steady course as parallel and eternally divided as train tracks. We passed and started to draw away to our separate destinations. I hadn't a clue who she was. Should I speak up? What would be the risk? So I turned and cleared my throat.

"I'm forty-four. I row a single." She stopped. She turned.

"Who are you?"

"Sara Hall."

She grinned. "I've heard about you. You'll do fine."

And life began anew.

She was Carol Bower, a woman whose doubles partner, Diana Post, had been forced by an emergency to stay in Philadelphia. She was Carol Bower, who needed to find a competitive female sculler in her mid-forties, a rare species even at this event, and needed to find her *right now*—the heats for the Women's C Double were in fifteen hours. What I didn't know was that Carol Bower was a 1984 Olympic gold medalist and former head women's coach, University of Pennsylvania. I wouldn't know this until just before I flew back to Boston on Sunday, ranked second in the United States in the Women's C Double. All I knew was that this moment on the long hot road was one of convergence: two strangers whose faces said, "I'm like you, alone in my boat. Shall we row our course together?" She asked if I had time on my schedule to row the doubles race.

"Let's go out for a few minutes to check the chemistry. You have time?" I didn't bother pretending I had somewhere else to go or someone else waiting. Sure, I said. So we trudged back down the road to the trailer from Philadelphia, carried oars to the beach and a new white Filippi double in the crooks of our arms to the water's edge, and launched. After a sequence of ten power strokes, ten easy, twenty power, twenty easy, Carol said, "We're going to be good." That was it. Back to shore. We shook hands and agreed when to meet the next morning.

At 10:00 a.m., Carol and I raced our heat in the National Championships with less than ten minutes practice. We had never rowed a course together, never executed a practice start, never drilled race strategies and stroke rates. As we sat at the start line, roll about to be called, Carol had leaned over and quietly told me the plan. "Three-quarter, half, half, three-quarter for the start. Ten high, then settle at thirty-three for the body. Sprint the last thirty. That okay with you?" I nodded. The flag dropped. We were off.

We flew. Twenty minutes later, we pressed through the crowd at the scoreboard to check the results of our race, one of the regatta's most popular and therefore most competitive events. I ran my finger down the sheet and there we were. As a result of our chance meeting on a hot road late yesterday afternoon, Carol and I had posted the fastest time in our heat, second-fastest time in all the heats. We would row the final on Sunday morning.

On Friday, I was eliminated in the heats of the B Single. On Saturday morning, I rowed a solid, but unsensational race in the C Single, placing fourth. Neither event was a defeat—simply rowing the single is always a win—but neither was a triumph. The lessons of this journey to California, however, didn't concern the single. They had everything to do with being "in this together."

On Saturday afternoon, I won silver in the Mixed D Quad for Pagosa Rowing Club from Colorado, of which I was now a member. In a swift stroke, or a hundred and twenty swift strokes, I was no longer in the land of the "Unaffiliated." Later that same afternoon I won another silver—in a PGRC Women's C Quad from Philadelphia, courtesy of an invitation, again by Carol, to fill the place of the missing Diana Post. Both events offered intense racing and seasoned competitors; both second-place wins were in boats in which our minutes of practice could be counted on our callused hands. If there was a message here, I don't think it was, "Don't bother to train, it doesn't make any difference," but rather, "When you make contact, you win."

Sometimes I wonder if my experience in Long Beach was a matter of God finally throwing up His hands and saying, like a teacher whose patience for the befuddled student has finally run out, *I'm tired of waiting so I'm just going to give you the answer: if you're brave enough to let go of what doesn't serve you, I will reward you tenfold with what does. Trust me.* If my no of two weeks ago was a necessary first step to letting go of the mistakes of my marriage, my yes three days ago had shown me the possibilities for the future—new and fruitful partnerships. If my swim to the middle of Lloyd Harbor released me from the medals that weighed me down, my lonely journey to Long Beach had brought me new medals, new friendships, new confidence. *Trust me.*

On Sunday morning, Carol and I launched the Filippi and stroked back and forth enough in the crowded warm-up area to be limber and ready to race. Our total practice time together, just over twenty minutes. The starter's voice echoed across the water: "Masters C Women's Double. Ladies to the line, please." Carol was calm and professional, but I was wound up, nervous as a racehorse fretting in the start gate. From the stroke seat of the Filippi, I would set the pace, locking onto a cadence that maximized our strengths. From bow, Carol would match my rhythm and steer us down the course, calling the offensives, signaling the final sprint.

Carol handed me a water bottle, then she put her hand on my shoulder. "Long and strong," she said. "We're going to be long and strong." We coiled, blades square, backs straight and braced for the load, heads up, eyes on the horizon. Then we were off the line in perfect unison, perfect intention. I could feel Carol's strength, and I could feel mine. I could feel Carol's balance and skill, and I could feel mine. I set the pace, and she followed, perfectly. She called the power move, and I responded, perfectly. Carol was experienced and controlled, and I fervent and instinctual—different as night and day, joined in the Race. We blazed down the course like a shooting star, the double perfect platform for the exercise of our strength and skill. From a *nothing*, we had become very much a *something*.

At eight hundred meters, my lungs were a desert, my legs on fire. As we launched into the final sprint, my heart seemed ready to burst. After years of shrinking to fit my husband's containment, of jumping and squeaking and scurrying to please, I finally saw that a true partnership is one in which the "vessel"—a boat, a friendship, a marriage—provides the structure in which each partner has the freedom and support to express his or her greatest individual strengths. In this boat, in this race, in this moment ten strokes before we crossed the line, we were both fully ourselves and "in this together." I didn't have to be alone anymore.

Chapter Fifteen

THE

BIG A

There's a great old Bing Crosby
movie I saw years ago in which Bing
and his friends all get together and decide to
put on a show. What I remember best is
their rampant and ingenuous enthusiasm, as if putting on a show were more
exciting than going to the moon or winning
the lottery. I remember longing for that kind
of enthusiasm, those kinds of friends, that
kind of consuming interest.

On Long Island, I had had warm
acquaintanceships based on play dates
and carpools, and a few close friends,
who remain in my life; but I had never, not
even before my marriage, had a circle of com-
rades, like the "kids" in Bing's showbiz crowd—
a group united and impassioned by shared
purpose. Until Boston, I had never before

experienced relationships in which my friends and I called each other on the phone to have long feverish discussions about some arcane aspect of our common interest—rigging, body angle, blade configurations—that would leave anyone else glazed with boredom. Never once had I thought of myself as belonging to a *gang*, a group with a magic handshake (in our case, a handshake extraordinarily firm).

At the Masters Nationals in Long Beach, I had been kindled with a new instinct to connect, to be "in this together." I found a perfect habitat in Boston. On Lloyd Harbor, I may have discovered myself to be a swan, but with the exception of my two months with Jeff, almost never saw any other swans. In Boston, I found the flock; in fact, I found a good portion of the entire species, just when I was most ready to join it, and all convened in what had the feel of an ancient migratory nesting ground: the Charles River.

When out-of-towners think of the Charles, they think of rowing. The river crawls with rowers, swarms with rowers, rings with the sound of coxswains' voices exhorting crews to "take it up two beats" and "give me ten more." In the early morning, a hundred or more scullers work the winding eight-mile stretch from the stone wall at the Science Museum down near the financial district to the Watertown dock above the marina in Newton (and neophytes are lured by the inviting arch of the lovely stone bridge just upriver of the Watertown dock where they row squarely onto the rocks).

Up and down its banks are the university boathouses and private clubs where rowers meet—private clubs like Riverside, an old gray-shingled Victorian with rambling porches and neat row of boat bays; and Cambridge Boat Club, blue and white pennants flying over the treacherous Cambridge Bend, nemesis of many Head of the Charles crews. One public facility, Community Rowing Incorporated (or CRI, as it's known on the river), offers some of Boston's surfeit of world-class coaches to the public for a modest fee. Anyone of any age, experience, and fitness level willing to get up daily at five can join the Charles's morning sculling fraternity within a week or two of showing up on the CRI dock in a T-shirt and sweats.

The rowing population of the Charles is widely diverse, but it falls primarily into two categories: those who are working, have worked, or will work to pay for someone's tuition; and those whose tuitions are currently being paid. In addition to town and gown, there are some subtle cultural differences loosely linked to age group and livelihood between the folk upriver, where the Charles is narrow and intimate, and downriver, where they must battle upstream through the chop of the open Charles Basin on windy mornings. I became an upriver sculler because upriver was where I found a public dock from which I could car-top the Sharrow when I first came to Boston in 1997; and a few months later, upriver was where I had the good fortune to be invited into a boathouse.

In the upper reaches of the Charles, up near the Eliot Bridge, the social landscape is distinguished by professors and sculptors, writers and entrepreneurs. Or as I heard someone say once, "Loners and owners." Upriver men have been known to wear tie-dyed T-shirts and compression rowing shorts that haven't compressed in years; even to sport full-grown beards. Upriver women are long on firm handshakes, short on nail polish. I have found the little band of men and women scullers I joined late my first summer in Boston to be a handsome and interesting group, but one for whom the most exacting eastern social conventions were either abandoned at birth or packed away with little cedar balls at some point with relief (or, like all my boiled-wool jackets, given to the Salvation Army).

I am proud to share with them certain characteristics of the species that from one perspective—the best perspective, I think—are worthy of admiration and emulation, but from another may be experienced as an irritant to those who love us. The easiest way to describe us is to relate the story my mother tells me every year on my birthday, even now when the number of birthdays is closing on fifty. The story never varies; it's always "The Delivery Room."

"Well," she begins, "you always were a stubborn thing, and you always did what you wanted to do, when you wanted to do it. On July 15, 1953, I'd been in labor for eight hours and was on the delivery table at Wesley Memorial Hospital in Chicago. Dear Dr. Dorr was there with his mask and his gown and the nurses were standing around waiting and getting impatient. We were ready for you to arrive, and thought we'd see the top of your head any time. But we didn't see the top of your head. We waited, and waited, and waited. Finally, Dr. Dorr said, 'Looks like the baby decided to go back.' I thought, Go back? Can babies do that? So I got up off the table, repacked my little valise, and went to the Pearson Hotel for the night. Apparently you had changed your mind and decided you wanted to be born another day. That's why your birthday is July 16."

I always loved the image: Dr. Dorr, dear Dr. Dorr, waiting philosophically, and my panting mother waiting less philosophically, for me to show up. I wonder if I became a single sculler either because my mother told me this story with exasperated admiration so many times that I shaped myself to an imagined ideal of stubborn single-mindedness, or because I really was congenitally stubborn and found the perfect vehicle to express myself in the single shell. What is most certainly true of scullers, especially single scullers, is that though they follow strict orders, they are their *own* strict orders. What some might call an indomitability of spirit, others might call a pernicious intractability—not just determination but infernal determination.

I have been privileged to claim the acquaintance of many such scullers. But in two Charles River friends, each very different from the other but both even more infernally determined than most, I found true comradeship. I think it's fair to say that in the last four years, my two friends and I have, like Bing Crosby and "the kids," put on quite a show. The first I met on a hot day in Syracuse, New York, in 1996. Her name was Carie Graves.

In 1996, the summer Jeff Schaeffer and I rowed together, he had encouraged me to go to the U.S. Masters Nationals, held that year in Syracuse, but warned me that "you better make lightweight or you'll have to race Carie Graves!" The tone of his voice told me I didn't even have to ask who Carie Graves was. What he then described so daunted me at the time that I had wondered if maybe I should go back to sorting bingo cards at the Beach Club. "She's six foot two, a hundred eighty pounds, and an Olympic gold medalist. Most powerful woman afloat."

Weeks before Nationals, then, I began eating scientifically to avoid the awful hubris of pitting my meager skills against this Amazon. At five foot nine, I can row lightweight (a hundred thirty pounds or less) if I eat carefully. Rowing is a miraculous weight management program in which if you want to maintain the same weight all you have to do is eat a breakfast of pancakes, bacon, hash browns, toast, orange juice, a bowl of oatmeal, and maybe some eggs. To lose weight, you cut out the bacon and the hash browns. So by mid-August, just before Nationals, I was within two pounds of one thirty. Then, in a perverse decision that confirmed everything my mother ever said about me, I changed my mind and decided to race lightweight in a younger category and heavyweight in my own, putting me at an age disadvantage in one and a weight disadvantage in the other, and placing me squarely (and very lightly) on the line with the dreaded Carie.

I had arrived at the race venue in Syracuse in a state of near meltdown. My car was filled with cranky, chocolate-covered children, skateboards, and overturned soda cans. Back then, I still rowed S4, which rode on top like a big gray arrow pointing first to McDonald's, then to the rest stop, then back to McDonald's for the forgotten chocolate sundae, finally to the shore of Lake Onondaga. Jeff ambled by as I unloaded the car and offered to introduce me to Carie. So, after the children disappeared to explore the vendor tents, Jeff and I wandered down the long line of shells to where a woman was rigging a single and disciplining a seven-year-old who'd apparently had it with rowing and rowers. She looked like an average mom, with nice brown hair in a ponytail and friendly brown eyes, but she was way taller than an average mom. She also looked way, way stronger. We shook hands with the crushing iron grip of oarsmen and women everywhere, and talked for a moment. Then she turned back to her riggers and I turned to find my three children, who were discovering ways to lose their appetites for dinner.

That evening, I took the kids out for pizza near the motel. We sat at a booth in the nearly deserted restaurant and had already ordered when I saw Carie across the room, tall and solitary but for her young son, Ben. The magnificent Carie, the intimidating Carie, the Carie who had been in *People* magazine. Was she too famous to sit at my greasy table? I walked across the room and invited her to join us.

By the end of the evening, we had discovered that we were born three weeks apart in 1953 and that, of the nearly one thousand competitors at the National Championship, we were two of probably not more than five female single scullers with young children. (A year later, in Boston, Carie told me that when she saw me pull into the parking lot that first day in Syracuse, with my old club single and three small children, she couldn't believe it. Another mother!) But more than that, we could laugh. And, of course, we were both passionate rowers. The only difference was that she had twenty-five years of experience, three Olympic Teams and two Olympic medals, seven National Teams, countless World Championship races, and over twenty years of being a groundbreaking women's coach. I had two summers of diligent amateur dedication and a total of three days of instruction.

We raced each other the next day. What I didn't know about the renowned Carie was that, while she was, and is, probably the most famous female sweep rower in America, she had just gotten into the single shell for the first time a few months before. The difference between sweep technique and sculling technique is enormous, so our playing field was leveled substantially by her inexperience as a sculler.

Our heat the next day came down to a duel. I had taken an early lead and remember seeing her launch an offensive at five hundred meters and feeling a welling of the same stubbornness that stumped Dr. Dorr and my mother. She would not get past me, Olympic Champion or not. She in turn used her own determination and physical power to wear away the margin between us. In the final sprint, we were neck and neck. When we crossed the finish line, we were so close neither could tell who had won. An article in *U.S. Rowing* reported later that she beat me by a tenth of a second. Our final took place a few days later in a howling gale and high chop—just like home. Almost no one, including Carie, had trained in the extreme conditions I had come to think of as normal. I came in fourth, she fifth.

In the months after Nationals in 1996 we talked on the phone occasionally, but it was when I moved to Boston that Carie and I reconnected. Carie was, at the time, head women's coach at Northeastern University, and after meeting on the river in singles for a few days, she invited me to bring the Sharrow to Henderson so we could train in our singles out of one location. Soon we started rowing a double every other day. In the double, a red Hudson heavyweight named *Flea*, we headed downriver every morning after my kids were in camp and her morning coaching chores were wrapped up. While I love rowing alone, and row alone often, rowing a double with another woman who both shared my interests and was also a mother of young children was heaven.

We talked and talked and talked—mostly about marriages and men—all the way down to the Massachusetts Avenue Bridge, where we "spun" the boat and talked some more before heading upstream at a good hard anaerobic threshold pace. The day after Princess Diana died, we discussed her life and death at length, or at least the length from the Eliot Bridge to the Weekes Footbridge, where we had to stop *Flea* to cry. By the end of each workout we had covered a lot of territory, and many mornings, adjourned to Starbucks to cover some more. We started racing the double the summer of 1997, my first summer on the Charles, winning the Cromwell Cup in Boston and the World Masters Games in Portland in 1998.

If rowing a double with Carie gave me the satisfactions of camaraderie, racing a double with Carie, much like racing with Carol Bower (who had been Carie's teammate in the 1984 gold medal Olympic eight), gave me extraordinary firsthand experience of someone whose spirit as a competitor and exacting standards in matters of sportsmanship as a coach are legendary. In the heat of a race, her thundering drive to win had the titanic relentlessness of a geological event—an earthquake or a volcanic eruption—a sphere altogether greater than that of petty human rivalry or shallow pride. I soon came to learn firsthand that on the racing scene Carie was both a force of nature and a towering righteous presence.

Our favorite race was one in which we placed fourth (though Carie insists with only the slightest grin that we won the race and were victim of a timing mistake). In an absurdly competitive little regatta in the backwater of the Connecticut as it flows through Putney, Vermont, we raced the Green Mountain Head in 1997, a month after I got back from Long Beach. It is an event that pulls out all the old Olympians with their battered boats, undiminished cardiovascular capacity, and daunting muscle tone. Our race, Women's Open Double, was a taste of heaven. Our path to the turning mark lay before us on the bright September morning like a carpet of stars and the trees of the thickly forested banks of the river carried the first fall leaves overhead like points of flame. We could hear the cheers of friends echoing across the water. A minute into the race, we locked onto a rhythm we could have sustained for all eternity, swinging in unison, blades breaking free in divine togetherness as we traveled our starry course. Carie told me later it was the best race of her life. That was saying a lot. I thought it was a little glimpse of what we might dare to expect if we are very, very good in this temporal existence.

My second summer in Boston I met a man who relished silence as much as Carie and I relished talk. Al Flanders came into my life when my friends Judy Davis and Henry Hamilton invited me to fill the number three seat of their quad at the famous Cambridge Boat Club—Henry in bow, Judy number two, me in number three, and Al stroke. The first time we rowed, I noticed when we got off the water that Al's right hand was covered with blood—nail gouges from a crossover thrown off by my imperfect balance in the boat. He hadn't said a thing. We rowed once or twice more as a foursome when Al showed up one morning without Judy and Henry. "Going to row a double this morning. That okay?"

Yes that was okay. Of course that was okay. I'd heard about Al Flanders a few days after I'd moved to Boston. He was one of those scullers whose preeminence is no longer discussed but simply as accepted as the fact that the river flows toward the sea. I had heard that Al, whose own physical strength was famous, was, like his friend and doubles partner Henry Hamilton, an advocate of the idea that might must serve balance, muscle serve grace. Thus he approached sculling as much an artist as an athlete. Al was, and is, the Master, though it always irritates him when I say this. "I am *not* the Master," he says. "*Henry* is the Master. I'm not that good."

Al is a man of few words. Very few words. He doesn't trust them, and he doesn't trust people who use them, especially those who use them in abundance. When you row with Al, you have to be quiet and listen—oh, not to him, but to the water sliding past the hull and the subtle *plash* of a blade as it enters the river like the quick incision of a good surgeon. If you start talking about how hot it was yesterday, or that the river seems low, or isn't the new dock great but what about all that goose poop, he won't say a thing, will simply give you a tired, long-suffering look that suggests you are a lower form of life. Of course, you are a lower form of life, because I believe Al to be an angel. A grumpy angel, an occasionally irritated angel, and sometimes an angel who suffers from the same occasional befuddlement of any man confronted with a woman's perspective. Not the kind of angel who sings sweetly, and certainly not, at six foot four, a beaming cherub. But Al nevertheless guides me wordlessly, leads me to the splendor of the world, but leaves it up to me to notice, perhaps doesn't even notice it himself. I would follow Al anywhere, and have.

So we rowed the double. That morning, and many mornings to follow. I thought I was quiet and deferential; he thought I was noisy and irritating as a gnat (and told me long after that he couldn't believe how bossy I was that first day, and how much I talked).

Rowing a double with Al was heavenly. I remember thinking that if I could ever feel such blessed togetherness with a man onshore, my life would be complete.

In the three years we've rowed together, Al hasn't really coached me; mostly he makes pointed remarks I can either ignore or take to heart. On the first morning we pushed off from the Cambridge dock in the double, for example, I was pleased not only to be rowing a lovely yellow Empacher with the Master, but also to be seen doing it. As we made our way downriver, I called gaily to Tom or Jay, Carol or Bonnie. After a minute or two of this, Al stopped rowing and shook his head wearily. "Let me know when you're ready to row," was all he said.

One day that first summer when I guided the double too near the riverbank, he noted, "Picnic time?" Another when my blades dug too deep, he said simply, "You fishing or rowing?" When we are ragged or tippy, he says, "Boat can't go fast if it isn't balanced." And "Can't balance without grace." Or just "Graceful, graceful."

Sometimes he tells me, "Your head's not in the boat," and he's right. I have often felt my mind start to wander from my stroke as if a crow roosting on my shoulder has lumbered from its perch to pursue a tasty bit of detritus onshore. In reality I don't move a muscle when my mind departs, flapping and greedy for something more exciting than endless Zen-like repetition, but the boat actually heels to port or starboard. When we race our quad, I make a point of focusing on the back of Al's T-shirt, resisting the impulse to look at the Vesper boat fifteen feet away with its cargo of champions, or the Fairmount boat mounting its assault from the stern.

The nature of a person like Al is that he, indeed, prods me to a state of grace, leads me into situations of terror and beauty without making the slightest deal of it. In fact, he seems often not even to have noted the extraordinary nature of what we have just experienced. "Hey, good row this morning," is as rhapsodic as he gets. One day after we rowed the double up a path into the sun, then back to Cambridge with a legato stroke lyrical as an aria, I waxed at length about the wonder of sculling. He got a faraway look in his eye. After a long moment, he said with more words than usual and without the slightest hint of irony, "You know, if my knee were in better shape I wouldn't row, I'd play golf. Now *there's* a sport!"

Sometimes he is like Superman, holding Lois Lane's hand so she, too, can fly over the rooftops and mountains, high over the North Pole. She never freezes or falls, and so far, neither have I.

One day we traveled upstream in our singles late in the low sun, only to have the sky turn first gray, then the ominous green of an impending squall. We were exactly between two bridges—the North Beacon Street Bridge and the Arsenal Street Bridge, a mile apart—when the storm hit like a full-blown hurricane. The wind was so violent that whole branches were suddenly torn from the trees growing thickly on each side of the river. Rain on the river's surface popped and jumped like water on a hot skillet and blew in torrents so heavy we could barely see the riverbanks thirty feet away. In less than a minute, water was spilling from our cockpits with every stroke.

And there was lightning. It lashed through the trees and struck at the sailboat masts on the Newton dock a half mile up, striking so close and so often that the air itself seemed charged and ready to explode. Jim Long taught me long ago in Huntington Harbor that the first rule of safety in rowing is, When there is lightning, get off the water! I screamed to Al over the howling wind that we had to get to shore. "No," he screamed back. "No place to stop, have to get to the bridge! GO, GO, GO!"

If there's one thing we know how to do, it is to go, go, go. We flew with the wind—like leaves, like Dorothy's farmhouse and the whirling haystacks. We were flung down the river with branches and bits of trash blown from nearby Soldier's Field Road. In the middle of the chaos I noticed with surprise a small wry voice coming from inside. It said, "God, if you think I'm wrong to want a better life, now is a good time to tell me." I didn't doubt for a moment that the answer might come with the next flash. Five seconds later, we were blown under the south arch of the Arsenal Street Bridge.

Then everything was still and warm. There was the trickling of the water flowing against the base of the abutments, the drip of rain falling like a beaded curtain from the edge of the arch, the rasp of our breath. We waited like a pair of trout hiding in an eddy under a rock, barely feathering our blades to stay perfectly still. We could see the branches fly, the rain pound, the lightning slash, but we couldn't hear it. Only trickles and drips and the muffled concussion of thunder like distant artillery, more felt than heard. We didn't speak. God had decided to remain silent; maybe I should be quiet, too.

The storm passed and we emerged from our arch fifteen minutes later to a river clotted with debris and the hiss of wet tires on Soldier's Field Road. At Henderson, where I keep my boat, I broke away. All Al said was, "Good row, Hall. See you tomorrow."

One summer night when my children were in Colorado visiting my parents and my husband was on a business trip, Al called to ask if I wanted to join a group to row singles that night. Row singles in the dark? What a question. Of *course* I wanted to row singles in the dark.

Rowing in the dark was nothing new to me—five in the morning is dark for all but the few months around June. But rowing at night seemed particularly thrilling. At eight that evening, I rowed the half mile to Cambridge Boat Club alone and hovered off the dock in the dark, waiting for them to arrive. The river was dark as the Styx, so dark that the distinction between air and water had disappeared and stroking through it was like rowing with my eyes closed. Soon they arrived in a blaze of headlights and in minutes had pushed off the dock to join me. We would go down to Riverside, where the river starts to widen, and back.

I steer with a mirror. It is a bike mirror, about an inch in diameter, mounted to my glasses. I got pretty good at it about four years ago when I'd had one collision too many and a friend told me that without it I'd never survive the Head of the Charles, at that point two weeks away. For two weeks I not only rowed with it, I cooked with it, drove with it, and did laundry with it, walking backward at a good clip from kitchen to stairs, hamper to laundry room. So, on this moonless night, I thought I knew where I was going—I could, after all, see the streetlights of roads and bridges in my mirror.

We rowed slowly round the Cambridge Bend, felt our way under the Anderson Bridge, and made the ninety-degree turn under Weekes Footbridge. Finally we had before us the Powerhouse Stretch to Riverside, a thousand meters of straightaway where we could really let loose. I looked in my mirror. There were the street lamps of the bridges and of Memorial Drive, like fairy lights at Christmas. There in the distance, too, were the lights of Boston, bobbing and twinkling enchantingly. Off we went at full throttle, ten strokes, twenty. Then Al shouted once: *"Sara!"*

What I had taken to be the enchanting lights of Boston were really the enchanting lights of a seventy-five-foot party boat filled with cocktail revelers and a dance combo not forty feet away, dead on my course under full steam. I was as invisible and as easily plowed under as an old buoy drifting in the dark. I pulled on port with a mighty haul and rowed the fastest five strokes of my life as the boat overtook me, bow towering overhead and just missing my stern. The boat swept past with a flash of pale faces and pearl necklaces, sound of a piano and tinkle of laughter, a whiff of perfume. Al waited for me in the dark on the other side. "Close call."

By the time I'd rowed with Al half a summer, we'd been in the eye of the tempest and gotten back alive, down the dark river, and returned to tell the tale. One morning at dawn, he took me to the Gates of the Beyond, the boat locks at the mouth of the Charles over which looms the three-hundred-foot tower of the new Freedom Bridge, a tower that looked uncannily like a giant cement A, New Times Roman.

We met on the dock at five-fifteen. "Somewhere new today" was all he said. When people first row with Al, they think they have to work hard to keep up. What they don't know is that for the first couple of miles, Al exerts virtually no effort. He rows in a state of silent attention to water's sweet, smooth demands. "You can't go fast if you try hard," he told me once (and didn't say another word for over an hour). The first time I rowed singles with him, I was pleased as punch to leave him in the dust during our warm-up. Finally he caught up and gave me a pitying look, as if I just didn't get it. This morning, we rowed together in silence, feeling the viscosity of the water, each of us hearing nothing but our gentle breathing, seeming to come from somewhere near our hearts.

We went under the Anderson Bridge. No one was up at Harvard's Newell Boathouse yet. Went under the Western Avenue Bridge, the River Street Bridge, past Riverside Boat Club and under the railroad bridge near the start of the Head of the Charles course. Al picked up the pace two beats. He didn't bother to tell me; I could feel it rowing beside him, blade tip to blade tip. We headed into the Basin, wide as a lake and bordered by a stone wall on one side and a grassy verge on the other. The sky overhead was low and gray, pressed like a damp sponge on the Massachusetts Avenue Bridge and, behind us, the spires of Harvard. As we slid into the dark under Longfellow Bridge deep in the Basin, an MTA train thundered overhead rattling the ancient stones and iron fretwork. Then we pointed our bows directly at the massive stone wall of the Science Museum—the end of the Basin, the end of the river. As far as I had ever gone. As far as I thought you could go.

Al pressed on, heading toward the old stone wall and the inevitable "spin" to turn our boats, drink some water, and start our journey upstream. What was new about this?

But we kept rowing, fifty strokes from the wall, now. Now forty. My angel didn't skip a beat. "Follow my stern, Hall." He appeared to be rowing directly at the wall at a pace undiminished, even accelerating now. I fell in behind. I would, as I said, follow Al anywhere, even into a stone wall. Twenty strokes to go, then ten. Anyone watching from shore would have held his breath and waited for the sound of impact, the splintering of carbon and breaking of oar shafts. Then suddenly, like the thrilling little door in the wall of the Secret Garden, there it was. I've been in this Basin fifty times and have never seen anything but an unbroken wall of stone. Five strokes. I was right on Al's stern, blades feathering in unison. Two strokes.

We went through the wall. Instantly we were in a passage so narrow we could barely fit the span of our oars between the high stones on either side. I didn't know where I was, didn't know where I was going. Twenty strokes, thirty, never slowing as we slid past the ancient stones and mortar. Then I could see open water ahead and we burst into an alien landscape of rusted dredging barges and pilings of a dimension fit to moor an ocean liner, thick with creosote and leaning askew. The noise was deafening—pounding of pile drivers and clanging of girders, the rumble of trucks overhead on the highway going to Boston with computer paper and galvanized pipes. There were old barges and workboats so dark and oily and massive that in our tiny shells and bright T-shirts we were two ruby-throated hummingbirds wandered far from the honeysuckle and the meadow, flitting and whirring through the rust and the clamor. Al pressed on. There were construction cranes at crazy angles on each side, and just ahead I could see the concrete A of the Freedom Bridge, imperious as Ozymandias.

The Freedom Bridge is the crowning glory of the Big Dig, Boston's eternal highway reconstruction project, and in rowing to the boat locks, we had rowed right into the heart of the Big Dig in a pair of thirty-pound racing shells. The Big Dig is both a tiresome joke to locals and one of those horrifying human attempts at immortality, like the Great Pyramids. It renders Boston's primary arteries into what appears to be a permanent state of disarray and commands a monumental expenditure of human resources. It appears to proceed at the speed of tectonic plates—legions of men transiting dawn to dusk, season to season, year to year, in pursuit of its completion.

On every side of us early shifts of construction workers in grimy uniforms and helmets leaned over catwalks and sat on girders like souls waiting in Purgatory. They drank coffee from Styrofoam cups and ate Dunkin' Donuts. Then they noticed us. "Hey, you guys lost?" "You nuts?" "Better watch out, gonna get squashed . . . " They laughed and waved. We waved back.

Then we arrived. All along Al was bringing me here, to the great gates at the foot of the Big A, the gates that lead to the other world, the gates of the lock. We pulled up at their base, insignificant in the face of their immutability, a wall of dark iron towering over our heads. Al called out: "Open the gates!" We waited for an answer but there was none. I wasn't sure what I expected—the thundering voice of St. Peter or the thin reply of an earthly lockmaster. Al called again, "Open the gates, we want to get through!" Again nothing. Then it occurred to me that the lockmaster must be accustomed to looking out his little shed and seeing the wheelhouse of a tugboat at eye level. At a height of three or four feet above the water we were puny as a pair of mosquitoes, and our call in the construction din just as insignificant. We waited, our hulls quiet in the oily water, our blades inches apart, our faces upturned expectantly for a signal from on high. We were so close to the other side, to the cry of the seabirds, the swells rolling all the way from Africa, the bottomless Atlantic. But this was not to be the day of passing through.

At last Al said, "Another day, maybe," and we turned, rowed back through the barges and the pilings, and found the way home to the river we knew.

Chapter Sixteen

RESOLUTE

In late August 1997, two months after
we moved to Boston, I was sitting on the floor
of the playroom choosing which plastic toys to
give to the Salvation Army and which to pitch
when the phone rang in the kitchen. I wondered if it was the plumber about the
leaky washer; certainly it wasn't a
social call—we had moved to Boston
only eight weeks before. No, when I answered
the phone it turned out to be a stranger, a crusty,
sixty-eight-year-old former Penn coxswain named
Bernard Tarradash. Bernie had a glass slipper in
nine medium. My size. The glass slipper was
a job in the rowing world. He told
me the name of his company
and I nearly choked on fairy dust. He
wanted to know if I might be interested in
part-time work representing Resolute Racing Shells.

"Murray thought I should give you a call," he said. "Thought you might be able to help us out." Enter the long arm of the river family. My husband's new boss in Boston was a devoted rower. The autumn before over dinner at a fancy restaurant in Manhattan (the kind where your food comes stacked in a tower), we had talked for an hour about rowing, much to my husband's apparent irritation. And now Murray had told his friend, Bernie, about me—Bernie, an investor in Resolute Racing Shells.

Resolute. *That* Resolute? I knew Resolute. Everyone knew Resolute. It was the hottest boat to hit the market since the first shell with sliding seats. With the collaboration of one of the top coaches in the nation—Steve Gladstone of Brown—and America's Cup boat builder Eric Goetz in Bristol, Rhode Island, Resolute Racing Shells had rocked the rowing world on its maiden voyage the year before with a dazzling win at Head of the Charles by the U.S. National Team. Coal black (it was, in fact, made of carbon), it had the radically snubbed bow, sheared transom, and lethal speed through the water that prompted reverent college crews to call it "The Darth Vader Boat" or "The Death Star."

Could I work with coaches to market the eight? Bernie asked. Could I help in the development of a single and bring it to the masters market? Could I create a marketing campaign and promotional materials for the product line? Could I come down to Bristol in the next few days and meet the Team? I paused for a millisecond, trying hard not to seem like one of those women in housecoats and curlers who open the door to find the Publisher's Clearinghouse guy standing on their stoop and holding a check for ten million dollars. I'd like to say that I thought long and hard about what my husband might have to say about me abandoning my sewing room for a boatyard, but I can't. I said, "How about tomorrow?" And what did my husband say? He couldn't afford to say much, at that point—the job introduction had come from his boss.

My interview was like the good part of a fairy tale (after the snakes and before the tempest). Eric Goetz, builder of America's Cup boats for Ted Turner and Bill Koch, among others, led the meeting in the Goetz boatyard conference room, littered with hull samples and blueprints. The walls were covered with photographs of winning boats with spinnakers flying and uniformed crews with bleached-out hair and dangerous-looking sunglasses manning the winches. Around the table were Goetz—softspoken, unassuming, in his mid-forties; Bernie Tarradash, who I later heard was referred to at his investment firm as "Mean Bernie," though I've always found him to be cordial and fair; and Misha Joukowsky, a primary financial backer of the company. Misha was young, headstrong, and very, very rich. He was keeping the ship afloat and on course.

We talked. We clipped on security passes and toured the yard, strolling by the Disney boat under construction, the French boat, the boat for Italy. (Months later when Goetz was building two America's Cup boats for the New York Yacht Club syndicate, we couldn't see the boats at all—they were built inside security tents.) I met the guys upstairs in "Z-Land," the territory staked out for Resolute, whose first prototype hull had been code-named "Z." Then they offered me the job. I remember wondering if somehow this was a case of mistaken identity, if maybe they had misunderstood who I was and where I'd been for the last decade. "You need to know that all I've done for years is drive carpools and do laundry. And row," I told them. They smiled. "We know about you," they said. "You'll do fine." Just what Carol had said. By the time I put my children on the school bus the next week, I was Vice President of Marketing for Resolute Racing Shells. It sounds quite grand, and was quite grand, but it was also part time—a plus for me with the demands of the children—and involved a great deal of hands-on work I found I enjoyed, replacing a skeg or rerigging a single for a particularly tall or short customer.

How did I get the job? In part it was because the company planned to build a single shell and sell it to the largest market—masters rowers, my home turf. It didn't hurt that I had just returned from Nationals with three silver medals. I had enough competitive exposure now that my presence in a Resolute single on the race course and at the race venues would bring it under the eye of those most likely to write checks for expensive boats with a competitive advantage— again, masters rowers. And I lived just over an hour from Bristol and could both come to the scheduled Monday morning meetings at the boatyard after I got the kids on the school bus (and be back by the time they got home), and respond to emergency calls from the boathouses in Boston for boats and parts. Finally, I didn't have an intimidating salary history; in fact, I had *no* salary history, and virtually no employment history either. A bonus for Resolute, which was still a new and speculative venture, not enthusiastic about paying the big bucks. So like the "forty-five-year-old sculler" Carol was looking for that day in Long Beach, there just weren't that many of us who fit the description. Most of all, though, Bernie had identified what turned out to be my greatest qualification for the job: the enthusiasm and love I brought to rowing.

Even so, the idea of filling Steve Gladstone's very large shoes was intimidating. Gladstone had been, and would be again, the most powerful and charismatic coach on the U.S. collegiate rowing scene, rivaled only by Harry Parker at Harvard. He had scoured the world for the right bodies to fill his boats at Brown and as a result had created a racing machine without peer. Gladstone had joined with Goetz the year before to combine his knowledge of high-performance rowing and Eric's virtuoso command of cutting edge composite materials in an attempt to build nothing less than the best racing shell in the world. They had launched their brainchild, Resolute, with Gladstone retiring from coaching to use his monolithic stature in the rowing community to market the boat. Then, after a year, he had a change of heart: he longed to return to his coaching launch, and left Resolute for U.C. Berkeley (where he has built yet another indomitable crew).

After Gladstone's departure, Resolute's sales were stagnant and rumor was rampant that the company would go under without his leadership and credibility. My job was to get it moving again, and quickly. I was hired the last week of August and my promotional campaign—creation of brochures for distribution, and banners, T-shirts, and hats for purchase—had to be in ready by the Head of the Charles weekend in mid-October, when I was also racing. I had to set up photo shoots, work with copywriters and printers, contact clothing manufacturers and embroiderers, hire a tent, contract with a graphics firm to create signage, and talk to every varsity crew coach in the country about "the Black Boat" during the six weeks following Bernie's call. And, of course, train for the most technically challenging endurance race in the world.

Though I was hired with the intention that my ultimate function was to promote the single, still in the first stages of design, I was also charged with marketing the eight to the college rowing world, a world entirely different from that of sculling and single shells, and masters rowers. Collegiate sweep rowing was alien territory to me: one in which credibility is measured in height, generally over six three; number of years rowed in men's varsity crews, generally four; and ability to schmooze coaches with beer and guy talk. Most of my competitors met the requirements easily. I didn't qualify on any count. So I didn't try. I was a woman, a mother, and a sculler with an extraordinary boat to sell and a willingness to be of service. That was all I could offer.

In my new job, I immediately came head to head with another company that had just launched an attack on Resolute with a less expensive lookalike and a very aggressive ad campaign. It turned out to be the company that had blown me off at the Canadian Henley the year before—Vespoli, the largest boat builder in the United States. For over a year I had reserved a special place in my heart for Vespoli, a place safely segregated from warm maternal or fuzzy kind feelings. And now here was Vespoli again, shooting across the bow of *my* boat, the Resolute. Four or five years earlier, I would have cowered in my kitchen. In the fall of 1997 however, I was in a confrontational kind of mood. I knew bullies and was no longer so willing to take them lying down.

While the sales representatives of the other boat manufacturers and I were cozily united in our enmity toward what we sometimes called "the Evil Empire," I had my own bone to pick—the attack on Resolute, and the affront to me a year before. One day in September, I wrote a reasonable little exegesis of various performance data and sent it to everybody in the universe via the rowing news group. I had no idea my aim was so good or that my little arrow was so sharp because darned if I didn't get a quick, dramatic response. Boston was soon aboil with coaches taking one side or another. I even heard a rumor that one influential Vespoli adherent was proposing more draconian methods of muzzling me—filing lawsuits, putting a stranglehold on the parts pipeline to coaches favoring the Resolute. I don't know that there was any truth to this; certainly no one filed suit. But it got my attention. The other reps had the sense to run for cover. I found myself facing Vespoli alone.

I was very frightened by the tempest I'd stirred up—these were big guys, powerful guys, angry guys—but I chose to hold my course. At the U.S. Rowing Convention in Hartford that December, an event attended by most of the coaches in the nation, I rented the display area directly across from the Vespoli booth, which was manned by the Vespoli representative I'd met in Canada and by Mike Vespoli himself. Neither greeted me warmly to the convention floor.

One of the selling points of the Resolute was its extraordinary stiffness and durability, which, according to our data, really did far surpass any other boat on the market. Eric and I had a strong sense, both from our numbers and from some exciting empirical research we had undertaken in the field, what our boat could take and what our competitors' boats could not. So, on the first day of the convention, I pulled out the white enamel stepstool I had brought from my laundry room and used it to climb on top of the overturned Resolute, suspended in its slings. Then, with Eric's blessing, I did the impossible: I jumped up and down, an outrage that would quickly have rendered any other boat, as my brother says, "carbon toothpicks." Then I did a little tap dance. Then I invited audience volunteers aboard to jump and dance with me. It was a knockout performance. The crowd gathered excitedly, lured by the sight of us hopping and skipping atop the almost sixty-foot racing hull, and soon the cavernous display hall was emptied of visitors—the rowing world was, literally, at our feet.

The college rowing world of school rivalries and crew hierarchies was strange and new to me, not just because I didn't know the protocols and procedures, but because team rivalry of any kind had never been part of my experience, and certainly not part of my own drive to win. It took me a long time to understand the haunted, cagey look coaches got when the names "Princeton" or "Penn" or "Washington" came up. I just didn't understand it. What I did understand, though, was that coaches and rowers not only needed backslapping and bravado, they needed taking care of. Like my son John. When he gets ready for a game, he psyches himself to win, but he also wants someone nearby to make sure he has his mouth guard and water bottle. I offered coaches the greatest service not only by selling them a competitive boat, but by checking that they had enough spare parts on the morning of the race, and offering chocolate chip cookies and cider at the venue.

I loved working with coaches, the vast majority of whom were decent and thoughtful, and didn't hold my inexperience against me as long as I answered questions accurately and got them the spare parts they needed on time. One Friday, in fact, the traffic was so bad on Storrow Drive that I used my Sharrow as a cargo ship, carrying parts down the river to Harvard in my tiny cockpit. To them, I was "the Resolute Lady," who could loan them a demo boat, or work out a time-pay plan, or make sure they had bearings for their wheels when they needed them.

I also grew fond of the other boat representatives whom I saw at regattas and conventions all over the United States—Alex Selvig, the Filippi rep who helped me with kind advice and a second pair of hands when I set up my displays; Kathy Williamson, who worked for Kaschper and gave me encouragement to take a strong stand at work and at home; and Bill McGowan, the Empacher king and former U.S. Rowing rep, who always gave me a bear hug and let me use his back porch in Brighton as drop site for our mutual embroiderer, Stella. We were an affectionate subset of the larger river community, always ready to lend a hand or share a sandwich. We even sent each other customers if we felt we couldn't meet special requirements or provide a last-minute boat for an out-of-town crew.

My entry into the river family in Boston had become a great source of friendship and support. That family expanded exponentially as a result of Resolute. I had an excuse to enter any boathouse, shake the hand and make a connection with any coach, rower, or boatman in the country, in the world. My family on the Charles expanded to everywhere boathouse doors rolled open every morning, everywhere anyone took a single from the top of an old station wagon and placed it in the water. Resolute was everything I could ask for. One of the tiny, sweet moments of my life was a morning when I rowed my single upstream and passed a college eight followed closely by a coaching launch going the other direction. The coach, whom I didn't recognize in hat and parka, turned toward me with his power megaphone and announced to all the world, *"Hellooooo, Sara Hall!"* Another was the day Harry Parker passed my single in his launch and lifted one finger in greeting. I belonged.

While Harry Parker and I didn't exactly become bosom buddies, I did sell him a boat. At my first meeting in Bristol as head of marketing, Bernie casually announced to the Team that I would be contacting Harvard to see if I could get a heavyweight boat into Newell in time for the Head of the Charles in mid-October. This was to be my first sales call. Harvard was, of course, Harry Parker. I, whose greatest sweep rowing triumph was rowing past CoCo's in an eight full of toymakers and grandmothers, was to persuade perhaps the most intimidating coach in the world to buy a Resolute.

I had been to Newell before. That summer, Bill McGowan, in his capacity as U.S. Rowing representative, had taken me on a tour of the university boathouses and introduced me to coaches and boatmen. At Newell I hadn't met Harry Parker, but did meet his legendary boatman, Everett Abbott. We became friends, joined by a common interest in the beauty of, of all things, wood. Newell had an abundance of the newest and best carbon hulls, but it also had some beautiful old wooden shells on the topmost racks, and I enjoyed hearing Everett tell me their history. By the time I made my Resolute sales call to Harry Parker, I had many times parked my Sharrow at the end of Newell's great dock and sought out my friend to talk about varnish or two-step adhesive marine paint.

I arrived at Newell on the appointed day and stopped by the boat bay to say hello to Everett. Then Harry Parker appeared. We went out to the broad dock and sat on a bench in the late morning sun. I felt ridiculously intimidated. But I looked him in the eye, as my father had taught me to do, and said, "There's nothing I can tell you about Resolute that you don't already know, and I'm not going to give you a sales pitch. All I can do is offer you a boat to try. How about it?" He looked at the river and thought for a moment. "Deliver it the end of October and I'll try it the last few weeks of the season." That was not the answer I wanted. Should I just say thank you? "Well, Mr. Parker, I have a boat coming off demo in a few weeks that can be rigged and ready to go the last week of September. I'd like to deliver it to you on October 1." He thought for a long minute, looking at the river. I imagined him toying with whether or not he was going to allow himself to accept my suggestion. He didn't. He said, "October 2."

I did deliver the boat on October 2, a rainy afternoon. I held my breath as his varsity crew took the Resolute off the trailer and swung its stern into the Storrow Drive rush-hour traffic to walk it through the vast crimson doors of Newell. Then I had enough sense to stay away and hold my tongue for the three weeks to follow (or maybe it was just my fear of Harry). Every once in awhile I would hear a report that Harvard was down in the Basin in the Resolute, and every once in awhile Everett would call for a spare part; but no one inside Newell or out could confirm whether or not Parker was planning to use the Resolute for Head of the Charles. We didn't know a thing until the day of the race, when Bernie, Eric, and I were standing in the chill of a gray October afternoon on the banks of Magazine Beach where I had rented a tent, waiting for the first boats of the Championship Eights to come up the river. A swell of commotion spread through the hundreds of spectators. Rounding the bend under full power was the Harvard Varsity Eight rowing the Resolute. We screamed with delight, jumping and slapping each other on the back. Harvard rowed the fastest collegiate time that day. Even then, it took Harry five months to order a boat. Tough customer.

For almost two years I got to know the face of American rowing and it got to know mine. I felt a profound sense of mission and a deep desire not to let down the coaches who counted on me, or Bernie and Eric who had had the faith to hire me. Often I did much of my Resolute paperwork and e-mails at 4:00 a.m.—there were, literally, not enough hours in the day. I trained on the river in the morning and made sales calls in the early afternoon before the children came home from school at three, when, after making the snacks and getting the news of school, I made my final sales calls to California, three time zones behind. I was exhausted. I was exhilarated. As the months passed, I increasingly felt a sense of mission. The central truth that emerged from my experience of Resolute was that I found I loved operating in the world *and* being a mother. I could talk carbon fiber with the World Champion one minute, and tie little shoes and head for soccer practice the next. If the back of my car was littered with beanie babies and rudder posts, beach towels and foot stretchers, I had never been so fully engaged, never felt so alive and connected to people who shared my interests.

Resolute offered me a new world; but it was not without cost. Certainly I was not unaware that my job was having a dramatic impact on my family. From the moment I mentioned to my husband that, with William going into first grade, I'd taken a part-time job, I knew to batten the hatches and reef the sails. I would never claim that I juggled my Resolute and family lives perfectly—it was all new territory to me and the children were understandably resentful of Resolute's demands on my time—but how could I have turned away from the world of which I was now a part? I was offered a world in which I would share in the daring experiment that was Resolute; a member of the Team. Could feel the brimming excitement of engagement in a noble endeavor, and feel it not just in the dim hours at the margin of day but a good part of the day, every day. For the first time in almost twenty years I found the satisfaction of expressing myself in the bigger world—not instead of being a mother, but in addition to it.

The timing couldn't have been better, or worse. When Bernie called, I was poised for change. Everything pointed to my ability and will to become more expansive in the world—my racing, my new friendships, my new willingness to lay it on the line. Our recent move from Long Island had severed old connections and habits and we were in a new land. For our family, this was the deciding moment. The time had come for my husband finally to back up last year's talk about spending time with the kids, and the time had come for me to stand up for myself. But although I felt ready for evolution, even revolution, my husband apparently did not feel the same. He seemed to want to pull out the blueprint of the old life and build it on new ground, like the colonist who builds a British country house in the tropics. Nothing was to change. There would be no problem as long as *he* was Master. But he was no longer Master. And even if he had been, there was a change in our lives the autumn of 1997 that had profound implications for me, and thus for my marriage: first grade.

Here's a quiz. What are the three most exciting days of a woman's life? Her wedding day? Yes. The day her firstborn is placed in her arms? Yes. The day her husband gives her a diamond necklace for their twenty-fifth anniversary? No. The day she sees her child graduate from college? No. No. No. It is the day her lastborn enters first grade, the day she gets some of herself back.

My sister Caroline, who has worked all her adult life, says that my attitudes and lifestyle are relics of another age. "First grade to most women," she says, "means nothing more than a reduction of day-care expenses." For stay-at-home mothers, though, it is different. For years, nursery school and baby-sitters had offered us tantalizing snippets of freedom here and there, just enough to go to the grocery store without a child begging for Cocoa Krispies or to the dentist without a wiggling toddler pulling on your sweater asking again and again: "When can we go home?" But the prospect of freedom seven hours in a row, five days a week? For the first time, we could get a job or pursue an interest, maybe even read a book cover to cover. It was unimaginable liberty. As one friend said, it was the end of the "toddler tunnel."

Rewarding but exhausting beyond description, the preschool years were ones in which our lives as individuals had been packed in a box and stored in the corner of the basement. (In the first decade of motherhood I really did have a box in the cellar filled with my writing saved from college days, jokingly labeled: "What's Left of Sara's Mind.") We wouldn't have the chance to wipe off the dust, open the lid, and see if the mice had eaten it or the flood of five years ago had rotted it away until our youngest had kissed us, taken his backpack filled with Big Chief paper and Crayola markers onto the bus, and gone off to first grade. If I was getting ready to give away the outgrown toys when Bernie called, it was partly to make room for "What's Left of Sara's Mind," about to be brought up from the cellar. His call came seven days before the start of first grade.

What did the job at Resolute mean to me? It meant not only a coming to the light at the end of the toddler tunnel, but a bringing into the light and giving a name to the person I had come to be in the dark hours of dawn on the water. It was a coming out, a making public of the fact that I was talented, I was capable, I had value in the world. For the first time, my rowing was not just Sara's obsessive little hobby, accommodated during the discarded hours no one claimed, but a job, a legitimate place in the larger world.

What did my job mean to the children? Though they knew from their sometimes reluctant participation in my regattas that I rowed, in my two years on the water my children had rarely seen me train because I did so mostly when they were either asleep or at school. I made their breakfast as usual, and except for the few weeks in the fall of 1996 when I'd coached a high school crew was at home when they arrived after school, as usual. In terms of impact on "vital services," the same was true for my husband. I may have been away from bed in the early dawn while he slept; but I was there at my post when he awoke, and there reading bedtime books to the kids when he came home from work.

My work schedule, Bernie had indicated, would hardly alter this; except for the addition of an hour of phone calling to the West Coast late in the afternoon after the kids ate their snack and were outside playing, and an occasional trip out of state. Everything could stay the same as far as my family was concerned. The difference for the children was not so much in the alteration of my mothering schedule but a shift in their perception of my role in the bigger world. Instead of saying, "Mommy makes curtains and builds bookshelves," it became, "Mommy sells racing boats." I hoped they would be proud of me.

It did not seem to be so for my husband. He had not, apparently, taken to heart the article I lifted from the orthodontist's waiting room and left conspicuously next to the toilet about the family structure and how it shifts when the youngest goes to school and the mother gets a job. He didn't demonstrate to me in any way I could perceive that he was "on board" with the approach to marital evolution it promoted. About how, after a period of resentment at my sudden lack of availability to do all the chores I'd always done at home, he would be pleased with my newfound confidence and assertiveness. How I would become a woman with interesting things to say at the end of the day and a new shine in my eye. How before long he wouldn't mind running the odd load of laundry, cooking a dinner once a week, even doing dishes on an equal time basis. How he would spend more time with the children as I had the occasional business trip or weekend seminar, and find he was enjoying them more than ever before, especially with me not always hovering and saying, "Oh no, we do it *this* way." And the children, in turn, would love getting to know their dad and be proud of their mother, who had become someone with a profession and not just a mommy.

It was supposed to be a win-win situation for everyone.

It might have worked that way if I had taken a job as a lunchroom aide or a substitute teacher, something more directly related to nurturing than speeding down a river in a single shell loaded to the gunwales with unidirectional carbon rudder/skeg assemblies. But I doubt it. It might have worked that way if I had used my experience of homemaking to get a job as a real estate agent (as did many of the women I knew back on Long Island), or my ability to listen to little voices tell me about their day and become a psychotherapist (as did some of my suburban acquaintances). But I doubt it. I didn't, however, want to be a lunchroom aide, a substitute teacher, a real estate agent, or a therapist. I wanted to live and breathe rowing, and spend my time with people whose competitive attitude and desire to make the boats go fast matched mine. That those people were mostly men did not escape my husband's attention, nor did it escape mine (though it was not nearly as compelling to me as the passion of shared interests). I had been starved of the friendship of men for nearly twenty years and reveled in the affection, respect, and admiration we shared. For my marriage, though, Resolute was the last straw.

Resolute offered me great opportunity. It offered him one as well. He could have been proud of me, could have encouraged me to try my wings; but, as I feared, he appeared to see them as the means to fly away. A fear and rage that I had escaped the cage was apparent in his remarks and in the atmosphere of hostility in our house, which escalated as my months at Resolute wore on. He began pointing out to the children that they were eating canned soup because Mommy didn't want to cook for them anymore. When, one day in September, I asked him if he would be willing to handle dinner one night a week, he looked at me as if I'd asked him to lick clean the bathroom floor. When I prepared to attend a Saturday morning race, instead of saying, "Hey, kids, let's go out for breakfast," he told them, in my presence, that their mother didn't have time for them in her busy life. Once, when I came home with a gold medal and the children gathered around me asking, "How'd you do, Mommy? Did you win?" I remember him saying to all three children as we stood there in the kitchen, his face flushed and angry, that my medal was the most expensive win in history. First he cited the cost of Mommy's boat, then the cumulative cost of Mommy's psychotherapy, then he told them I was "ruining the lives of you three children. Great job, Sara!" Imagine how our children felt, children who just wanted to be proud of their mother.

The children had been a convenient means for my husband to keep me tightly leashed, a leash whose twitch I felt every time he mentioned the word "selfish" in a certain tone. My own fear that maybe he was right and I *was* somehow negligent and unnatural to want to row on a Saturday morning at seven instead of five, leaving the children "crying for Mommy and starving for breakfast," always brought me to heel. A less brainwashed woman will wonder why he couldn't pour the cereal himself and tell them, "Mom's busy right now; let's have a special time with just us." My unconscious acceptance of his notion of motherhood was the choke chain that tightened with every move I made toward the larger world.

Things spun out of control rapidly after I took the job at Resolute. It was frightening to stand up to my husband and sickening to face the sarcasm at the breakfast table in our big house in the pretty town: bitter remarks over our orange juice and eggs. One morning he even asked me pointedly in front of the children if I was taking steroids, something lost on seven-year-old William, but not on athletic ten-year-old John, or Janie. (As he must have known, once the seed of the idea was planted, my indignant denials couldn't completely uproot it from their minds.) The children seemed stupefied, almost dazed, and I had the sense that they were beginning to keep their heads down, figuratively and literally. Some days it was hard to keep the sureness and confidence in myself that I was doing the right thing, risking that, in the desire to hurt me implicit in his accusations, it would be the children who suffered.

Will women forgive me when I ask, "Does a woman deserve to be a person as well as a mother and wife?" I still suffer from my years lost in my husband's world. I know the answer in my head, but I still don't always know it in my heart. My husband's voice, his lovely voice, still echoes in my head sarcastically every time I get a baby-sitter or make grilled cheese sandwiches and canned soup for dinner again. Still, more than three years after Bernie's call, I have to ask, What do I deserve? What is reasonable? I'm ashamed that every woman seems to know the answer to this but me, to whom it is as elusive as a deer moving in the dimmest twilight on the edge of a forest. I strain to memorize its shape and heft before it disappears. Sometimes even now I cannot simply say, *This is what I want, this is what I feel, this is what I deserve.*

Yet, as the very air we breathed at home grew thick with anger, I could feel near me a source of strength and faith, a hand on my shoulder and a voice. *Long and strong.* It was near on the day I saw the single for the first time. Near the day I said goodbye to my medals, and on the Mother's Day when I faced the waves. Near on the day I said *no,* on the day I met Carol, and the day Bernie called. Surely the voice I heard was telling me not to give in to fear, not to succumb to doubt.

God was near as the black clouds gathered on the horizon in

autumn of 1997 and when the storm howled in 1998. Even on the worst nights, when I felt I was helplessly watching my husband's anger, I knew He was there, because the more I was willing to remake my life, the more I was given the tools to do it—love, fervor, even fury. Most of all, the faith to let go and move on. Surely I was doing something very right, because in the months of 1997 and 1998 when I needed the strength to see that I had a right to exist in the larger world, when I had to hold my course and drive to the finish, Resolute was there.

Chapter Seventeen

FIRE

AND WATER

In Boulder, we learned about
water in the third grade—about the
"Watershed," which was everywhere, immutable
and invisible. The Watershed was a grand plan
mapping the destiny of every raindrop, every
day, every year forevermore. It was
neatly bisected by the Continental Divide,
running the spine of the continent—an invisible
line (though I always imagined it to look like metal
garden edging) that sent any given raindrop across
the prairie to the East, where everyone came
from, or to the West like the pioneers,
through the desert with the mighty Colorado.
Where we lived, on the dry bed of an ancient sea
filled with trilobites and clam shells and tipped
into foothills by the thrust of dark granite,
we could look west to the Divide

every morning, wreathed in clouds and often covered with snow. Our parents sometimes took us up the long mountain pass so we could step over the line with a little ceremony, going from the half of the continent that was home to the half that was not. It bore the stamp of the Highest Authority, this imaginary line in the dirt on Loveland Pass—a hydrological Great Wall of China, thrillingly final. There was no indecisiveness in its dictates, no possibility of negotiation, no "sometimes the rain is in a New York state of mind." I loved that.

I decided to leave my husband on January 28, 1998. It was a decision that was as simple and final as stepping over the Divide. I had met my mother and sisters on the island in the Abacos off the coast of Florida where they had held their mother/daughter reunions for the seven years preceding this one, seven years in which I "couldn't get away." This was the year I got away. We would walk the beach, ride old fat-tire bicycles, and talk and talk over the strange food we liked (strange, at least, to our children at home)—veggie burgers and lentil stew with seaweed and tofu. Talk about our children and our lives, about Annie's jazz class and Mother's new Mozart sonata, about Caroline's book. And, when and if I was ready, about marriages. My mother and sisters were wise enough not to greet me with what they had thought for nearly two decades. "Don't you see? How can you stay with him?" Each day, we walked and talked and laughed together. Each day, I walked on the beach at dawn. My mother had sent me out alone the first morning. "This is a wonderful place to put your life in perspective," she told me.

One day just before sunrise, I stopped in my tracks, faced the sea, and answered a voice that asked, "What are you going to do?" I said, "I'm going to leave him." Just like that, like crossing the Continental Divide—as simple and easy as taking one little step, as difficult as years of climbing up long scree fields and hacking through stands of brush to get to the point where I could see the other side.

I have never looked back since that one little step, and never stopped walking. There has been no second thought, no regret, no hint of a nagging voice saying, "You could have made it work; maybe you could have tried harder." If there is any sorrow about the death of my marriage, it is that I have felt no sorrow, only profound relief. That, and regret that I didn't do it sooner. If in our culture we decry the ease with which couples end their marriages, I'm here to say that, at least for me, it wasn't so. My marriage had the malignant tenacity of Rasputin—there seemed no end to its ability to cling to life. To leave my husband was a decision that took less than a second and more than fifteen years. A watershed decision.

Two weeks after I made it, on an afternoon when Janie and John had just been put on the plane to my parents in Boulder and William was at a friend's house for the afternoon, I sat in the car with my husband and looked him calmly in the eye. I said three words: "I'm divorcing you."

We may have learned about water in the third grade, but we also learned about the fire that sweeps the forests with a swift and terrible hand and opens the hard seedcases to start afresh. In the three years since I said, "I'm divorcing you," I've come to know all its uses—the punishing fire, the destroying fire. The transforming fire. I know the fire that glows in my kitchen and renders all the hard, cold stuff in the larder warm and soft for my children's little tongues, the fire in the furnace that makes the radiator smell like dust on the first cold November day. I know the fire that burns me to ash on the race course and leaves me at the finish scoured and new—like a stand of pines under a wide Colorado sky. I know the fire that burns the heretic and the disobedient woman—the one with a dangerous will who holds in her hand the flaming sword or the forbidden wisdom or the simple truth, the witch or the saint. I know the fire in the night that crawled through the hallways and up the staircase of our stricken house, trying the doors, testing the hinges, curling through the cracks, raging with an explosion of windows and crashing of timbers. I know the incandescent wafting of burning curtains like angels' wings, like a soul departing. Our house like a torch, bright and terrible. Our house near the stout stone church in the prosperous little town, satisfied and orderly. Our house with the four white pillars that said, "I am forever." No one could see the flames, hear from the tidy street the crack of glass and collapse of roof beams, but we were on fire for seven months in 1998.

I had thought that when I told my husband it was over, he would be sad and angry, maybe break the china and throw some furniture, then pack a bag and decamp to an apartment to seethe with anger and seek out allies with whom he could exchange bitter stories of feminine perfidy. We would put the house on the market and begin the process of dividing the life we had built, each walking away with a share to build again. The children would live with me—they had spent so little time with their father over the years, and, ironically, the weekends and evenings they were with him now would be far more time than they had ever had before. Surely there would be vengeance—in a history where everything was my fault and none his, he would feel himself to be the injured party—but I wasn't prepared for the indiscriminate power and sheer magnitude of the conflagration.

When I said my three words, it was as if I had dropped a match into a well of fuel concealed under the brick and fieldstone foundation of our lives, ignited a kind of emotional environmental hazard. The edifice that we had built—our grand house, our three children with their jumpers and khaki pants, trusting eyes, all the furniture and fixtures of our lives—was not to be spared. The buried tank was so vast and volatile that nothing would be left after it had spent its fury, nothing but scorched earth and charred remains. My three little words, delivered so calmly, brought to life a terrible energy that had been safely contained by the rigid form of our marriage, buried beneath the trappings of civility, held in check by my compliance.

The first night, after the china hutch was overturned, the plates broken, William and I slept at a friend's house. The second we spent at home, a night in which my husband's anguish was so intense that I held him when he cried, as I would hold anyone in such pain. By the third night, his sorrow seemed to have disappeared, and I have not seen it since. That's when I smelled smoke. A close friend to whom I had spoken of our breakup the day before called me a few mornings later to say she feared I was in danger. "You've got to get out," she said. "I've seen him with you and I have this feeling about him. I think he might hurt you."

My family had "this feeling" about him, too. By the time the children returned from Boulder, my parents were afraid. "Come to Colorado where we can protect you," they said. "Bring the children and come." But I was intimidated by the law and my husband's experience using it. I worried that if we bolted, he would get a judge to haul us back where we would be captive. This was a mistake. I've learned over the last three years that, in a sort of reverse discrimination, the abused woman with strong nerves is penalized; there's a perception that if she were really threatened, she would panic and run.

But most of all I didn't leave because tearing the children from their house, their school, their pets would have frightened them. I could handle it. After all those mornings on a howling harbor, if I had anything, it was an ability to face adversity with a steady hand and a strong heart.

I really believed that my husband would leave. His life seemed built around not only the need to control but the need to save face, so I assumed he would be too angry and embarrassed to stay with the woman who had rejected him. But he didn't leave, and soon it was clear he had no intention of leaving. The very sight of me seemed to fan the flames, to stimulate and excite him into an ecstasy of rage. Soon I came to the conclusion he planned to have us all burn together, as a family.

One time he called from a business trip to leave a message about how he wanted to lie in bed with me and "look into my deep blue eyes." At other times he shrieked on the phone: "Selfish bitch!" or "Sick cunt!" I came to believe that these were two sides of the same thing.

I was frightened. My family—my parents, brother and sisters— were frightened for me. Some days I didn't know how the children and I could stay in the house another moment. Yet my attorney at the time advised me to stay. I understood that to leave could mean the loss of the children—an inconceivable thought.

I had moved to a room in the finished attic of our big house, and every night before I got into bed, I wedged a chair under the doorknob. As I lay in the dark I knew he could easily burn me out, literally light the house afire and burn me in my bed high above our manicured lawn. I thought about the children in their warm beds below me and wanted to run downstairs, pack their little school backpacks with clothes, and drive away with them. Anywhere.

Then one afternoon in April, two months after I had said my three words, I looked out the narrow window next to the front door and saw a blue Chevy station wagon with Colorado plates pulling into my driveway.

My father's seventy-year-old brother, Uncle Tucker—Robert Tucker Hall—is a prize possession in my family. My sisters and I, in particular, adore him, as do our children to whom he is a familiar and beloved member of each household. Since his divorce in the early nineties, he has been the favored houseguest in all our families. He drops by for months at a time, bringing his power saw and his tool-box, building a much-needed sun porch or renovating a bathroom, or simply sitting quietly in the living room with his thick books on history (he has joined the library in all our towns). When the children come home from school, he often puts down his book and sits with them at the kitchen table to help with homework or design a boat or an airplane to be made from wood scraps. The toy is usually finished by dinner.

Uncle Tucker's quiet presence in our houses is not only not a burden, it is an asset so precious that my sisters and I have, at times, fought over him. More than once I've called him at Annie's house only to have Annie say, only slightly in jest, that she won't put him on the phone unless I promise not to try to lure him away. It isn't that Tucker has no will of his own; it is that he is happy to be where he's needed, and generally he is needed by all of us.

Never had he been needed more than in the spring of 1998 in Boston. The afternoon he arrived, I put my face on the shoulder of the old green Shetland sweater the children and I knew so well from all his visits, and for the first of what would be many, many times, heard him say, "Go ahead. You could use a good cry." By dinnertime he had moved to the attic room next to mine, and after we got the children fed and tucked in, we talked late into the night. Tucker made all the difference. He made it possible to endure the terror of that house. He stayed with me in the attic through the rest of the fire: five months.

By the time he arrived, the house seemed seething and alive. Often I was awakened from a dead sleep when the lights in the attic snapped on with a glare at two in the morning. When I turned them off, they would come on again ten minutes later. Someone was awake. Someone was waiting by the switch downstairs, waiting in the dark for me to close my "deep blue eyes" again. One time when Tucker and I climbed the steep, spiral staircase to the attic at the end of the day, the lights snapped off as we were midflight. I felt my way back to the second floor and we began to climb again. The lights snapped off again. I was frightened not so much of falling in the dark—we knew the stairway "with our eyes closed"—but of the sense that someone was waiting, willing us to miss a step.

Night after night the phone line went dead from dark to morning, coming on again just before my husband left for work. And sometimes the house actually seemed to crack and collapse around us: one morning as Tucker slept, an ironing board crashed on me as I walked through the door of the second floor to get the children ready for school. The ironing board had been carefully arranged and fell as the door from the attic was opened.

The narrow back stairway I used before dawn to go rowing was blocked one day. The stairway descended next to my husband's room and I made a habit of going down it in the dark, stepping on the outside edge of each tread: I was certain the hall light and sound of creaking would wake him and I was afraid of a confrontation. One morning as I crept down from the attic, my foot caught on a large trash bag filled with heavy material, a bag that had been positioned on the steepest part of the twisting stairway, nowhere near the wide ground-floor landing on which it was normally placed on garbage days. I just caught the banister before I fell headlong. One night at bedtime as I lay reading a story to William, metal watering cans suddenly began bouncing down the nearby stairway as if thrown from below again and again. Later the exterior wall behind William's bed cracked with the report of what sounded like rocks thrown against the siding. Our son was only seven.

Our big house felt calculating and malevolent and a sense of disaster filled every room. The overwhelming anger that consumed it left a trail of debris: the framed photograph of my grandfather smashed to the floor in a litter of glass; the sculpture Carie had given me for Christmas torn apart and left in pieces on the floor. I reeled in panic. The children looked frightened and dazed. Tucker stayed calm. What would the children and I have done without his sanity and strength in that house?

One weekend in May 1998, I went to New Jersey on Resolute business while Tucker went to New Hampshire to visit one of his four sons. Janie stayed at a friend's house and my husband took the boys on a trip to Long Island. I returned late at night, driving up from New Haven through Hartford. The radio crackled with news of tornadoes and heavy downpours in the area between Hartford and the Massachusetts Turnpike, and as I turned east on 80, the wind accelerated and the wipers couldn't keep up with the rain. After a few miles I was in the middle of a storm so violent that my car was being thrown from lane to lane. I stopped under an overpass. Here were semis and big vans and passenger cars, all hiding from the elements under the shelter of the bridge, headlights barely piercing the rain.

The lights of my dashboard glowed green and the car rocked in the wind. I remember feeling warm and safe in the wild night under a bridge with strangers.

At midnight, I turned off my headlights and rolled quietly into the long driveway of our house, gleaming under a full moon with its shining slate roof and multitude of black windows. I could see my husband's car in the driveway and knew he and the boys were inside asleep. I couldn't make myself get out of my car, climb the steps, and walk into the dark house alone. My hand wouldn't reach for the door handle. After a few minutes, I backed out of the driveway and waited until dawn.

There was no proof of anything and, other than Tucker, no witnesses except the house itself. Sometimes I realized in a rare moment of calm that if my fear often felt unbearable, my husband's torment must have been terrible. In spite of everything that had happened, now and in our long history together, some small part of me had always sensed that, between the two of us, on the deepest level, *his* was the greater neediness, *his* the greater fear, and both of us had been victim of it. Now his very flesh seemed to be consumed by intolerable agony; he must have lost forty pounds in the first two months of the disaster.

He wandered like a soul afire, upstairs and down, in the hallways, the living room, the dining room. I remember him yelling at me, sometimes in front of the children—"*Sick, sick, freak. You selfish freak!*" The nakedness of his feelings was awful in the middle of the flowered upholstery and the books, the magazines on the coffee table. He looked for all the world like a bomb victim who remains miraculously upright in spite of mortal wounds, stumbling through the rubble, delirious. I was thankful the children soon began spending most of their time in their rooms.

One night I stood on the front lawn looking at the moon. When

I turned back to the house, I saw him standing in the French door of the second story, overlooking the front door and the busy road. He stared down at me, his face as angry as I'd ever seen it. He looked like a man crucified—arms outstretched on the frame of the door, the lights of passing cars illuminating his torso like lightning. I'm sure he thought I was the one with the hammer and nails, just like his first wife.

I called the Domestic Abuse Hotline again and again. Get a restraining order, a 209A, they said. Come to the shelter. I ended up at the police station again and again. They were helpless: until he actually raised a hand and struck me, they couldn't get him out. I'm sure my husband knew this—he had lunged to grab me one night and I watched him snap his hands to his sides at the last instant as if I were a hot stove. The only time he actually went at me it was with his car, which veered at mine, then veered away at the last moment. It was on an empty street just west of town. There were no witnesses. One police officer offered to come to court with me to help me get a protective order, but without a broken nose or a black eye there was no protection. "But what if he kills me?" I asked my lawyer. *Then* I would get protection.

Then, suddenly, he stopped wandering the halls. He had found a new interest. One morning as I got the children up and dressed, he seemed to make a point of letting me see him in his bed, probing and marking a thick red book with a firm hand. It was the *DSM-4*: the *Diagnostic and Statistical Manual of Mental Disorders*.

It's been centuries since men have been allowed to dispose of troublesome women at the stake. We sleep peacefully in these enlightened times secure in the knowledge that a Devil-fearing mob won't pound on our door and haul us off to the pyre. We're fooling ourselves. The mob is still there, the faggots dry and ready for the torch. It's just a different kind of fire.

If strong women, uncooperative women, rabble-rousing women have always prompted some men to fear that an army of us will get out of control, take power, then modern man has a neat new stake to which we can be securely lashed while someone runs to get a match: psychopathology. You would think that judges, communities, and friends would groan with boredom when yet another abandoned husband claims that the wife who was normal just last week has suddenly been possessed by a new kind of Devil—mental illness. But society's lurid interest in the whole idea of "the woman possessed," especially a woman as thrillingly and literally close to the bosom of the family as a wife and mother, remains unabated, combining as it does the allure of scandal with the special titillation found in the spectacle of public humiliation—always an easy sell.

Now, three years after the fact, I've heard of many, many cases of women who were good mothers and members of the community finding themselves condemned when they leave angry husbands. Their reputations go up in smoke as they are diagnosed by their husbands as having a Borderline Personality, or an Obsessive-Compulsive Disorder, or a Manic-Depressive Disorder. Some spouses throw in homosexuality and drug addiction to round out the picture of pathology (and it is interesting to note that the idea of a wife "turned gay" seems to be both the ultimate insult and the ultimate comfort to a rejected husband). At the time it happened to me, I had no idea this was commonplace. All I knew in 1998 was that friends from Long Island and Boston started calling to say, "You need to know what he's telling people . . . "

I had heard my husband tell our children that a famous psychiatrist at McLean Hospital had diagnosed me as suffering from a Borderline Personality Disorder. By all reports the psychiatrist was no fool, and had to know that to diagnose me as an anything without having seen me as a patient was grounds to have his license yanked, so it is fair to say that the famous doctor had nothing to do with any kind of diagnosis. That appeared to be no deterrent to my husband. The news of my "illness" seemed to spread like wildfire, along with rumors that, in addition, I routinely beat the children, and was now both gay and possibly on drugs, maybe even performance-enhancing drugs. According to loyal friends, my husband was burning up the phone lines with a convincing sincerity. Apparently he was sick with worry and just wanted to have me brought in and placed in a treatment program that would address the awful symptoms of my disease, a program that would restore me, once again, to the family, the wonderful wife and mother I had been.

This message surely suggested a number of ideas titillating to our close community from church, club, and school, a community whose juiciest scandal had been the time one of its members, the head of an exclusive social organization and loud proponent of "the American family," had been caught kissing another woman at his wife's fortieth birthday party. Suddenly the mommy who had yearly bought the prizes for Pet Night at the Beach Club was an outlaw needing to be rounded up and restrained, possibly with a straitjacket. I was a danger to my spouse and children; yet my husband, in his compassion, still loved me. And finally I had succumbed to the virus many men fear to be incubating in the bloodstream of woman—a virus of irrationality, amorality, and most of all a kind of fierce and feral *selfishness* that had violently erupted and torn our lovely family asunder.

I found out over many months that my husband had prepared a series of long documents superbly crafted in their use of innuendo. They were apparently distributed to a number of people, including, occasionally, me; he sent me copies of much, or what I assumed was much, of what he disseminated. Sometimes even now I awake from a deep sleep to the ringing of my fax line and the whir of the machine spitting out his anger, page after page. In them, and in conversations that made their way back to me, he created a masterful account of my devolution, meticulously gathering the threads of incidents that occur in the life of any woman, in any family, and mingling them with outright fiction. This slender stuff he wove with terrifying skill into a vivid and compelling tapestry of dysfunction. My friendships with women my mother's age, he insinuated, were suspiciously age-inappropriate. My firing of a baby-sitter became evidence of propensity for personality conflict (he failed to mention that I let her go after discovering that she had a police record). My disagreement with a class mother about a proposed lavish teacher gift became my inability to maintain interpersonal relationships, and my complaints that I couldn't lose the last five pounds of "baby weight" while breast-feeding became evidence of a deep postpartum depression.

And there was my history of physical brutality toward the children. Like the time I got really irritated and broke a plate on the floor one night when the kids continued to scream and Rollerblade around and around the kitchen after I'd called them to the dinner table a dozen times. This became Sara hurling crockery at the children's heads. And the time I caught one of the boys smearing a pot of lip gloss over a windowpane and took him firmly by the arm, sitting him on the bed for a "talking to." By the time it got back to me, the account of this event was almost unrecognizable—it seemed I'd swung the child round by the arm and flung him to the floor with "fury," "force," and "frenzy."

Some of his written accounts were typed on official-looking paper in the bottom margin of which was printed, "Personal and Confidential: Patient Privileged Materials," as if it had been written by the famous psychiatrist himself, and throughout there was a sprinkling of psychiatric terms: I suffered from a "fractured reality," and was proficient at "splitting" and "projection." Even the court-appointed psychologist, in an interview with me during the course of the divorce, turned to a page from one of my husband's "documents" and, reading, asked me gently to explain my admission to the hospital with emotional problems during my last pregnancy. My husband had apparently managed to suggest that the emergency hospitalization of a six-months-pregnant woman with blood gushing from her vagina was really a confinement in a psychiatric ward. In writing, phone calls, or personal visits, he contacted friends, neighbors, baby-sitters, therapists, counselors, ministers, school personnel, anyone who would listen, concentrating enormous energy on his campaign. By the end of

August 1998 he was no longer putting on a blue suit and commuting to his new job in Boston.

Perhaps most painful to me during this campaign was the use he made of the tender, secret things I had told him—the sorrow I had felt as a teenager that my female body was affected by the DES, the trauma I had felt at the hands of the rancher as a thirteen-year-old. Even the therapy I had gotten to deal with it, and later, the therapy I had sought to manage the anger at my husband for his treatment of me during my last pregnancy were presented as indications of disease. That I sought support from a therapist again during this chaotic and frightening period was, not unpredictably, cited as evidence that I was the one who was sick.

The issue of the rancher struck deep. Though I knew that the rancher had nothing to do with the breakup of my marriage—it had far more to do with the fact that I married a man like my husband in the first place—having this issue laid bare in public was extraordinarily painful. A child who suffers the trauma of sexual abuse suffers enough. For my husband to make me suffer again, and so very publicly, felt like more rape. Sometimes I imagine that if all vengeful spouses used the kind of information my husband did to attack their wive's fitness as mothers, our kitchens would be filled with decent women weeping and clutching their children. I write my secrets—the DES, the rancher, the visits to a therapist—because I know my secrets are *their* secrets. My outrage *theirs*.

What could I do? At first I felt as trapped as a deer facing a wall of flame. There is no defense against this kind of assault except to be resolutely sane. I couldn't run into the streets either in Boston or Long Island tearing my hair and yelling, "I'm not crazy! It's not true!" My friends didn't believe him for a minute. But the women to whom I wasn't particularly close, and their husbands, must have heard the concern and anguish in my husband's beautiful, reasonable voice and were inclined to believe what our society is predisposed to think anyway—that I was another female gone haywire with hormones and midlife crisis.

I knew the damage was serious when a friend from our new community called to say she was at a cocktail party and when the subject of rowing had come up and she mentioned my name, someone said, "Oh, isn't she the woman who turned gay and deserted her husband and kids?" I knew when another friend said that a mother in her daughter's class had called her and asked if it was true I was on drugs. I knew when a woman who had welcomed me into the church on our arrival last summer, an elder of the congregation, snubbed me in the grocery store, turning her back on me with a long look and an angry sniff when I greeted her by name. And when friends from Long Island called to say *they* had gotten calls from members of the Beach Club who had heard I was mentally ill and beat the children, and was it true, I feared he had burned any bridge to the community where I had spent so many hours with the other mothers talking about ear infections and teething, rocking our newborns in their plastic baby seats, and wiping ice cream off sticky toddler hands.

My friends did what they could. I did what I could, which was to act as sane and normal as one can do living in a collapsing house. But effective as my husband's offensive was, he miscalculated. If his intent was to strike the blow that would bring me to my knees, he struck, in a sense, after I had already left the battlefield.

Even when a Xeroxed copy of the intimate, personal diary I kept of my thoughts and nightly dreams, a little cribbed blue spiral notebook which had disappeared months before, was slid with sly satisfaction across the deposition table marked as a court exhibit by my husband's attorney with the questions, "Do you recognize this? Is this your handwriting?" I was able to calm the urge to vomit. But what did I really have to fear, I told myself. Can a woman be condemned for her dreams? (The answer, even in our new millennium, is *yes*.)

If all of this had happened five years earlier, when my only value outside motherhood was the role I played in the life of our community, his campaign might have destroyed me. But now I had much, much more. I had my rowing and the companionship of the river community; I had useful, exciting work in Resolute; and I was discovering old friendships from Long Island and new ones in Boston that, in my present adversity, were not disappearing but deepening.

In the face of what looked like a defeat, I found a victory. My real friends became more supportive than ever, and I erased from my address book those acquaintances who chose to believe his witch-hunt rhetoric (though not without pain). And though it was devastating to feel pilloried, my children penalized, in our new community before I had a chance to shake hands, I did make friends. The parents of Janie's best friend were of inestimable value to me, and to Janie during this period. They offered her their stable home and warm affection for all the months of the fire, a period when, in addition to her experience of the chaos at home, Janie was entering the confusion and turmoil of adolescence. And in one friend, a new neighbor, I found a champion.

My neighbor took up my cause and went into the streets carrying my flag. One of her sons had rowed varsity at Harvard, the other at Dartmouth; she had plenty of the river family running through her veins. After decades serving on church committees and championing causes, she was not going to stand by and watch me tarred and feathered. She took the trouble to get to know me and the children, and Uncle Tucker, in a time when I was becoming a pariah, then wrote an article about me and my rowing for the local paper—a full-page article, with a large photograph. The day after the article came out, my children came off the bus bursting with news. "My teacher put the newspaper article on the bulletin board *all day!*" William said. "My hand is tired from signing autographs and my friend says his mom really wants to meet you," said John. I cannot thank my neighbor enough for the gift she gave my children: pride in their mother for that day.

As soon as the first rumors began to make their way back to me, it was evident my husband was launching a custody campaign. It was ironic that he would fight for the children given that, other than the occasional field trip and hockey game, he had appeared to show little interest in fathering over the years. His plan seemed clear to me. He would sway public opinion while manipulating the children with ceaseless subtle and not-so-subtle disparagement of me.

To see parents in intense conflict is terrifying for children. For ours to hear their father say to them, as he did many times in my presence, that Mommy is sick in the head and that she might hurt them must have been devastating. In front of me he suggested to them frequently that as a result of my "illness," I no longer wanted to be their mother. "Mommy has divorced the family," I remember him telling them in the explanatory tones of a science teacher discussing photosynthesis, and I heard him communicate to them in myriad ways that I no longer loved them. My rowing, of course, was presented as the pathological obsession for which I deserted them. In any other family, I would have been praised for my dedication and perseverance and held up as an example for children to emulate. "Don't worry, I don't think Mom is going to do anything to hurt you today," I remember him saying as I helped one of my sons get dressed for school one morning. A few minutes later he returned to the bedroom. "I want to make sure Mom isn't beating you."

How, I often wondered, would anyone ever sort reality from his masterful "spin"?

Tucker knew what was going on, but my husband seemed to be working hard to impugn Tucker as well. Both Tucker and I remember one night overhearing my husband say goodnight to the boys before they came upstairs to us. He said the usual I love you's and nighty-nights, then he told them to make sure Tucker was sober and, especially, "make sure Tucker doesn't touch you." It was common knowledge in my family (and thus known to my husband) that Tucker had had an alcohol problem in the late sixties, and that he had successfully addressed it by 1974. To weave that shred of truth with the accusation implicit in the "touch" remark was profoundly unfair and damaging to Tucker in the boys' eyes, and thus damaging to the boys, who trusted and relied on him. Another night my husband strongly implied to me, in front of William, an accusation that Tucker and I were conducting an incestuous relationship nightly in the attic.

I worried sometimes that no one would ever believe the story of what went on under our large slate roof, and often when I lay in bed at night I wondered if I would live to tell it. I bought a microcassette tape recorder. One day I told my husband, with the recorder visible and running, that I would be taping all our interactions. It didn't faze him in the slightest; indeed, it became evidence of my "paranoia."

When each of my children was a baby—a baby just old enough to roll over or sit up, maybe four or six months old—I used to dream that they were at the foot of my bed and were just about to roll off and fall to the hard floor. I would wake myself lunging to catch them before they fell. I remember how my heart banged, how frantic I was to keep them safe. So, if anything has nearly broken my spirit since the winter of 1998, it has been my inability to protect the children. For my husband to attempt to undermine their trust of me, a trust that might have carried them through the fire, was child abuse as surely as if he had poisoned their morning Cheerios. Sometimes I drove down Route 20 gripping the wheel and praying for God to protect them. Certainly it was increasingly clear to me that I could not.

Janie moved out. She was too overwhelmed by a conflict that even the lock she asked me to install on her door couldn't keep out. In the spring of 1998, she started spending more and more time with the family of her best friend, until late in the spring she simply packed a bag and moved to their house. She never spent another night in her room. She was thirteen, and when she came to live with me in my own house on Elm Street months later, she was no longer a little girl. During those months, my husband demanded that she come home, but she refused. He ordered me to order her back, but I could not (and in this, luckily, Janie's decision was supported by the therapist we had consulted on her welfare). She was safe. How did it happen that a thirteen-year-old girl felt compelled to flee her own home? Where were the courts? Isn't the law supposed to protect women and children?

If I was held captive in the big house first by my unwillingness to uproot the children, then by the hope that my husband would leave, and finally by my belief that the victim's advocacy and court system would act to protect us, at last I really was a prisoner. I should have grabbed the children and run when I had the chance. I had contacted the Department of Social Services (DSS). The intake officer confirmed that what I described was abuse and wanted to initiate an investigation. My attorney at the time, however, told me that the DSS had a reputation for botching investigations so badly that the children could end up in foster care. He convinced me to rely on the courts and I listened.

After my repeated pleas for court intervention and in the face of my perception of threat to the emotional and physical welfare of a woman and her children, the court finally issued an order in June 1998. Uncle Tucker was beside himself when he heard about it and I remember his response. "You mean to tell me you're supposed to live in the attic. He lives on the first floor. The children live in the middle, and every night just as they're going to bed, the custody responsibility switches? My God, how could any sane judge think this is a solution?"

It was madness. The arrangement virtually guaranteed the perpetuation of conflict, ensuring that the children would witness an emotionally violent confrontation every night just when they were most tired and vulnerable. The first rule of domestic conflict is to defuse the situation, not stack the dynamite and flick the lighter.

Is there anything positive that can be said about Probate Court? Only that it is perfect in one respect. In Probate Court, I found a perfect replication of the emotionally abusive relationship; it's all "gaslighting." He whose attorney can fabricate the version of reality that looks most convincing wins. It's a storyteller's paradise, and my husband had a great deal of experience recounting his sad story of my decline and an attorney whose attention to veracity was often overwhelmed by his zeal. My parents and Uncle Tucker, who went to court with me occasionally, remember hearing that my husband's attorney described me as "foaming at the mouth" and a "victim of incest." They were flabbergasted. "Can he simply lie like that to the judge?" they asked, angry and incredulous. My father was as ashen and tight-lipped as I have ever seen him. I understand that my husband's attorney offered to write the judge and withdraw the incest remark, what he called his "misstatement," long after the court orders were issued and the damage done.

I found Probate Court to be unimaginably flawed. I have come to believe it is intrinsically flawed. The decisions that emerge from it represent a futile attempt by judges to apply principles of a judicial system founded on objective truth, solid as a rough red brick, to a situation in which the only reality is the emotional truth of "the parties," a truth quivering, complex, protean, fatally subjective. And the evidence of the house—the flickering lights? the rigged doors? the phone lines dead? Like Ingrid Bergman, pale under the gaslights, it was impossible for me to prove. The Probate process for me, and I believe for many others, is steeped in sorrow and produces nothing but more sorrow. We, and all the stricken souls talking anxiously and weeping quietly on the hard wooden benches outside the courtrooms, needed a doctor, not a judge. I've experienced three miscarriages in my life as a mother. In this fourth, the miscarriage of justice, I lost any faith that "the system" could recognize and rectify something it seemed to have no power to see, something I myself hadn't seen clearly for almost two decades of marriage. There was no vindication to be found, at least not in the tall, worn building on the other side of the river.

What, after all, *was* justice in the conflagration in which we found ourselves? A judgment that shames and punishes a man surely already burnt in the flames of his own inner hell? One that would reduce him to rubble, dishonored and stripped of his children? Is that what I wanted? Is it a judgment that leaves me fat and smug with vengeance, owner of the children and the money, ruler of him as he once ruled me? Would that serve me, to see him grovel? Would it serve the children, who need, most of all, two healthy, productive parents who provide safety and love? Didn't I owe it to them to be such a parent?

How was the energy of *my* rage to be spent, a rage accumulated in silence over all the years of my marriage and the last months of ceaseless assault to decency and dignity? Was it to be spent locked in eternal battle with the man who had already tormented me for nearly half my life? Was he worth it? Sometimes I felt like Dorothy, sweeping back the curtain to find the great Wizard nothing but a frightened man, an organism in reaction—hardly a magnificent moral opponent. Sometimes it even occurred to me that my husband's "campaign" wasn't based in angry guile, but in a sincere and deluded conviction. Would I waste my life trapped in mortal combat with such a foe? Was I to become one of those divorced women who spend their days consumed in anger and their nights dreaming of revenge, prisoner again, this time of my desire to "get even"?

In directing my anger against him, or against the courts, or against the people who believed his rhetoric, I would waste my resources engaged in the same struggle I'd risked my life to leave behind. In allowing myself to be drained by endless bloody skirmishes over nameless hillocks—who's right and who's wrong; who had the upper hand today and who will have it tomorrow; who screwed whom out of whatever (money, visitation, having the children for the Christmas vacation)—wouldn't I squander the gift of this fiery energy, the energy of my own rage? How would I use my fire? The choice was mine: to punish, to destroy, or to transform? How could I build an honorable life for me and my children, a life in which, "every day in every way," we serve the shred of the divine with which we've been blessed?

This was the question on which everything swung. In an ultimate court—one much, much higher than the red brick building on a grimy city street I knew so well—what does winning look like? Was my award to be cinders or gold, enslavement or freedom? The answer came from the center of the fire, because the center of the fire was where I found myself for seven long months in 1998: *If you're brave enough to let go of what doesn't serve you, I will reward you tenfold with what does. Trust me.* I had heard it before and I would hear it over and over in my life, like a prayer or a perfect stroke.

In Boston, in the summer of 1998, I turned my rage to power, my fear to faith. As the weeks of the summer unfolded and the horror escalated, I didn't succumb. In fact, the greater the adversity, the more strength and conviction I found to overcome it. And as I got stronger and stronger, more and more certain of my course, I got faster and faster on the water.

The more I endured at home, the faster I got. The more I was assaulted by gossip and innuendo, the faster I got. The more the court failed my family, the faster I got. The more my husband tried to frighten, intimidate, disparage, shame, humiliate, threaten, the faster I got. Sometimes during the two years since that terrible summer I have thought that the speed I found in racing in 1998 was God's assurance that He was near, that I had the strength to make it through, like a strong hand on my shoulder. *Long and strong. We're going to be long and strong.* Where else could I have found the amazing grace that kept me balanced when my world was spinning off its axis? Certainly I have never felt closer to Him than in my little boat during that dark time.

What does winning look like? I know the answer. It looks like a woman who lets go of her demons and takes her strength into the world. In the summer of 1998, I won virtually every sprint race I entered. The Riverside Sprints. The Cromwell Cup. The Maine State Championships. The Diamond State Regatta (site of my first Thirty-five-Year-Old-Guy Start two years earlier) not only in my own age category, but my races in all three age categories. I was in the fight of my life and I was getting nothing but stronger. On the race course, I was no longer vulnerable to my husband's ability to undermine me. On the race course, there was no self-doubt. No vacillation. No surrender. I was a flaming sword, honed and ferocious. I was fire on water.

Early in August I wrapped up the Sharrow, loaded it on the trailer for the long trip over the plains and across the Divide to the Pacific, and readied for the final showdown, the premier masters athletic event in the world, attended by ten thousand athletes, eleven hundred of them rowers.

The World Masters Games.

Chapter Eighteen

THE

FINAL

I get shivers every time I see my boat
leave Boston on a trailer, bound for a distant
city, speeding through the night alongside the
boats belonging to my friends. I love to think
of its slender white hull going seventy miles
an hour over the prairie, through the
mountains, skirting big midwestern
cities. There is a sense of destiny about
it—my little vessel going so fast, bow breaking
through the winds, shaking off rain squalls, sometimes waiting quietly in the early evening at a rest
stop just as the last glimmer of light fades from
the western horizon, while the truck fills with
gas and the driver, my friend Alex, buys a
bag of the little boxed apple pies he
loves to eat on the open road.

When the boats are loaded, the hands

shaken, and the engine started, a part of me is afraid I will never see my boat again, and I want to run to the corner and look after the trailer one last time before it disappears up Charlesbank Road in a flutter of tail flags, want to say one last farewell before it heads west for the Mississippi and beyond. Another part feels the excitement and trepidation of knowing that the next time we meet will be in a distant, unfamiliar place. I will search a field near some far-off city for the trailer from Cambridge, filled with shells and oars, lawn chairs and bicycles, until I lay my hand once again on the flank of my little craft.

I will open its faded yellow cover with the ragged red flag and see the lovely gleaming whiteness of its hull, the varnished beauty of its wooden seat deck whose grain still speaks of green leaves and summer storms—the language of the sunlight and the stars. I will lift my boat, tracks worn with thousands of strokes, riggers nicked by thousands of miles of bouncing in trailers, and carry it down to unfamiliar waters. I will take up my much-worn oar handles, with the blood in the grooves of the rubber from all the times I've miscalculated my crossover when I'm tired, and look for the rhythm I love.

I know my home river—every bridge, every turn, the spot where the heron stands in the spring, the place above the railroad bridge where the flock of white geese look like scattered toys in the early morning while they sleep, heads under wings. But now I'm on someone else's home water, and I wonder if the skill and strength I found in all the dawn hours on the Charles, the reverence I felt every time I pushed away from the dock to meditate on water and blade, are here. Have I brought with me in my black canvas bag the mornings when the mist of my breath hovers like a spirit, and the water is thick and dark, holding my blades like the sleepy embrace of a lover, when the moon is a smooth white river stone hanging over the turret of the boathouse like a talisman?

I have a friend who says that rowing is a prayer. She lectures to clergy and laypeople about spiritual practice, and sometimes we talk in the little room high under the eaves of her old gray house, the electric heater panting on the floor, a litter of books and papers everywhere. I take the rocker and she the desk chair. We've talked about my rowing, and she has said that for me it engages all my body and soul—rhythmic, aspiring, worshipful.

If rowing is prayer, then racing is a gospel meeting. We rise up and sing to heaven, hearts afire. We praise God, breathing in blasts, moving in cadence. Maybe I'm the only one who feels this way, but I don't think so. Others tell of a mystical togetherness in team boats called "swing." If this isn't communion, I don't know what is. For me in the summer of 1998, I felt communion even in my single—a loving hand was always resting on my shoulder. *Long and strong.*

I race to sing praise and honor the gift I've been given.

In August 1998, my boat left Boston for Oregon and the World Masters Games, the most competitive masters event in the world, conducted once every four years in a host city. I could have been sending my boat to Melbourne or Budapest or Moscow, but this year the city that had won the bid was Portland, so it was to Portland that I flew five days after my boat headed west, my bag full of racing unisuits and enough homemade granola for a week. I was to meet my father at the airport there.

After all the years of helping my brother compete around the world, my father had never seen me race, and he wanted to be there for me. I was to discover that he had a wonderfully quiet, instinctual sense of purpose, always making it about my quest, never about himself, and I think we were both grateful that, at last, here was opportunity for him to protect and support me in my dearest desire. It wasn't too late for us. He was here, and this was the big one.

I had come to race a double with Carie Graves for Pagosa Rowing Club; a mixed quad for Cambridge Boat Club with Henry, Judy, and Al (whose seat was filled at the last minute by Chris Ives when Al had to stay in Boston); and a women's quad from Portland Boat Club. And, of course, the single.

The World Masters Games is an event open to anyone over the age of twenty-seven with the desire to test him- or herself in international competition. Athletes, many of them former elite champions, had trained long and hard in dozens of sports from over a hundred countries in preparation for these games, bringing all their skill and experience to Lake Vancouver, near Portland. When I arrived at the airport, the sheer quantity of masters athletes pouring off flights from around the world radiated an almost tangible wave of vitality. (There had been an amiable fifty-year-old rugby player on my flight whose narrow seat could barely contain his boundless enthusiasm for his sport and relish for the upcoming battles.) Portland itself was awash with pennants and posters advertising the events. There were television interviewers in the street, and athletes of every age from twenty-eight to upward of eighty filled sidewalk cafés and restaurants.

The games were a very big deal. In the months preceding August I had heard of pre-games training camps for rowers to fine-tune technique and hone starts, and I knew from friends around the country that old rivals from Russia and Germany, Bulgaria and Great Britain were heading west for a rehashing of pecking orders. Camps were out of the question for me—I was still running Resolute's marketing, and my life at home was chaos. I had been coached once a week earlier in the summer by Kathy Keeler, who was, like Carie and Carol Bower, another rower from the '84 Olympic eight; but after Kathy left on vacation in July, I hadn't had the time for more coaching, so I assumed that I didn't have much of a chance to medal. My record of wins was satisfying, but it was confined mostly to the East Coast and Canada (except for the three silvers at the Masters Nationals in Long Beach), and these competitors would be the best in the world. No, I would go and do my best, and get Resolute some exposure in the international market, though with only the men's heavyweight hull in production, I planned to race my own Sharrow single.

I had decided to race the open weight single event where the fastest times would be clocked, in spite of the fact that I was currently under one thirty and qualified as a lightweight. I wanted to go up against the biggest and fastest women my age in the world, and this was where they would be. It was a decision much like the one at Masters Nationals in Syracuse. Dear Dr. Dorr and my mother would have been exasperated and proud.

Most people say that success depends on a winning attitude. In fact, just a few days ago I overheard a woman, a former Olympic athlete, say on the dock to someone, "You'll never win unless you believe you can." My approach certainly didn't look like anyone else's idea of a winning attitude—entering a race in which my chances of success were small and which I assumed I would lose—but my idea of winning was different from theirs. My win had always been, and I hope will always be, simply to race my race in accordance with my own three rules: do my best, love my competitors, and feel the rhythm. If I followed them in Portland, I would win no matter when I crossed the finish line. I didn't have the time or energy to think about anything more than that.

Dad and I stayed in the same hotel as Carie and her family. My children were in their father's custody that week, so it was just the two of us. But Carie had her parents, her brother, and her three sisters—a judge, a graduate student, and a publicist—whom she had assembled as a four-woman crew, Team Graves. They had trained in Boston and San Diego alternatively for the last year, and were celebrated in tremendous media coverage—cover articles in *USA Today*, feature articles in glossy magazines. In all, with the Team Graves four and our doubles race impending, there was a festival air and sense of family reunion about everything—lots of running back and forth to talk strategy and drink another cup of herb tea. Yet I found I wanted time for quiet, time just to be with my dad. We had a lot of catching up to do.

We rarely joined the big athlete dinners, but found an out-of-the-way Chinese restaurant round the corner where we ate almost every night, picking at our spring rolls and talking about our family. It was ironic that this monumental event, at which everyone was at a fever pitch of preparedness and excitement, was the first chance I'd had to let down my defenses and enjoy a sense of peace and calm in the more than six months since I'd told my husband I was leaving him. The pressures of international competition were downright soothing compared to bedtime in Boston. At last, after all these months, I could spend a night under a roof that felt safe.

The day after our arrival, I rigged my boat and tried the course, a thousand-meter buoyed straightaway on a large lake near Portland, behind which Mount St. Helens towered, covered with snow even in August. Landmarks were easy—I soon found points to which I could point my stern in the race to be dead center in my lane. The warm-up area was well marked and orderly, and the race officials efficient. They even carried cases of bottled water to toss to competitors after their races. The course didn't seem to have any surprises. After running it once, I returned to shore to rest in the shade with my father and friends.

It seemed like a dream, this regatta. After the horror at home, the calm of the grassy park next to the water was a balm, our picnic table piled high with bananas and plastic gallons of fresh water an oasis. On every side of me were people who loved what I loved. They tinkered with their rigging and talked quietly, testing the pitch on their oarlocks and cleaning their seat tracks with greasy bits of old towel. Friends and supporters, like my dad, brought bags of deli sandwiches and spread towels, set up low chairs in the shade where we could rest and eat. All day I rowed, or talked to friends, or went exploring in the nearby mountains with my father. Being around nice people, kind people, reasonable people made me nearly weep with relief. Maybe I really had died and this was heaven.

The second day, I went into the heats for the single. I had looked on the sheets and found no one I knew in my race; the competitors were virtually all Australians, Russians, and Europeans. Rowing out to the line, I checked them out. Except for one woman from the West

Coast, I was the only American, and all the competition had come a long, long way for this race. Their boats gleamed, but the loveliness of my Sharrow quickened my heart, and that would surely be worth at least a half a length over a thousand meters. They looked very big and very ready.

We greeted each other as well as we could in our various languages, and, as always, there was a sense of shared mission between us. Though their unisuits were bright, I had chosen the dull black unisuit I had bought on the day I raced the Canadian Henley, my first win. Also, the single wasn't a race in which I wanted to wear a team logo. My experience of the single had to do with worship, not club loyalty. In the minutes remaining before the start, my competitors warmed up with a polished precision. So did I. I felt very light but very, very alive. Then we were called to the line.

I had nailed every start that summer. At the beginning of the season, I developed my own start sequence: a series of six very quick, light strokes that lifted my boat and shot it like an arrow. In every race I was getting out ahead in the first thirty meters. This morning on Lake Vancouver was no exception. I was on, no question. By five hundred meters, I was decisively in the lead; by eight hundred, I had it in the bag. Crossing the line, I knew I had made it to the final, two days away. Dad met me when I pulled in to shore, ready to take my oars and help me carry my boat. My father is a master at acting calm and collected, but he was pretty excited. "Oh, you were so smooth, so smooth. You looked like you were hardly working," he said with a grin.

Twenty minutes later, the heat times were posted and Dad and I wandered over to the scoreboard. We already knew mine was the fastest time in my heat. We searched for the sheets with the overall heat results for the Women's C Single. Dad found them. "Look, Sar!" There it was in black and white. Mine was the fastest time in all the heats.

Lord, I thought. What do you have in mind here?

For all that day and the next, I wrestled with fantasies of glory. I would go home, World Champion, and all the Beach Club would reel in wonder, all my town would fall at my feet wanting to know me, my husband would gnash his teeth and boil in bitter bile, and my children would brag about their mom to all their friends. Oh, the triumph, the revenge! I was reminded of the days when I first started winning and my medals possessed me, when I could feel their intoxication working on me like shot of liquor and I had to resist taking them out for just another look. But what triumph? What revenge? Doing my best, not being the best. That's what I train for, that's what I race for. To enjoy the thrill of winning is fine; to fall in love with being best is futile—you can't be best forever. And foolish—best *what*? Nevertheless, my heart pounded and my stomach lurched whenever I let myself realize that winning was a real possibility.

What does winning look like? In Portland in 1998, it looked like forgiving myself for my temporary medal lust, and leaving it bundled tightly in a tote bag under one of the picnic benches onshore. I would go onto the race course with my three rules and a little boat. That's how I would race. That's how I would live. Whatever happens, happens.

Like the night before the Albany race, that night I had more dreams of wild water, of stroking into the teeth of the wind on that stormy Mother's Day in Lloyd Harbor, of being blown downriver like a leaf in the violent afternoon squall that summer with Al, of rowing alone next to the dark stones under the Longfellow Bridge in the high chop of the Charles Basin. I had the same lightheaded, nauseated feeling I'd had in Albany, the same sense of total commitment, same sense of impending birth. But now, two years later, I'd left my husband and was embarked on my new life. After hours of fitful dreams I gave up on sleep and went to the hotel pool around 4:00 a.m. The water was warm as a bath and everything was dark, except for a single underwater light that made the pool a jewel in the chill night air. I floated, looking at the stars and picking out constellations, feeling the water against my fingers. My hair fanned and rippled and I closed my eyes.

What peace there was in the dark of that dawn, the water a quiet caress like mermaid sisters gathered round and lacing their arms in the Girl Scout sling—hands to wrists—to hold me afloat. "Look, we're together," they seemed to say. "We're home." I floated for a long, long time. Then the sky began to lighten in the east and the stars faded. My time. Time to race. At six, I dressed in my plain black suit. My father asked if I could have any breakfast and I tried to eat half a bowl of cereal. Then I gathered our sunscreen, a jug of water, and bunch of bananas, all the stuff for just another day, and headed out for the race of my life.

There are few tools available to the competitive sculler—body, boat, two oars, and a Stroke Coach. At its best, the Stroke Coach gives me useful performance feedback, stroke rating and elapsed time (mine even had a sort of speedometer). At its worst, the Stroke Coach tells me I'm wrong again and what I thought was a rating of thirty-two was really a thirty, what I thought was faster wasn't nearly as fast as yesterday, and what I thought was a snappy, crisp cadence was too low. Most people row with a Stroke Coach; everybody races with one.

In the spring of 1998, I had unsnapped my Stroke Coach one day and pulled from the Sharrow's cockpit all its wires and magnetic pads, taped in place like the sensors of an EEG machine. I decided I didn't care to hear anyone telling me what was right for me, even this little electronic box. I would trust my feelings—for the water, for the cadences of my body and instincts. If I won, I won; if I lost, I lost. So far I had won. Today, as I balanced my boat on my head waiting in line to be cleared through the safety inspection and get my bow number, I could see the empty bolt holes in my upside-down foot stretchers where the Stroke Coach had been mounted. I laughed. At last here was real evidence of insanity.

We passed inspection and my father helped me to the shore with my oars. Once again, like every other race day, I wanted to throw up. I think maybe Dad did, too. I closed the ports and opened the oar-locks. Dad handed me my oars, one by one, and gave me a thumbs-up and a little smile. I settled into my seat and laced into my shoes. Then he told me he loved me.

The world was new and bright with early sun. I felt my boat move graceful as a hunting bird as we skimmed the lake heading north to the start, blades beating like a pair of strong wings, free of all the encum-brances of earth. What a gift—all of it. For the sky, for the water, for the beauty of my boat and the blessings of my body, for the gift of my competitors, I gave thanks, every stroke. Down the course to the warm-up area, approaching the start line. Every stroke . . .

At 8:38, we are called to the line. There is a light tailwind, but the sky is cloudless and the mountain in the distance looks closer in the clear morning. The Russian whose time was closest to mine in the heats is on my right. I found out later through an interpreter that she is a former Soviet Olympic sculler and two-time European champion. I can see her face, lined by years on her river, half a world away from mine. Her eyes are serious and calm. She rolls up to the catch once and checks to make sure her blades are square, then she rolls back down. To my left is a big Australian. I make sure my stern is securely in the stake boat attendant's hands and pull slightly on starboard to realign my bow down the lane in the slight breeze. Then we wait.

Finally, all six of us roll slowly up to the catch, legs compressed, oars buried and square, eyes on the horizon. The roll is called, the flag raised. There is a long pause. I find myself holding my breath and silently saying my prayer: *Oh my God, thank you for this chance, thank you for this race* . . . Then the flag drops, and everything that is still, waiting, breathless, explodes into action.

My start is there. Total connection. Three strokes, four strokes. I am out front. Find the rhythm, feel the blades biting the water, lock-ing on the water. Feel the breath filling my chest. Listen to my heart beating the message I don't need a Stroke Coach to tell me: I have strength, I have life, I have love. Three hundred meters. I'm in the lead. I'm burning with a bright fire that sends this little boat with every stroke. The other three scullers are well behind and the Australian has dropped behind now as well. It will be just me and the Russian who is at my stern, down a boat length, matching my rate stroke for stroke. Here are the voices: my coach, Kathy, inside my head booming through her megaphone, "Drive! Drive to the finish!" Al, saying in his calm, dry way, "Are you fishing or are you rowing?"

By five hundred I am well out front, the Russian two boat lengths behind. I can see the muscles of her back working, and sense her coiling for a power move. I coil and move at the same time. We accelerate together, like osprey hunting together on the harbor. Suddenly I feel as connected to her as if we are tied by an invisible cord, as if we can feel each other's movements and intentions. We are fighting for the greatest speed, and we are inspiring each other to find it—at once opponents and partners. She is beautiful in the bright water, big and sleek and powerful. I am light and sharp.

Then at eight hundred meters my port blade catches. My momentum is lost, my balance thrown. I have a millisecond to make a decision. Will I spend the rest of my life saying to myself, I might have won if my blade hadn't gotten trapped on that one stroke. Will my life be about a mistake? What does winning look like? Decide. *Now.* It looks like leaving the mistake in my wake, finding my rhythm again, and moving on. It looks like letting go. *Trust me.*

The Russian had closed on me with the missed stroke. I lock on to the water with my war sword, the Edge, and let loose the rage of these forty-five years and the exultation of this day of days. Fifty meters to go. I am out ahead again. There is a hand on my shoulder, *Long and strong.* Thirty meters. There are voices of a chorus—"Feel the rhythm, feel the strength of your mermaid's tail, feel the beauty of this day, this hour, this moment when you transcend all your sorrows and give the best you have to give with these hands, this body, this heart." Five meters. Three meters. I cross over.

I have a lot to be thankful for. Ironically, it is the man who was my husband and who is the father of my children who deserves the greatest acknowledgment. If I feel gratitude toward my opponents for their willingness to test my courage and strength, then my husband has done no less. In fighting for my freedom from him I have had to dig deep for the resources that might, in another circumstance, have remained as hidden as a vein of gold beneath a rocky hillside.

I have found untold riches. A new connection to my family—my mermaid sisters; my brother, still a hawk; my wise mother who knows about letting go; and the loving father I have finally found as a grown woman. The fellowship of friends and community that has deepened from the mundane to the profound. Most importantly, the passion for my rowing that has connected me to the divine within myself. Sometimes I wonder if my life with my husband hadn't been so bitter, the river water might not have tasted so exquisitely sweet. Finally, I've found a voice in the world that might have remained forever buried under sorrow and laundry had it not been sparked to life by our conflict.

Even my ability to write this book arose from the experience of my marriage and separation. In these last two years, the necessity of making my voice heard in daily logs, memoranda, and impassioned letters has forced me to face the keyboard for the first time since college. In fighting for my children, I have found a voice to express my mind and heart. It's a hell of a cure for writer's block. As Christiane Northrup said in her wonderful book on physical and emotional healing, *Woman's Bodies, Women's Wisdom*, "Rage transformed is power. Rage transformed is strength." Rage transformed is also voice.

The challenges of these years have also affirmed a connection to God that gives shape to all my experience of the world. What serves Him serves me—it is the litmus test for every decision. Our endless struggle with ego and control, both within ourselves and in relation to others, is a diversion that serves us ill. In "killing the sparrows," we squander our energy and our precious time on earth, and all of us must find the source of courage that allows us to loosen our hold and follow the calling of a greater imperative. *Trust me.*

My husband also deserves my gratitude for giving me the opportunity to be a mother and experience the inestimable blessing of our three children. Perhaps now is payback time. Although I have deplored my husband's methods for trying to take the children from me, in my most philosophical moments I also recognize the opportunity implicit in the custody we share—the chance for him to be a father involved in their day-to-day lives. In the end, I believe our sons will have seen the example of a woman who would no longer tolerate abuse, and they will also have seen a father who fought hard for his share of them.

These are hard lessons for them, but better than the alternative—boys who might model their behavior on what they saw for so many years, boys who might become men whose controlling behavior prevented them from ever knowing the love of a woman, who might have married and divorced again and again, becoming more and more bewildered and embittered. And the lesson of their father's battle to own them? After the years in which they sometimes described Daddy as someone who "talked on the phone all the time, yelled a lot, and flew around in airplanes," their father is at last deeply involved in their daily lives. I'm convinced that the children offer him, as they offer all of us, the chance to be fully human. In them, he has the opportunity of a lifetime: three human beings who want nothing more than to love him and be loved by him. Thus it comes around. My life is rich with love. Maybe his can be, too. If my experience of him has allowed me to find my "best," perhaps in the children we created together, he can find his.

I once read a novel about a man who was convinced that something magnificent would enter his life to redeem him and define his mission on earth. He waited a lifetime for it to happen, rejecting the love of a good woman because she might divert him from his yet-to-be-discovered mission. The irony was, she was the "something magnificent"; their love his redemption.

Shortly after the purchase of the single in 1996, my husband and I were driving home one afternoon when we saw a delta of airplanes low overhead and a sign for an air show. We followed the placards into a dirt road that led to an airstrip, and parked in a soggy field. In fifteen minutes, the loudspeaker announced, a famous husband-and-wife aerobatic team would perform. We ate popcorn and looked at the planes until the clouds broke and the husband and wife taxied onto the strip and took off in tandem, each in a little blue airplane with stubby wings.

I remember standing next to my husband on the wet field, both of us turning our faces to the sky to watch the pair, who performed their balletic routine with breathtaking grace. They swooped, inches apart in frighteningly tight formation, rolling and spinning in perfect togetherness. Then they split apart to perform their own virtuoso loops and dives, each claiming a quadrant of the vast sky. Together and apart, together and apart they flew. As I watched, I realized there was no hope for us. Realized it with a cool, sad, absolute certainty. We might remain husband and wife until we were "parted by death," as we had pledged so many years before; but as a team we were done. Or maybe as a team we'd never begun.

I wasn't angry, I wasn't triumphant. I didn't think about lawyers and divorce court. I looked at my husband's face still tipped toward heaven, his hand shading his brow. I'm convinced he never realized then, or in all the years of our marriage, that his redemption was standing next to him.

If you are brave enough to let go of what doesn't serve you, I will reward you tenfold with what does. How I've been rewarded.

What was His plan when I won the World Masters Games? I think it was that my gold medal (and, as Jeff might say, it's a real whopper) gave me the chance to write about my win, on the water and off, a win I hope will inspire and encourage women searching for their voices, their strength. It was fitting that I found my publisher three months after the World Masters Games through the Mommy Network. Over Thanksgiving weekend 1998, my dear college friend Suki Fredericks and I were sitting in the kitchen of her farmhouse in Leicester, Vermont, talking about what we really wanted to do "when we grew up." Our children played Monopoly in the next room. "I'd like to write a book about how rowing has changed my life," I said. "Well," said Suki, "one of the fathers at the kids' school is an editor. Maybe we should give him a call." It was one of those moments in which fate balanced on tippytoe. I could have said, "Sure, maybe sometime." What I said was, "Let's call him right now." He was home, he wanted us to meet, and an hour later, on the street in front of the dimestore, he asked me to send him a proposal.

Thus, in letting go not only of my painful marriage but of the rancor that might have poisoned the life to follow, I have been rewarded with both a mission and the means to pursue it, and the warmth of friends and family.

I live on a quiet street with Janie; the boys go back and forth on a weekly basis from my house to their father's. Tucker comes to visit for months at a time. The day I won in Portland, I vowed never to spend another night under the same roof as my husband. After two weeks in Colorado with my family, the children and I returned to Boston and moved into a hotel until I could take possession of an apartment in a pleasant old two-family house. Tucker stayed to help me fix it up. The dire legal consequences I expected as a result of my defiance—my escape from the big house—quickly evaporated, though my husband and I have revisited the courthouse many, many times since then. In my new life I have no pillars, no fireplace, no large lawn, and only one bathroom. I have never been happier. I have freedom and a life abundant with love and possibility.

The legal process winds its way forward at a snail's pace—our courts are uniquely designed for the party who *can't* let go. We recently went to trial, and as the hours and days ground past, I listened to my husband's litany. In the end I can't really say why he thought what he thought, felt what he felt, did what he did; but if I am convinced of anything, it is that my "feminine pathology" is, was, and has always been his reality.

In the process of preparing for trial, my attorney asked me to get the original boathouse logs of the last five years to prove how much time I really had spent on the water. Even though I knew the answer, I was still amazed at what I found. In my five years of rowing, my average water time was just less than an hour a day during the season—about as much time as any other mother might devote to a brisk daily walk. As I listened to my husband weave his tale, I rested my right hand on the boathouse logs. What is real? I thought. My husband's beautiful voice telling his own truth, or these daily accounts of dozens of mornings enjoyed by dozens of people—mornings when we roll back the heavy boat bay doors to see the river wreathed in mist and lay our oars on the dock. When we balance the gossamer lightness of our shells overhead and carry them to the water once again. Here was all the truth I'd ever need.

My mother sent me a worn typewritten page a few months ago. It was a parable entitled "What Do Women Want?" and told the story of Sir Gawain and the Witch. The page had obviously gone from hand to hand, and my mother couldn't remember where she had gotten it, only that she knew she wanted me to see it, then pass it along. I'm passing it along now.

Once upon a time a hideously ugly witch was terrorizing King Arthur's realm, and the only thing that would placate her was marriage to Sir Gawain, Arthur's handsome and stalwart knight. Arthur reluctantly asks Gawain if he will make this ultimate, or penultimate, sacrifice for the good of the kingdom. He agrees and is married to the witch the next day. On their wedding night, as Gawain girds his loins for the ordeal ahead, the witch appears before him and makes an unusual offer. "I have the ability to be a beautiful maiden half the time, the witch you see before you the other. I will give you your choice. Would you prefer me to be witch by night and beautiful maiden by day, or ravishing maiden by night and the hag you see before you by day?" Gawain thinks for a long moment, then gives a reply to which every man would do well to pay attention. "It is not for me to decide, my wife. The choice is yours and you must please yourself. I will happily abide by your decision." The witch turns in an instant into the most beautiful maiden Gawain has ever seen. She smiles.

"For your answer, wise husband, you shall have maiden by day *and* by night." And they live happily ever after.

What does winning look like? It looks like a river, cool and sweet, calm and deep, smelling of cut grass and the apple blossoms that almost touch my shoulder as I row my little Sharrow round the long bend past Eliot Bridge, past the next dock, under the next bridge, leading me to the east where the river widens and readies to join the sea. It looks like a moment one afternoon at the World Masters Games when I met the women from Portland Boat Club with whom I was to race a D quad. Here's our boat, they said, and I looked at the beautiful old wooden Staempfli resting on slings, and at the brass plaque on its bow. A friend had given me a poem early the spring before, a poem called "The Journey," by Mary Oliver, the Pulitzer Prize–winning poet. I have carried the poem with me everywhere since. Engraved on the brass plaque of the Staempfli was its name: the *Mary Oliver*. We raced the *Mary Oliver* in a hilarious, joyous lopsided race (her rudder was slightly askew) to a silver medal.

Sometimes God is so obvious.

Acknowledgments

bove all I wish to thank my extra-ordinary family, who have given me their loving and unconditional support always, but especially during the months of "the fire": my parents, Richard and Patricia Hall; my brother, Richard L. Hall; my sister Anne Hall Hudnut; and most especially, my sister Caroline Hall Otis, who brings her intelligence and loving heart to the world as a life coach, and to me as both sister and diligent "front-line" editor in the early stages of this book. My three siblings and I make a hell of a quad. In addition, I thank my uncle, Robert Tucker Hall, to whom this book is dedicated, and who knows how much my children and I owe him for his wisdom, love, and calm presence.

I'm lucky. My experience in the last few years has shown me not only the true nature of victory but of friendship. On Long Island, my friends François and Marie Paule Bogrand, Anne Brower DuBosque, Bea Hanson, Kathy Pavlakis, Alison Tung, and Terry Walton stood by me in tough times. In Boston, I can never thank the following enough for their support of my children and me: Judy Barclay and David St. Mary, Gary and Patty Leroy, Betty Lou Marple, Melissa Patterson, Sarah Rossiter, Janet Sharp, and Bob and Bettye Freeman, who gave us shelter. Thanks, also, to my dear friends Ellen Brennan in San Francisco and Suki Fredericks in Leicester. Others who lent their invaluable support are James Dalsimer in Boston, and the staff, directors, and supporters of Sanctuary for Families in Manhattan, specifically Executive Director Carolyn Nash; Clinical Director Beth Silverman-Yam; and board members Dudley delBalso and Eileen Jachym. And thanks to Emily Wharton in Stonington, who led me to them.

The rowing community is too large and too dear to me to acknowledge adequately in these brief pages, but I especially wish to thank the following members of my immediate river family: on Long Island, Peter Bisik, Marge Dole, Jim Long, Rich McLaughlin, and Tom Thompson; and in Boston, Everett Abbott, Jay Bragdon, Ted Benford, Judy Davis, Al Flanders, Marie Hagelstein, Henry Hamilton, Kathy Keeler, Linda Kennett, Kathy Kirk, Craig Lambert, Bill McGowan, Jerry Murphy, Pete Peterson, Alison Sanders-Fleming, Jeff Schaeffer, Alex Selvig, and Carlo and Susie Zezza. I also wish to thank Northeastern University and the coaches at Henderson Boathouse—Buzz Congram, Evans Lionel, Joe Wilhelm, and boatman extraordinaire Rick Schroeder. Many thanks to all the Resolute crew in Bristol, especially Eric Goetz and Bernie Tarradash. Across the country, I send gratitude and warm regard to Carol Bower and Vicki Valerio in Philadelphia, and Meg and Gary Schoch in Vachon Island, Washington. Most importantly, I want to acknowledge Carie Graves, who deserves all the laurels she can carry, and she can carry a lot. She has been a loyal friend, a superb doubles partner, and a woman whose strength and courage have inspired thousands of women, including me. And special thanks to the Nike Corporation for its unstinting support and sponsorship of the 1998 World Masters Games.

In addition, I want to express profound gratitude to those who took a chance on me: my editors at W. W. Norton—John Barstow, who supported this project from the moment we met in front of the dimestore in Middlebury, Vermont; Alane Mason; and especially Helen Whybrow, whose understanding of my mission and ear for the music of language has made writing this book a joy; and my agent, John Taylor "Ike" Williams of the Hill & Barlow Agency, who added an unknown, unpublished housewife to his list of luminaries on the belief that my story was of value to women and the world.

Finally, I convey a grateful hug to the friend who has given me the haven of his loving arms for over two years—David Bunting.